THE
COMPLETE BOOK
OF
DESSERTS

THE
COMPLETE BOOK OF
DESSERTS

By ANN SERANNE

FABER AND FABER
for
THE COOKERY BOOK CLUB

This edition published 1967 by
The Cookery Book Club
9 Grape Street, London, W.C.2.
for sale only to its members
Printed in Great Britain by
John Dickens & Co Ltd, Northampton
Originally published 1964 by
Faber & Faber Limited

To my dedicated editor and constant friend

CLARA CLAASEN

Preface

No lunch or dinner is complete without dessert. Whether it is an elaborate cake, a luscious pastry, a soufflé, crepes, cream or custard, a single small sweet biscuit, or a dish of fresh berries—dessert is to the dinner what an epilogue is to a play.

It is truly unfortunate, in this day of great awareness of waistlines, that many people soothe their consciences by foregoing the dessert course to a meal on the basis that, if they give up the sweet, they will lose weight. No premise is more inaccurate, and I, for one, who love desserts and prefer a slice of hot pie with whipped cream for breakfast to a bowl of cereal or bacon and eggs, can attest the fact. I weigh no more today than I did when I left college and came to New York. I am five feet eight inches and still slip easily into a size twelve!

Regardless of the number of books devoted to the subject of obesity, there is only one logical answer to the diet problem, and that is to eat small quantities of a variety of dishes each day. Our bodies need a little sugar each day as much as they need adequate amounts of protein, minerals, and vitamins.

Sugar is an essential ingredient in a baby's formula, and I believe it is just as essential to the well-being of the grown man and woman.

In addition to being a partner in a business devoted to the pleasures of the table, I raise Yorkshire terriers as a hobby—exquisite little creatures with long flowing coats and known at Westminster as "the floating terriers." They are given a tiny piece of lump sugar each day to help them digest the large quantity of fat needed in their diets to make their coats luxurious and glossy. They are a trim, active, spirited, healthy lot of dogs, and I have yet to pay a doctor's bill for anything more than protective shots or help in whelping.

But this is not a book on diet or on dogs. It is a book that explains the basic principles of mastering the fine art of making desserts. More conscientious effort has gone into the creating and fashioning of desserts than has been put into many more important and serious subjects, yet, strangely, not many books have been devoted to desserts. Dessert recipes follow as a meager contribution at the end of a cookbook, trailing far behind the fish, meat, vegetables, and salads. This proportion is out of proportion, for knowing cooks don't need a cookbook to cook the rest of an average meal. They can improvise and take many liberties with other dishes, adding to a ragout, subtracting from or substituting in a casserole. But not so with the dessert. When it comes to a custard we must know just how many egg yolks are needed to thicken a cup of milk, and just how long and at what temperature we can cook it without the egg curdling. We must know precisely the amount of gelatin required to stiffen a pint of fruit juice to produce a delicate jelly. If we overestimate, the jelly will taste like rubber. And when it comes to fine pastries creative instinct is not going to do it; the straight and narrow path of correct proportions and technique must be strictly followed.

The Complete Book of Desserts explains the basic principles of mastering the fine art of making desserts and gives you accurate recipes for all the fine desserts that we have inherited from the great chefs of the world. Many of these are classic European desserts. Where I thought it would be of particular interest, I've noted the European name as well as the American. Try a new one of these excellent desserts on your table each day and see how much additional pleasure you will give your family. Desserts are not only good for the morale, they are good for you.

ANN SERANNE

TABLE OF

Contents

Recipes for items printed in small capitals can be located by consulting the Index.

PUBLISHER'S NOTE

No attempt has been made to adapt this edition for the English (or rather non-American) cook as it is felt that although some of the terms used may not be those to which she is accustomed, their meaning is generally clear. It should, however, be remembered that: where 'all-purpose' and 'cake' flour are referred to, ordinary plain flour is to be used; 'cornstarch' is cornflour; 'confectioner's sugar' is icing sugar; 'shortening' is any suitable type of fat and, incidentally, a raisin in America is usually a sultana in England. Some ingredients may not be easily obtainable in this country but substitutes can, in most cases, be found—i.e. black treacle for molasses, walnuts for pecans, plain wholemeal biscuits for graham crackers, etc. The measures used are, of course, standard American cup measures and it is now possible to buy, for a few shillings, American measuring cups; at the time of going to press they are obtainable from Selfridges Ltd., Oxford Street, W.1. Use of such measures is strongly recommended for the sake of speed, simplicity and accuracy, but the following simple conversion table is given as a guide:

CONVERSION TABLE

Approximate Equivalents for 1 American Cup

Breadcrumbs { dry	4 oz.		Nuts	4½ oz.
{ fresh	1 oz.		Oats (rolled)	3 oz.
Coconut	3 oz.		Peanut Butter	8 oz.
Cornflour	4½ oz.		Rice	6¼ oz.
Cream—double	8¼ oz.		Suet (chopped)	4½ oz.
Dried Fruits	6 oz.		Sugar (brown, caster,	
Fat	8 oz.		granulated)	7 oz.
Flour	4 oz.		Sugar (icing)	4½ oz.
Milk { condensed	10¾ oz.		Syrups and Honey	11½ oz.
{ evaporated	9 oz.			

1 American pint = 16 fluid oz.
1 English pint = 20 fluid oz.
1 cup liquid = 8 fluid oz. (1½ gills)

Equipment and
General Techniques

In almost any profession, certain basic equipment is essential to the operation of the business. Additional equipment may increase the scope of the business, open new avenues, or contribute to the speed and efficiency of the operation. And so it is in the field of cooking. Certain basic equipment is necessary to allow one to roast, fry, poach, and stew. Certain other equipment enables the homemaker to produce a greater variety of dishes more quickly and easily.

For basic dessert making, everyone should have:

1 set mixing bowls
1 or more liquid measuring cups
1 set cups for dry measurement
1 set measuring spoons
1 or more wooden spoons
1 slotted spoon
1 pancake turner
Several spatulas of different sizes and flexibility
1 egg beater
1 cheese or nut grater
1 flour sifter
2 sieves, one large, one small

1 pastry brush
1 rolling pin
1 pastry blender
Pastry cloth and cover for rolling pin
1 or more rubber spatulas
2 or more round 8- or 9-inch cake pans
1 or more 8- or 9-inch square pans
1 loaf or bread pan
1 shallow 9- ×12-inch pan
1 muffin pan
1 pie pan
2 cooky sheets
1 or more baking dishes
6 custard cups
1 9-inch tube pan
1 double saucepan
Kitchen scissors
Vegetable parer
Waxed paper
Aluminum foil

To enlarge your repertoire, you should have some or all of the following:

1 or more decorative molds
1 or more tube molds or savarin pans
1 or 2 spring form pans of different shape and size
1 torte ring
Fluted tart pans with removable sides
Tartlet pans
Doughnut cutter
Biscuit cutters
Assorted cooky cutters
1 charlotte mold
Baba molds
A variety of pastry tips and bags
A cooky press
1 small crepe pan
1 omelet pan
1 steamed pudding mold with tight-fitting cover

A pastry wheel
2 whisks, one medium, one balloon
Fluted paper cup liners
Cheesecloth
Parchment paper
Rosette irons
A Swedish krumkake iron
Cornucopia tubes
Piqué knife for fluting lemons
A deep-fat fryer
Griddle and waffle irons
An ice-cream freezer

For greater efficiency and speed, you must have:

An electric blender
An electric rotary beater

GENERAL TECHNIQUES

Throughout this book I have tried to explain in detail the techniques that apply to each individual category of dessert making. There are, however, some techniques that apply to dessert making in general. I include them here.

CREAMING BUTTER AND SUGAR

Hand Creaming: Let butter soften to room temperature. Put into mixing bowl and gradually beat in the sugar. Continue to beat until mixture is light and fluffy.

Electric Beater Method: Remove butter from refrigerator about 1 hour before needing it. Warm mixing bowl by rinsing in hot water; dry. Cut butter into ½-inch pieces and put into bowl. Add sugar and beat at moderate speed for several minutes, stopping occasionally to scrape mixture from sides of bowl back into path of the beaters.

MELTING CHOCOLATE

Chocolate of any kind burns easily and must be carefully watched as it melts. Use chocolate pieces or cut squares of chocolate (each is

1 ounce) into small pieces. Put them into a small saucepan, set saucepan over steaming—not boiling—water, and cover saucepan to keep out moisture. Let stand for about 10 minutes.

If a small quantity of liquid is called for to be added to the chocolate you can heat the mixture directly over low heat, providing you stir constantly and do not let the mixture boil. This method takes only a couple of minutes.

WHIPPING CREAM

Whipped cream should be double in volume, fluffy, and smooth. This means that as much air as possible must be beaten into the cream, and this is accomplished more successfully by hand whipping than by an electric beater. The cream must be as cold as possible. Chill the bowl and also the beater or beaters. In summertime, when cream is often difficult to whip, especially if the weather is humid as well as hot, I pour the cream into the bowl, insert the whisk, and put all in the freezer for about 20 minutes.

To Hand Whip: Use a whisk and beat leisurely at about 2 strokes per second for 2 to 3 minutes, or until cream is fluffy and stiff.

To Whip with Electric Beater: Begin at low speed and gradually increase to moderate (never use high speed for whipping cream). Circulate the bowl or use a rubber spatula to push the stiffening cream from sides of bowl into the beaters.

SOFT WHIPPED CREAM, or *Crème Chantilly*

Beat cream only until a dollop dropped onto a plate will retain its shape in a soft peak.

STIFFLY BEATEN CREAM

Continue to beat a few seconds after the soft peak stage is reached. Be careful not to overbeat or you may end up with butter.

STORING WHIPPED CREAM

Empty cream into a fine sieve and place the sieve over a bowl to catch any of the milk liquids that usually exude. Store in refrigerator where it will keep well for several hours.

TO FLAVOR WHIPPED CREAM

Just before serving, fold in 2 tablespoons per cup of fine granulated or confectioners' sugar and 1 or 2 teaspoons vanilla, rum, brandy, fruit spirit, or a sweet liqueur.

BEATING EGG YOLKS AND SUGAR TO THE RIBBON STAGE

When a recipe specifies that eggs or egg yolks and sugar should be beaten until very thick and pale in color, this means they must be beaten until a small amount lifted up and poured back takes some time to level out. This is known as "the ribbon stage," and it can be accomplished by hand beating or by an electric beater. Since we are trying to achieve consistency as well as volume, an electric rotary beater does the job extremely well in about 5 minutes at high speed.

Electric Beater Method: The eggs must be at room temperature. Rinse the bowl with very hot water and dry. Add eggs and sugar and beat at high speed for about 5 minutes, or until a spoonful of the mixture takes some time to level out when poured back. The mixture will triple in volume and will be thick enough to hold the air beaten into it when flour or butter are carefully folded in.

Hand Beating: Set the bowl containing the eggs and sugar over steaming water and beat rapidly with a wire whisk for 2 to 3 minutes or until tripled in volume and thick enough to take some time to level out when a spoonful is lifted up and poured back.

BEATING EGG WHITES

Egg whites beat to greater volume if they are at room temperature. They will not thicken if they contain the slightest particle of egg yolks or grease of any kind. The bowl in which they are beaten and the beater itself must be thoroughly clean.

The old-fashioned method of hand beating is still recommended as the best way to beat egg whites to the greatest volume, and you won't find any French chef who will beat them any other way. To hand beat you need a large balloon whip, about 5 inches across so that it can keep the whole mass of egg whites in constant motion.

Copper bowls are excellent, otherwise use glass or stainless steel. Never use aluminum, as it is apt to discolor the egg whites, giving them a gray tone.

To Hand Beat: Have egg whites at room temperature. Empty them into a clean, round-bottomed bowl about 9 inches in diameter and 5 to 6 inches deep. Add a pinch of salt. Begin beating with a circular motion about 2 strokes per second until the eggs are foamy. Then increase speed to about 4 strokes per second and increase the diameter of the circular motion to incorporate as much air as possible. Keep turning the bowl so that the entire mass of egg whites is gathered up by the whisk in each motion. Test for stiffness by raising the whisk upright. When the egg whites do not run from the whisk but form soft peaks, the egg whites are stiffly beaten. Do not beat any longer as you will only lose the air beaten into them and the egg whites will lose their glossy appearance and become dry.

Electric Beater Method: Either a stationary mixer or a hand rotary beater may be used. If using the stationary kind you must constantly push the egg whites from the sides of the bowl back into the path of the beaters. For this use a slim rubber spatula or bottle scraper. Begin beating at a slow speed for about 1 minute or until egg whites are frothy. Gradually increase speed to medium and begin testing for stiffness as soon as the egg whites begin to mound up on the sides of the bowl.

VANILLA BEAN AND FLAVORING EXTRACTS

To use a vanilla bean, cut off a small piece and add it to the liquid being heated for a dessert. Use about 1 inch for each 2 cups of liquid. It may be served in the cream or custard or removed. If removed, dry it carefully and add it to a canister of sugar that is reserved for dessert making or for flavoring fruits. Keep adding sugar and stirring as you use it. Several pieces of vanilla bean will impart a mild vanilla flavor to the sugar for as long as six months.

FOR A STRONGER-FLAVORED SUGAR

Blend 1 vanilla bean, cut into pieces, and 1 cup sugar in an electric blender for about 1 minute. Let stand in a tightly closed container for about 1 week, then strain.

TO FLAVOR COLD DESSERTS WITH VANILLA BEAN

Split a piece of vanilla bean and scrape out the pulp and seeds. Stir it into the other ingredients.

FLAVORING WITH EXTRACTS

When adding vanilla or other extracts to a dessert, the ingredients must be cool. Since extracts all have an alcohol base, the alcohol evaporates readily from hot ingredients and the flavor is dissipated.

ORANGE, LIME, OR LEMON SUGAR

Combine ½ cup sugar with the grated rind from 1 orange, lime, or lemon. Store in tightly closed containers and sieve before using.

ORANGE, LIME, AND LEMON FLAVORINGS

Either the juice or rind, or both, may be used. If using rind, remember that a little goes a long way. Grate only the colored portion, for the white is unpleasantly bitter. If you grate it on a diagonal you will find that not as much will adhere to the grater.

If only the juice is used, store the half rinds in a covered jar in the refrigerator to use when needed, or grate and combine with sugar to make ORANGE, LIME, or LEMON SUGAR.

To Make Julienne Strips: Remove only the thin colored portion of the fruit. This is very easy if you use a vegetable parer. Cut it into very thin strips with kitchen scissors. Before using, pour boiling water over the strips and let them soak for 10 minutes to remove any bitter flavor. Drain and add to other ingredients, or use for a garnish.

GLAZED ORANGE OR LEMON PEEL FOR GARNISH

5 lemons or 3 large oranges	1 cup granulated sugar
1 quart water	⅓ cup water

Remove colored portion of lemon or orange skin with a vegetable parer. Cut into thin julienne strips. Simmer in the quart of water for 10 minutes, or until tender. Drain and rinse in cold water. Dry on paper towels.

Combine sugar and ⅓ cup water. Bring to a boil and boil rapidly to the thread stage (230° F.). Remove syrup from heat and stir in the peel. Let peel soak in the syrup for 30 minutes, or until ready to serve. Drain and use. If you store the peel and syrup in the refrigerator it will keep for several weeks.

ALMONDS

Whole, blanched, blanched slivered, or toasted almonds can be purchased in almost any supermarket throughout the country, but are more costly than if you prepare them from the whole nut.

To Blanch Almonds: Cover shelled almonds with boiling water, simmer for 1 minute, and drain. Rinse in cool water and the skins will slip off easily.

To Dry Almonds: Spread blanched almonds in a baking pan and heat in a 350° F. oven for 10 to 15 minutes.

To Shred Almonds: Almonds are easier to shred if they are freshly blanched and slightly warm. Use a sharp knife to cut each one into several pieces from pointed end to base. Spread on baking sheet or pie plate and dry in a 350° F. oven for 5 to 10 minutes.

To Pulverize Almonds: Blend ½ cup at a time of dry blanched almonds on high speed in an electric blender for about 20 seconds, or pound in a mortar with a pestle, adding a little of the sugar specified in the recipe.

To Toast Almonds: Roast blanched almonds on a baking sheet in a preheated 350° F. oven, stirring frequently, for about 30 minutes, or until lightly browned.

To Sauté Almonds: Melt 1 tablespoon oil or butter in a frying pan and when it is foaming add ½ cup whole, halved, or shredded blanched almonds and cook over moderate heat, stirring constantly, until browned on all sides. When nuts are the right color, remove from heat but keep stirring for another minute or so, as the almonds will continue to brown from the heat of the pan.

Almond Paste: This may be purchased in many food shops throughout the country, especially at Christmas time, or may be made by pounding blanched almonds to a paste in a mortar and kneading in the oil that is extruded in the pounding. It should be pounded until very smooth and free of any hard particles.

Almond Milk: Put ½ cup dried blanched almonds and 1 cup water into container of the electric blender. Cover and blend on high speed for about 30 seconds until liquid is milky and nuts are pulverized. Strain and squeeze through cheesecloth. Or pound nuts and water in a mortar. Use 2 parts almond milk to 1 part milk or cream in making creams and custards. The original French *Blanc-Manger* was made with almond milk.

COCONUT

Coconut Milk may be made in the same way as almond milk. Put ½ cup diced fresh coconut and 1 cup water into container of the electric blender. Cover and blend on high speed for 30 seconds. Strain into a bowl, pressing with back of a spoon to extract all the milk.

Grating Fresh Coconut: Many a scraped knuckle is saved through an electric blender. Grate ½ cup at a time peeled, diced fresh coconut meat in an electric blender on high speed for 5 seconds.

PULVERIZING MACAROONS

Break macaroons into small pieces and spread on baking sheet. Dry in a very slow (200° F.) oven for about 1 hour, or until lightly browned. Let cool and crisp. Then pulverize ½ cup at a time in an electric blender, or pound in a mortar. Store in tightly closed jars and it will keep for many weeks. Use in place of praline.

CARAMEL

Caramel is simply sugar cooked until it turns brown. It is used as a coloring, a flavoring, and to coat dessert molds.

In a saucepan combine 1 cup sugar and ⅓ cup water. Bring to a boil over moderate heat, shaking pan occasionally until all sugar is dissolved. Do not stir. Let boil, watching carefully, until it turns gradually from light gold to dark caramel color. Do not let it get too dark or it will become bitter. Remove immediately from the heat and set pan into another pan containing cold water to stop the cooking and to prevent it from darkening further.

CARAMEL SYRUP

Make caramel, as above, and cool. Then stir in ⅓ cup water and heat to simmering, stirring constantly, until caramel is dissolved.

PUREES, FRUIT

Purées may be easily made by pressing berries or soft fruits through a sieve or food mill or by blending in an electric blender.* Hard fruits such as apples or quince, or dried fruits such as apricots should be cooked with a little water until soft, then strained and puréed. The consistency depends entirely on the amount of juice the fruit itself contains. If the purée is too thick, it may be thinned with water or fruit juice. If too thin it must be stirred and cooked over moderate heat until enough of the moisture has been cooked away and the purée is thicker.

Purées should be sweetened to taste with fine granulated sugar and may be flavored with brandy, rum, or any desired liqueur.

PRALINE POWDER

¾ cup sugar
¼ cup water

¼ teaspoon cream of tartar
½ cup blanched almonds

In a small heavy saucepan combine sugar, water, and cream of tartar.

Cook over low heat until sugar is dissolved.

Add almonds and cook over high heat, without stirring, until syrup and almonds are the color of dark molasses.

Immediately pour into an oiled cooky sheet to cool.

When cool, remove from sheet and crush in a mortar. Or blend about half at a time on high speed in an electric blender for 10 seconds.

Store in a tightly closed moistureproof container.

Hazelnuts may be used in place of almonds.

* Purées made in the electric blender from fruits containing seeds (such as raspberries) or hard cores (such as apples) should be strained before using.

CHAPTER 1

Baked and Steamed Puddings

THE pudding is an extremely British article of food. And it is to John Bull that credit must be given for creating the greatest of all puddings, the plum pudding—which grew in stature from its humble origin of spiced fruit porridge, called *la groute*, to the fruit-filled luxury that it is today.

In the days of William the Conqueror, *la groute* must have been considered a palatable concoction, for its inventor, Robert Argyllon, was rewarded with a fine estate, the Manor of Addington—probably wrenched from the unwilling hands of some Saxon churl. But cooking in medieval times left much to be desired: *la groute* was simply compressed into a ball, tied in cotton or linen, and boiled.

It was around 1680 that the first plum pudding as we know it appeared in gastronomic history, and today no Christmas or New Year's repast is complete without this royal dish steamed in a mold and served in a blaze of rum or brandy.

There are many other types of puddings, less complicated to compose than the plum, that make delicious, satisfying, and hearty desserts and we couldn't agree more with Joseph Barber who, in his charming book, *Crumbs from the Round Table*, advised, "Married ladies who love your lords, give them puddings."

BREAD PUDDING

8 slices bread, trimmed	3 cups hot milk
4 tablespoons (½ stick) butter	⅔ cup sugar
	2 teaspoons vanilla
½ cup light (sultana) raisins	4 eggs, lightly beaten
Cinnamon	Cream, plain or whipped

Butter bread generously and cut each in quarters, making 32 squares.

Cover raisins with hot water and let stand for 10 minutes, then drain and dry.

Cover bottom of a baking dish 10×6×1½ inches with 16 squares of buttered bread. Sprinkle with cinnamon and the raisins. Cover with another layer of buttered bread and sprinkle again with cinnamon.

Stir sugar and vanilla into the hot milk. Gradually stir in eggs. Pour egg-milk mixture over the bread. Place pan in a larger pan containing 1 inch hot water and bake in a 325° F. oven for 40 minutes, or until custard is set and bread is browned on top.

Serve with plain or whipped cream. *Serves 4 to 6.*

OLD-FASHIONED BREAD PUDDING

1½ cups diced stale bread	¼ teaspoon salt
3 cups milk	1 teaspoon cinnamon
2 eggs, beaten	½ cup raisins
½ cup sugar	LEMON or JELLY SAUCE

Soak bread in the milk and empty into a buttered 1-quart baking dish.

Combine eggs, sugar, salt, and cinnamon and stir into the bread mixture.

Stir in raisins.

Put dish in a pan containing about 1 inch hot water and bake in a preheated 350° F. oven for 45 minutes, or until almost set in center.

Serve with lemon or jelly sauce. *Serves 4.*

INDIAN PUDDING

1 quart milk	½ teaspoon ginger
2 tablespoons butter	¼ teaspoon cloves
⅔ cup yellow corn meal	2 eggs
⅓ cup all-purpose flour	½ cup molasses
1 tablespoon sugar	1½ cups cold milk
1 teaspoon salt	Heavy cream and brown sugar
1 teaspoon cinnamon	

Scald the quart of milk and stir in the butter.

Combine corn meal, flour, the tablespoon sugar, salt, and spices.

Beat eggs lightly and stir in molasses. Gradually stir in the mixed dry ingredients and stir until mixture is smooth. Gradually stir in the hot milk.

Pour batter into a well-greased 6-cup baking dish and cool to lukewarm.

Bake in a preheated 325° F. oven for 4 hours. At the end of each hour pour over ½ cup of the cold milk until all the 1½ cups have been added. Do not stir.

Serve hot with heavy cream and brown sugar. *Serves 6.*

CRUMB CAKE PUDDING

1 cup dry cake crumbs	3 egg yolks, beaten
½ cup milk	1 cup peach preserves
¼ cup butter	1 cup chopped nuts
1 cup sugar	Whipped cream

Soak cake crumbs in the milk, adding a little more milk if necessary to completely moisten them. The amount depends on the dryness of the crumbs.

Cream butter and sugar until light and fluffy.

Stir in egg yolks and the soaked crumbs and mix thoroughly.

Stir in preserves and nuts.

Turn into a buttered 1-quart baking dish and bake in a preheated 300° F. oven for about 1 hour, or until firm.

Serve with whipped cream. *Serves 4.*

QUEEN OF PUDDINGS

3 cups fresh bread crumbs
2 cups hot milk
¼ cup sugar
Grated rind of ½ lemon
2 tablespoons butter
2 egg yolks, lightly beaten

1 teaspoon vanilla
2 tablespoons strawberry
  preserves
2 egg whites
2 tablespoons sugar

Empty crumbs into a buttered 1½-quart casserole.

Combine hot milk, the ¼ cup sugar, lemon rind, and butter and stir until butter is melted. Stir in egg yolks and vanilla.

Bake in a preheated 325° F. oven for 30 minutes.

Remove from oven and spread strawberry preserves over top of pudding.

Beat egg whites until stiff, gradually beat in the 2 tablespoons sugar, and continue to beat until the meringue is thick and glossy. Spread meringue over pudding.

Return pudding to oven and bake for 15 minutes longer, or until meringue is golden. *Serves 6.*

DATE PUDDING

½ cup graham cracker
  crumbs
1 teaspoon double-acting
  baking powder
¼ teaspoon salt
2 eggs
½ cup sugar
1 teaspoon vanilla

¾ cup chopped walnut meats
¾ cup chopped almonds
  (not blanched)
1½ cups pitted, chopped
  dates
CUSTARD SAUCE or whipped
  cream

Combine cracker crumbs, baking powder, and salt and set aside.

Beat eggs and sugar until sugar is dissolved. Stir in vanilla, nuts, and dates. Stir in cracker crumb mixture.

Pour batter into a well-oiled or -buttered baking dish 6×10×1½ inches and bake in a preheated 325° F. oven for 50 to 60 minutes.

Cut into squares and serve hot with custard sauce or whipped cream. *Serves 6.*

PRINCE ALBERT PUDDING

6 ounces dried prunes
⅓ cup butter
¼ cup sugar
2 eggs, separated
¼ cup milk

1 teaspoon grated lemon rind
1 cup cake crumbs
1 teaspoon double-acting
baking powder
SABAYON SAUCE

Cook prunes according to directions on package. Remove pits and cut prunes in half. Line a 4-cup greased mold with the prunes.

Cream butter and sugar together. Beat in egg yolks and milk.

Stir in lemon rind, crumbs, and baking powder.

Beat egg whites until stiff and fold in.

Turn batter into prepared mold. Cover and steam for 1½ hours. Unmold and serve hot with sabayon sauce. *Serves 4.*

STEAMED FIG PUDDING

⅓ cup flour
½ teaspoon double-acting
baking powder
¼ teaspoon cloves
⅛ teaspoon nutmeg
¼ teaspoon salt
1 cup ground suet
⅓ cup sugar

2 eggs, separated
½ pound figs, chopped
1 teaspoon grated orange rind
½ cup bread crumbs
¼ cup milk
2 tablespoons brandy
ORANGE SAUCE

Sift flour, baking powder, cloves, nutmeg, and salt into a bowl.

In another bowl cream suet and sugar together until smooth.

Stir in egg yolks, figs, orange rind, and crumbs.

Stir in dry ingredients alternately with milk and brandy.

Beat egg whites until stiff and fold in. Pour into a buttered 6-cup mold and steam for 1 hour. Serve with orange sauce. *Serves 6.*

BOILED SUET PUDDING

1½ cups whole-wheat bread
crumbs
1 cup beef suet, chopped and
free of strings
Grated rind of 1 orange
1 cup flour
1 cup sugar
½ teaspoon salt

2 teaspoons double-acting
baking powder
1 cup pitted, chopped dates
2 eggs, lightly beaten
¼ cup milk
2 teaspoons vanilla
1 tablespoon brandy
BRANDY or HARD SAUCE

In a large mixing bowl combine bread crumbs and suet. Stir in grated orange rind.

Combine flour, sugar, salt, and baking powder and stir into the bread crumb mixture. Stir in dates.

Stir in eggs, milk, vanilla, and brandy.

Generously butter a clean square of muslin and dust it with flour.

Turn pudding mixture into center of cloth, gather up corners and edges, and tie securely, making sure room has been left in the "bag" for the pudding to swell.

Half fill a pot large enough to hold the pudding with water and bring to a boil. Gently lower pudding into the boiling water, cover, and simmer for 3 hours, replenishing the water with more boiling water as needed.

Remove pudding to cake rack to drain.

Turn out on a large serving dish. Sprinkle with granulated sugar. Pour over a few spoonfuls of heated brandy and ignite. Take blazing to table and serve with brandy or hard sauce. *Serves 6.*

APPLE PANDOWDY

15 medium apples, peeled, quartered, and cored	1 cup all-purpose flour
1 cup sugar	1 teaspoon double-acting baking powder
2 teaspoons cinnamon	¼ teaspoon salt
1 teaspoon nutmeg	4 tablespoons shortening
½ teaspoon cloves	1 egg, lightly beaten
4 tablespoons butter (½ stick)	¼ cup cold milk
⅔ cup dark molasses	Heavy cream

Slice apples into a large buttered baking dish 10 inches in diameter and 3 inches deep, sprinkling each layer with the sugar mixed with the spices, and dotting with butter.

Pour molasses over the apples.

Bake in a preheated 400° F. oven for 45 to 50 minutes, basting apples occasionally with their own juice.

When apples are almost tender, combine flour, baking powder, and salt.

Cut in shortening and stir in egg and milk, making a soft biscuit dough.

Remove apples from oven and drop the dough in spoonfuls around edge of dish in a ring.

Return dish to oven and bake for about 15 minutes, or until biscuits are baked and lightly browned.

Serve hot with heavy cream. *Serves 8.*

DUTCH APPLE PUDDING

2 *cups sifted all-purpose flour*	¾ *cup milk*
3 *teaspoons double-acting baking powder*	⅓ *cup brown sugar*
	1 *teaspoon cinnamon*
½ *teaspoon salt*	½ *teaspoon nutmeg*
2 *tablespoons sugar*	2 *cups thinly sliced apples*
¾ *cup butter*	*Heavy cream*
1 *egg, lightly beaten*	

In mixing bowl combine flour, baking powder, salt, and the 2 tablespoons sugar. Cut in ½ cup of the butter.

Combine egg and milk and stir into the flour mixture, stirring only enough to make a soft dough.

Mix remaining butter, brown sugar, cinnamon, and nutmeg. Spread this mixture in bottom of an 8-inch square cake pan.

Cover brown sugar mixture with apple slices.

Spread dough evenly on top of apples.

Bake in a preheated 350° F. oven for 1 hour.

Serve hot with heavy cream. *Serves 6.*

APPLE BROWN BETTY

6 *tart apples, pared, cored, and diced*	2 *tablespoons butter*
	Juice and grated rind of 1 lemon
1⅓ *cups fresh bread crumbs*	
¾ *cup sugar*	⅓ *cup water*
1 *teaspoon cinnamon*	HARD SAUCE or FOAMY SAUCE

Spread half the apples in a buttered 1½-quart casserole.

Combine bread crumbs, sugar, and cinnamon. Sprinkle half this mixture over the apples and dot with half the butter. Repeat with remaining apples, crumbs, and butter.

Sprinkle with lemon juice and rind, add water, cover, and bake in a preheated 375° F. oven for 45 to 60 minutes.

Serve with hard sauce or foamy sauce. *Serves 6.*

APPLE CRISP

6 large tart cooking apples, peeled, cored, and sliced
½ cup orange juice
1 tablespoon lemon juice
1 cup sugar
1 teaspoon cinnamon
¾ cup flour
¼ teaspoon salt
6 tablespoons shortening or butter
Cream, whipped cream, or HARD SAUCE

Arrange apple slices in greased baking dish.

Pour the orange and lemon juice over apples.

Combine half the sugar with the cinnamon and sprinkle over apples.

Combine flour, remaining sugar, and salt and cut in shortening or butter with a pastry cutter or 2 knives, and sprinkle over apples.

Bake in a preheated 350° F. oven for 45 to 60 minutes, or until apples are tender and crust is crisp and golden.

Serve warm with cream, whipped cream, or hard sauce. *Serves 4.*

APPLE PUDDING

3 tablespoons flour
1 teaspoon double-acting baking powder
¼ teaspoon cinnamon
Pinch salt
1 egg
¾ cup sugar
1 teaspoon vanilla
1 teaspoon grated lemon rind
½ cup chopped walnuts
4 medium apples, peeled, cored, and diced
Sweetened whipped cream

In a small mixing bowl combine flour, baking powder, cinnamon, and salt.

In large mixing bowl beat egg. Gradually beat in sugar and continue to beat until light and fluffy. Stir in dry ingredients, vanilla, and lemon rind.

Fold in walnuts and diced apples.

Turn mixture into a buttered 9-inch layer cake pan and bake in a preheated 350° F. oven for 40 minutes.

Serve hot or warm with sweetened whipped cream. *Serves 4.*

APPLESAUCE PUDDING

A 1-pound can applesauce	Pinch salt
3 egg yolks	⅓ cup sugar
1 teaspoon lemon rind	½ teaspoon vanilla
2 teaspoons lemon juice	Cream
3 egg whites	

Beat together applesauce, egg yolks, lemon rind, and juice.

Beat egg whites and salt until foamy. Gradually beat in sugar, 1 tablespoon at a time.

Stir in vanilla.

Fold half of the meringue into the applesauce mixture.

Turn into a greased baking dish and top with remaining meringue.

Set dish in pan containing 1 inch hot water and bake in a preheated 325° F. oven for 30 minutes. Serve with cream. *Serves 4.*

PUDDING SANS SOUCI

2 apples, peeled, cored, and diced	1 teaspoon vanilla
4 tablespoons butter	⅓ cup sugar
3 tablespoons flour	3 eggs, separated
¾ cup milk	SABAYON SAUCE

Sauté the apples in 2 tablespoons of the butter until soft and golden.

In saucepan melt remaining butter. Stir in flour. Gradually stir in milk and cook, stirring, until sauce is smooth and thickened. Stir in vanilla and sugar.

Beat egg yolks until creamy and gradually beat in the hot sauce mixture.

Fold in sautéed apples.

Beat whites until stiff and fold in gently.

Turn mixture into a 6-cup mold. Cover and steam for 40 minutes. Remove from kettle. Let stand 5 minutes, then unmold.

Serve with sabayon sauce. *Serves 4.*

BOILED APPLE DUMPLINGS

6 small tart cooking apples
2 cups flour
½ teaspoon salt
2 teaspoons double-acting
  baking powder
6 tablespoons shortening
⅓ cup milk

6 squares linen
Strawberry preserves
6 tablespoons fine granulated
  sugar
Confectioners' sugar and
  heavy cream

Peel and core the apples.

Combine flour, salt, and baking powder. Cut in shortening, and stir in milk to make a soft dough.

Turn dough out on floured cloth and knead about 10 times to make a smooth dough. Roll out and cut into 6 squares large enough to cover the apples.

Place an apple in center of each square. Fill each apple with strawberry preserves and sprinkle each with 1 tablespoon sugar.

Wet edges of the dough and fold together with points overlapping on top. Press edges together securely.

Dip linen squares in boiling water, spread out, and flour well.

Place an apple in center of each linen square and tie securely, leaving enough room for dumpling to swell.

Place dumplings in a pot of boiling water, cover, and boil for ¾ hour.

Remove dumplings from cloths and place on hot serving platter. Serve with confectioners' sugar and heavy cream. *Serves 6.*

HOT FRUIT COBBLERS

Sliced cooked apples, peaches,
  plums, or berries
Sugar to taste
Pinch salt

1 teaspoon vanilla or 2 table-
  spoons rum
Biscuit mix
Heavy cream

Butter a square baking dish and fill half full with fruit.

Sprinkle with sugar to taste, salt, and vanilla or rum.

Make drop biscuits according to directions on a package of biscuit mix and drop by spoonfuls on top of the fruit.

Bake in a 425° F. oven for 25 minutes.

Serve hot with heavy cream.

PLUM PUDDING

1 pound suet, ground
½ cup blanched almonds
½ cup currants
½ cup seeded raisins
½ cup light (sultana) raisins
½ cup chopped apple
¼ cup chopped dried figs
¼ cup chopped pitted dates
¼ cup candied cherries
¼ cup chopped candied orange rind
¼ cup chopped candied lemon rind
¼ cup chopped citron
1 cup brown sugar
½ teaspoon salt
¼ cup chopped preserved ginger

1 teaspoon cinnamon
1 teaspoon nutmeg
½ teaspoon cloves
½ teaspoon mace
Juice and grated rind of 1 orange
Juice and grated rind of 1 lemon
3 cups dark rum
1½ cups fine dry bread crumbs
¾ cup flour
6 eggs, lightly beaten
Fine granulated sugar
¼ cup rum

In a large bowl mix suet, nuts, fruits, rinds, sugar, salt, ginger, and spices.

Moisten with orange and lemon juice and 1 cup of the rum.

Cover bowl with waxed paper and let marinate in refrigerator for 10 days, adding a few tablespoons rum and tossing the mixture each day.

The day the pudding is to be served, stir in remaining rum, bread crumbs, flour, and eggs, and turn batter into a well-buttered 10-cup decorative mold, filling mold ¾ full.

Tie metal foil or a heavy buttered cloth over top of mold and place mold on a rack in a pan containing water that comes to 2 inches of the top of the mold. Cover kettle and simmer for 5 to 6 hours.

When ready to serve, turn pudding out onto serving platter and sprinkle with fine granulated sugar. Pour over ¼ cup warm rum, light the rum, and serve the pudding ablaze. *Serves 12.*

APPLE COBBLER

3 medium tart cooking apples, pared, cored, and diced
¼ to ½ cup sugar
1 tablespoon grated lemon rind
¼ teaspoon nutmeg
¾ cup water
1 cup flour

1½ teaspoons double-acting baking powder
¼ teaspoon salt
½ cup sugar
¼ cup (½ stick) butter
½ cup milk
1 egg, lightly beaten
2 teaspoons vanilla
Cream

In saucepan combine apples, from ¼ to ½ cup sugar, depending on tartness of apples, lemon rind, nutmeg, and water. Bring to a boil, stirring.

Cover tightly, reduce heat, and simmer for 10 minutes, or until apples have begun to soften.

In mixing bowl combine flour, baking powder, salt, and sugar.

Cut in butter with pastry blender or 2 knives.

Mix milk, egg, and vanilla and add to flour-butter mixture.

Stir gently just until dry ingredients are moistened.

Pour hot fruit and syrup into buttered baking dish 11×7×2 inches; spoon the batter over top of fruit.

Bake in a preheated 375° F. oven for 30 minutes, or until done when tested with a pick.

Serve warm with cream. *Serves 6.*

BLACK CHERRY PUDDING

A 1-pound can dark sweet cherries
1 cup sifted cake flour
1½ teaspoons double-acting baking powder
¼ teaspoon salt
½ teaspoon cinnamon

¼ cup butter
⅔ cup sugar
2 eggs, lightly beaten
¼ cup milk
¼ cup hot water
1 teaspoon vanilla
Whipped cream

Heat cherries and juice to boiling point and empty into a buttered 1-quart baking dish.

Combine flour, baking powder, salt, and cinnamon.

In mixing bowl cream butter. Add sugar gradually and cream together.

Beat in eggs. Stir in flour mixture alternately with the milk and water, beating until smooth after each addition. Stir in vanilla.

Pour batter on top of the hot cherries and bake in a preheated 400° F. oven for 25 to 30 minutes, or until cake tests done.

Serve warm with whipped cream. *Serves 4 to 6.*

FRESH CHERRY COBBLER

3 cups sour pitted cherries
1 cup sugar
1 cup water
1 tablespoon cornstarch
2 tablespoons water
1 tablespoon butter
1 teaspoon cinnamon

1 cup sifted all-purpose flour
¼ teaspoon salt
1 teaspoon double-acting baking powder
3 tablespoons shortening
½ cup milk
Heavy cream

Heat cherries with the 1 cup sugar and 1 cup water until almost boiling.

Mix cornstarch with the 2 tablespoons water and stir into fruit mixture. Cook, stirring, for 3 minutes.

Pour fruit and juice into an 8-inch square baking dish.

Dot with butter and sprinkle with cinnamon.

Combine flour, salt, and baking powder. Cut in shortening. Stir in milk to make a soft drop-biscuit dough.

Drop dough by spoonfuls over the fruit and bake in a preheated 400° F. oven for 30 minutes.

Serve hot with heavy cream. *Serves 6.*

FRUIT ROLY-POLY

2 cups sifted all-purpose flour
½ teaspoon salt
2 teaspoons double-acting baking powder
6 tablespoons shortening

⅔ cup milk
¼ cup melted butter
Fruit combination as listed below

Sift flour, salt, and baking powder into a mixing bowl.

Cut in shortening.

Stir in milk to form a soft dough.

Turn out dough on floured pastry board and knead gently about 10 times.

Roll dough out into a rectangle about ¼ inch thick.

Brush surface with melted butter, spread with filling, and roll up jelly-roll fashion.

Transfer roll to an oiled baking sheet, seam side down.

Brush with melted butter.

Bake in a preheated 400° F. oven for 25 to 30 minutes.

Slice warm and serve with cream. *Serves 8.*

FRUIT COMBINATIONS

1 cup diced apples mixed with ½ cup raisins, 1 teaspoon cinnamon, ½ cup granulated sugar, and ½ cup brown sugar.

6 peaches, peeled and sliced, ½ cup sugar, 1½ tablespoons lemon juice, and 1 teaspoon grated lemon rind.

1 pint blackberries, ½ cup sugar, and ½ teaspoon cinnamon.

1 pint blueberries, ½ cup sugar, juice and grated rind of 1 lemon.

1 pint gooseberries, ¼ teaspoon ginger, and 1 cup brown sugar.

APRICOT ROLY-POLY

1 cup finely chopped dried apricots
½ cup seedless raisins
½ cup brown sugar, firmly packed
¼ cup granulated sugar
¼ cup broken walnut meats

1½ cups water
4 tablespoons lemon juice
2 cups biscuit mix
⅔ cup milk
¼ teaspoon nutmeg
Heavy or whipped cream

In a saucepan combine apricots, raisins, half the brown and the granulated sugar, walnut meats, half the water, and half the lemon juice.

Cook over medium heat for 15 minutes, stirring occasionally.

Prepare biscuit dough according to directions on package, using the milk for liquid.

Turn dough out onto lightly floured pastry cloth and roll into a rectangle about ¼ inch thick.

Spread filling to within ¼ inch of edge and roll up like a jelly roll, starting at one long side. Slice crosswise in 1½-inch-thick pieces and arrange the slices cut side down in a greased 8-inch square pan.

Combine remaining water and lemon juice with remaining brown sugar and the nutmeg. Bring to a boil and simmer for 5 minutes.

Pour half the syrup over the roly-polies and bake in a preheated 350° F. oven for 45 minutes, or until pastry is lightly browned, basting occasionally with the remaining syrup.

Serve hot or warm with heavy or whipped cream. *Serves 6 to 8.*

PEACH PUDDING PIE · *Auflauf*

¼ cup brown sugar
2 pounds peaches, peeled, pitted, and sliced
½ cup sifted all-purpose flour
¼ teaspoon salt
½ teaspoon double-acting baking powder

2 eggs, separated
2 tablespoons water
½ cup granulated sugar
1 teaspoon vanilla
Whipped cream

Sprinkle brown sugar in bottom of a buttered 1½-quart baking dish. Top with the peaches.

Combine flour, salt, and baking powder.

In mixing bowl beat egg yolks and water until light, and gradually beat in sugar. Continue to beat until mixture is thick and pale in color.

Stir in dry ingredients.

Beat egg whites until stiff but not dry and fold into egg yolk mixture. Add vanilla.

Spread batter over peaches and bake in a preheated 350° F. oven for 35 minutes, or until cake tests done.

Serve hot or warm with whipped cream. *Serves 4.*

BAKED PEACH DESSERT

1 cup sifted cake flour
1 teaspoon double-acting baking powder
¼ teaspoon salt
½ cup sugar
½ cup butter
1 teaspoon grated lemon rind
2 eggs

⅓ cup milk
4 peaches, peeled, halved, and pitted
⅓ cup sugar
½ teaspoon cinnamon
¼ cup chopped pecans
Whipped cream

Combine flour, baking powder, and salt.

In mixing bowl cream together the ½ cup sugar, butter, and lemon rind.

Beat in eggs.

Fold in dry ingredients alternately with the milk.

Spread half the batter in a greased 8-inch square pan. Arrange peaches on top and cover with remaining batter.

Sprinkle with the ⅓ cup sugar, cinnamon, and pecans.

Bake in a preheated 350° F. oven for 50 minutes.

Cut into squares and serve hot with whipped cream. *Serves 6.*

RASPBERRY SLUMP

2 *pints raspberries*	⅓ *teaspoon salt*
1 *cup sugar*	¼ *cup sugar*
1 *cup flour*	½ *cup milk*
1½ *teaspoons double-acting baking powder*	2 *tablespoons melted butter*

Rinse berries and empty into bottom of a 1-quart baking dish.

Sprinkle with the 1 cup sugar.

In mixing bowl combine flour, baking powder, salt, and the ¼ cup sugar.

Stir in milk to make a smooth batter.

Stir in butter.

Pour batter over berries in dish and bake in a preheated 375° F. oven for 45 minutes. Serve hot. *Serves 4.*

HOT COCOA PUDDING

1 *cup sifted all-purpose flour*	½ *cup milk*
2 *teaspoons double-acting baking powder*	2 *tablespoons melted butter*
½ *teaspoon salt*	1 *cup chopped nuts*
¾ *cup sugar*	1 *cup brown sugar*
6 *tablespoons cocoa*	1¾ *cups hot water*
	Whipped cream

Combine flour, baking powder, salt, sugar, and 2 tablespoons of the cocoa in a mixing bowl.

Stir in milk and melted butter and mix until smooth.

Stir in nuts and spread batter into a buttered 1-quart casserole or baking dish.

Sprinkle surface with the brown sugar and remaining cocoa.

Pour hot water over the batter. Do not stir.

Bake in a preheated 350° F. oven for 40 minutes.

To serve, cut cake into squares and serve with some of the sauce from the pan.

Top with whipped cream. *Serves 4.*

STEAMED CHOCOLATE PUDDING

¼ pound (1 stick) plus 2 tablespoons butter
⅔ cup sugar
5 egg yolks, lightly beaten
2 tablespoons rum
3 ounces semi-sweet chocolate, melted
⅔ cup ground blanched almonds

⅔ cup ground toasted hazelnuts
3 tablespoons fine dry bread crumbs
½ cup light (sultana) raisins
5 egg whites, stiffly beaten
Whipped cream or CHOCOLATE SAUCE

Cream butter and sugar until light and fluffy.

Beat in egg yolks, rum, and melted chocolate.

Fold in nuts, bread crumbs, and raisins.

Fold in egg whites.

Butter a 2-quart pudding or melon mold and dust with sugar.

Pour in batter, filling mold no more than ⅔ full.

Cover mold and place in a kettle containing a few inches of simmering water.

Cover pot and steam pudding for 1½ hours, adding more simmering water if necessary.

Remove pudding from steamer. Let stand 10 minutes, then turn out on serving platter.

Serve immediately with whipped cream or chocolate sauce. *Serves 6.*

LEMON CUSTARD PUDDING

¼ cup sifted all-purpose flour
1 cup sugar
¼ teaspoon salt
2 teaspoons grated lemon rind

¼ cup lemon juice
2 eggs, separated
1 cup milk
Whipped cream

In mixing bowl combine flour, sugar, and salt.

Stir in lemon rind and juice.

Beat in egg yolks and milk.

Beat egg whites until stiff and fold into the batter.

Pour into a buttered 8-inch casserole.

Place casserole in pan containing about 1 inch hot water and bake in a preheated 350° F. oven for 40 to 45 minutes.

Serve warm with whipped cream. *Serves 4.*

SWEET POTATO PUDDING

2 eggs
1 cup brown sugar
1 cup cream
2 cups grated sweet potatoes
¼ cup melted butter
1 teaspoon grated lemon rind
1 tablespoon lemon juice

¼ teaspoon ginger
¼ teaspoon cloves
¼ teaspoon salt
⅓ cup raisins
½ cup chopped nuts
Cream

Beat eggs until light and beat in sugar.

Stir in cream and remaining ingredients.

Turn mixture into a greased shallow 1-quart baking dish. Bake in a preheated 350° F. oven for 30 minutes. Stir with a spoon and continue to bake for 15 minutes longer. Serve hot with cream. *Serves 4.*

MADEIRA PUDDING

1 cup mixed chopped candied
  peels
¾ cup Madeira wine
½ cup butter
⅓ cup sugar

3 eggs
1 cup flour
Pinch salt
MADEIRA SAUCE

Soak peel in Madeira for 1 hour. Drain and reserve the liquid for madeira sauce.

Cream together butter and sugar.

Beat in eggs. Fold in flour and salt.

Alternate layers of peel and batter in a greased 4-cup mold.

Cover and steam for 2 hours.

Unmold and serve hot with Madeira sauce. *Serves 4.*

LITTLE CHOCOLATE PUDDINGS

1 cup milk
2 squares (2 ounces) unsweetened chocolate
1 tablespoon butter
1 tablespoon dark rum
1½ cups sifted all-purpose flour

¼ teaspoon salt
1½ teaspoons double-acting baking powder
1 egg
1 cup sugar
Whipped cream

In a small saucepan combine milk, chocolate, and butter.

Cook over low heat until chocolate and butter are melted and mixture is smooth. Stir in rum and cool.

Combine flour, salt, and baking powder.

In mixing bowl beat egg until light and gradually beat in sugar.

Stir in dry ingredients alternately with the chocolate milk mixture, mixing after each addition until smooth.

Divide batter into 6 buttered 6-ounce custard cups and cover with aluminum foil.

Place cups in pan containing 1 inch warm water and bake in a preheated 350° F. oven for 50 minutes, or until toothpick inserted in center comes out clean.

Remove foil and cool 5 minutes. Turn out on serving dish and serve warm with whipped cream. *Serves 6.*

CHAPTER 2

Creams and Custards

THE "boiled" custard is one of the few really great recipes that England gave the world, and from it can be made a limitless number of delicious desserts.

Actually, there is no such thing as a "boiled" custard, for the sweetened mixture of milk and eggs can never be heated to the boiling point or it would curdle. Custards may be stirred over direct heat until the mixture coats the spoon, but a safer method is to cook it over steaming water for about 8 minutes, stirring constantly. Custards may be baked in a moderate oven in a casserole dish or in a piecrust. A common fault is to overbake, and most recipes specify to bake "until a silver knife inserted in the center comes out clean." This is erroneous, for a custard continues to cook from its own heat after it is taken from the oven. A knife coming out clean when inserted into the custard *two inches from the outer edge* is a better barometer to the degree of doneness and will assure a beautifully smooth, fully cooked dessert, whether it is served warm or cold.

Either one or two eggs are used to thicken a cup of liquid, one making a very thin custard, more suitable as a dessert sauce than a dessert, and two making a heavier, richer consistency. Two egg yolks may be used in place of one whole egg, and brown sugar or shaved maple sugar may be used in place of regular granulated. The liquid may be milk, fruit juice, or wine, or a combination of these, giving a wide variety in the flavors of a basic custard. And from these basic flavors and basic recipes stem a multitude of delicious desserts for the enjoyment of your family and guests.

ENGLISH CUSTARD · *Crème Anglaise*

1½ cups milk	3 egg yolks
1 one-inch piece vanilla bean	1 teaspoon flour
⅓ cup sugar	

In saucepan scald milk with vanilla bean.

In another saucepan combine sugar, egg yolks, and flour.

Gradually stir hot milk into egg yolk mixture and cook over low heat, stirring constantly, until cream almost reaches a boil, but be careful not to let it boil.

Discard vanilla bean and stir cream over cracked ice until cool and thick. *Serves 3*

COFFEE CUSTARD · *Crème Anglaise Café*

Substitute half light cream and half strong black coffee for the milk.

CHOCOLATE CUSTARD · *Crème Anglaise Chocolat*

Stir 2 ounces (2 squares) semi-sweet chocolate, melted, into the hot cream.

SOFT VANILLA CUSTARD

2 cups milk	1 teaspoon vanilla
6 egg yolks	Fresh or preserved fruits, jam,
4 tablespoons sugar	or jelly, optional

In small saucepan heat milk to steaming.

In top of double saucepan beat egg yolks and sugar until sugar is dissolved.

Gradually whisk in hot milk and cook over simmering water, stirring constantly, until mixture becomes consistency of rich cream and coats the spoon. Do not let water in lower saucepan boil.

Stir in vanilla and pour into serving dish or individual dishes.

Serve hot or cold and top, if desired, with fresh or preserved fruits, jam, or jelly. *Serves 4.*

BAKED CUSTARD

3 cups milk
6 egg yolks
6 tablespoons sugar
Pinch of salt

1 teaspoon vanilla
FLAKY PASTRY, optional
Nutmeg

In saucepan heat milk to steaming.

In mixing bowl beat egg yolks, sugar, salt, and vanilla until yolks are thick and pale in color.

Gradually beat or whisk in the hot milk.

Pour mixture into buttered baking dish or pie plate lined with flaky pastry and sprinkle surface with freshly grated nutmeg.

Bake in preheated 350° F. oven for 35 minutes, or until blade of a silver knife comes out clean. *Serves 6.*

THE QUEEN'S CUSTARD · *Crème à la Reine*

3 cups hot milk
3 tablespoons sugar
8 egg yolks
1 teaspoon vanilla
3 tablespoons curaçao

6 egg whites
6 tablespoons sugar
½ teaspoon vanilla
Real or candied violets,
   optional

Combine milk and 3 tablespoons sugar and stir until sugar is dissolved.

Beat egg yolks with rotary beater and gradually beat in the hot milk. Flavor with 1 teaspoon vanilla.

Strain or pour into a buttered 2-quart baking dish and bake in a preheated 350° F. oven for 45 minutes, or until a silver knife blade comes out clean.

Remove dish from oven and pour the curaçao over the surface.

Beat egg whites until stiff and gradually beat in the 6 tablespoons sugar, 1 tablespoon at a time. Beat in the ½ teaspoon vanilla. Spread half the meringue over the custard. Decorate with remaining meringue, pressing it through a pastry bag with a fluted tube. Return dessert to oven and bake for 15 minutes, or until meringue is a delicate brown. Garnish with violets if desired. *Serves 8.*

CARAMEL CUSTARD • *Crème Caramel*

2 cups milk
4 eggs
4 tablespoons granulated
sugar

1 teaspoon vanilla
¾ cup brown sugar

In small saucepan heat milk to scalding.
In mixing bowl beat eggs and granulated sugar until sugar is dissolved.
Gradually beat in hot milk.
Add vanilla and set aside.
Sprinkle brown sugar into bottom of a buttered baking dish. Place dish over low heat until sugar is caramelized, watching carefully that it does not burn.
Pour in custard mixture.
Set dish in baking pan containing 1 inch hot water and bake in a preheated 350° F. oven for 40 minutes, or until a silver knife blade comes out clean. Serve hot. *Serves 4.*

APPLE CUSTARD • *Crème aux Pommes*

2 cups milk
4 eggs, separated
4 tablespoons sugar

2 cups applesauce, sweetened
to taste

In saucepan heat milk to scalding.
In top of double saucepan beat egg yolks and sugar until sugar is dissolved.
Gradually whisk in hot milk and cook over simmering water, stirring constantly, until custard coats the spoon.
Chill both custard and applesauce.
Mix applesauce and custard together lightly.
Beat egg whites until stiff and fold into the apple custard.
Chill until ready to serve. *Serves 6.*

PINEAPPLE CUSTARD • *Crème aux Ananas*

1 fresh pineapple
1 cup pineapple juice from
the pineapple

½ cup sugar
3 eggs, separated
Whipped cream

Grate pineapple and strain juice from pulp. It should measure 1 cup.

In small saucepan combine pineapple juice and sugar.

Bring to a boil and simmer for 10 minutes.

In mixing bowl beat syrup gradually into egg yolks.

Return mixture to saucepan and cook over low heat, stirring, until custard coats the spoon. Cool.

Put pineapple pulp into bottom of serving dish.

Beat egg whites until stiff.

Fold beaten egg whites into cooled custard and pour over pineapple.

Serve topped with whipped cream. *Serves 6.*

WHITE WINE AND SHERRY CUSTARD · *Flan au Vin*

1 cup white wine	2 tablespoons heavy cream
2 tablespoons sugar	2 teaspoons sherry
4 egg yolks, lightly beaten	

In small saucepan heat white wine and sugar, but do not boil.

Stir in egg yolks and cook, stirring constantly, over low heat until mixture coats the spoon. Be careful not to let it boil.

Stir in cream and sherry and pour into serving dish.

Serve hot or cold. *Serves 2.*

WHITE WINE CUSTARD · *Flan au Vin*

½ cup sugar	5 egg yolks, beaten
2 cups white wine	Brandied cherries

Add sugar to wine and heat over simmering water until sugar is dissolved.

Stir hot wine gradually into egg yolks.

Strain into individual custard cups or into a 3-cup mold.

Put cups or mold in pan containing 1 inch hot water and bake in a preheated 350° F. oven for 20 to 30 minutes, or until blade of a silver knife comes out clean.

Cool, chill, and serve very cold with brandied cherries on top. *Serves 3.*

RASPBERRY CUSTARD • *Crème aux Framboises*

1 cup milk
2 tablespoons sugar
3 egg yolks, beaten
1 cup raspberries, fresh or
   frozen

Sugar to taste
Sherry
Whipped cream

Scald milk. Cool a little and stir in sugar and egg yolks.
Strain mixture into 4 small soufflé dishes.
Put dishes in a pan containing 1 inch hot water and bake in a
preheated 350° F. oven for about 15 minutes, or until set.
Cool.
Crush raspberries and force through a fine sieve.
Mix raspberry purée with sugar to taste.
Pour 1 teaspoon sherry over custard in each dish, add a layer of
raspberry purée, and serve topped with whipped cream. *Serves 4.*

STRAWBERRY CUSTARD • *Crème aux Fraises*

4 eggs, separated
1 cup hot milk
3 tablespoons sugar

1 teaspoon vanilla
2 cups heavy cream, whipped
2 cups crushed strawberries

Beat egg yolks until light and mix with hot milk and sugar.
Stir over low heat until custard coats the spoon.
Remove from heat and stir in vanilla.
Cool.
Have serving dish, custard, whipped cream, and strawberries all
very cold.
Beat egg whites until stiff and fold into whipped cream.
Fold in custard, then the strawberries.
Turn into serving bowl and serve immediately. *Serves 6.*

LIQUEUR CUSTARD • *Crème au Liqueur*

1 cup hot milk
Pinch salt
2 tablespoons sugar
3 tablespoons Chartreuse,
   Cointreau, curaçao, or
   crème de menthe

4 egg yolks
2 tablespoons heavy cream

Combine hot milk, salt, sugar, and liqueur.

Beat egg yolks and cream lightly.

Pour hot milk gradually over egg yolk mixture, stirring constantly.

Cook over low heat, stirring constantly, until mixture coats the spoon.

Pour or strain into serving dish and serve hot or cold. *Serves 2.*

ZABAGLIONE

> 6 *egg yolks*
> ½ *cup sugar*
> ⅔ *cup Marsala*

Beat egg yolks and gradually beat in sugar and wine.

Put mixture over simmering water and beat with a whisk until custard foams up in pan and begins to thicken. Do not overcook.

Spoon into sherbet glasses and serve warm. *Serves 4.*

VANILLA CREAM IN POTS · *Pots de Crème Vanille*

> 2 *cups heavy cream*   6 *egg yolks*
> 3 *tablespoons sugar*   1 *teaspoon vanilla*

Heat cream and sugar over simmering water.

Beat egg yolks lightly and gradually beat hot cream into them.

Add vanilla and strain into small cream pots.

Put pots in pan containing 1 inch hot water and bake in a preheated 350° F. oven for about 15 minutes, or until silver knife inserted comes out clean. Do not overbake.

Chill before serving. *Serves 6.*

CHOCOLATE CREAM IN POTS · *Pots de Crème au Chocolat*

Substitute 4 ounces (squares) sweet chocolate, melted with 1 tablespoon strong coffee, for the sugar.

COFFEE CREAM IN POTS · *Pots de Crème au Café*

Substitute 1 tablespoon coffee extract for the vanilla.

BURNT CREAM · Crème Brûlée

2 cups heavy cream
6 tablespoons granulated
sugar

6 egg yolks
2 teaspoons vanilla
½ cup light brown sugar

Heat cream over simmering water and stir in granulated sugar.
Beat egg yolks until light in color and gradually stir in hot cream.
Stir in vanilla and pour or strain into a 1-quart baking dish.
Put dish in pan containing 1 inch hot water and bake in a pre-
heated 325° F. oven for 35 minutes, or until silver knife blade comes
out clean. Do not overbake.
Cool, then chill.
Before serving, cover surface of the custard with light brown sugar.
Set dish on a bed of cracked ice and set under the broiler until
sugar is brown and melted. Watch carefully, for sugar burns easily.
Serve immediately, or chill again and serve cold. *Serves 6.*

MOLDED CARAMEL CUSTARD · Crème Renversée au Caramel

1 cup heavy cream
1 cup milk
1 one-inch piece vanilla bean
3 eggs
2 egg yolks

½ cup sugar
1 cup sugar
⅓ cup water
Whipped cream

Heat cream and milk with vanilla bean.
Beat eggs and egg yolks with the ½ cup sugar until well blended.
Discard vanilla bean from hot milk and gradually stir milk into
egg mixture.
Heat the 1 cup sugar in a heavy saucepan until melted.
Gradually add water and boil until syrup turns light brown.
Pour syrup into a 1-quart ring mold and tip mold until inside is
coated.
Let the syrup (caramel) set, then pour in egg mixture.
Set mold in pan containing 1 inch hot water and bake in a pre-
heated 325° F. oven for about 35 minutes, or until silver knife blade
comes out clean.
Cool, then chill.
To serve: Unmold and serve with lightly whipped cream. *Serves 4.*

FRENCH CREAM • *Crème Française*

Make MOLDED CARAMEL CUSTARD in a charlotte mold, coating the mold with the caramel. Chill. Unmold and garnish with rosettes of whipped cream.

PEARS JOINVILLE • *Poires à la Joinville*

Make MOLDED CARAMEL CUSTARD in a ring mold. When cold, unmold on chilled round platter and fill center with sliced pears cooked in VANILLA SYRUP flavored with lemon juice. Cover pears with a pyramid of whipped cream and decorate with whipped cream tinted a delicate pink and pressed out through a large fluted tube. Surround by a ribbon of APRICOT SAUCE flavored with kirsch.

PEARS BORDELAISE • *Poires à la Bordelaise*

Poach fresh pears in red Bordeaux wine flavored with cinnamon. Chill, drain, and sponge dry. Dress pears in a pyramid in center of a ring of MOLDED CARAMEL CUSTARD. Just before serving, mask pears with the cooking syrup bound with a little apple jelly, strained and chilled. Garnish with a border of grapes.

PEARS CECELIA • *Poires à la Cecelia*

Make MOLDED CARAMEL CUSTARD with the caramel in a ring mold. Chill. Unmold on chilled serving platter. Arrange in the center a dome of quartered pears, cooked in VANILLA SYRUP and chilled. Coat pears with the cooking liquid, reduced and colored pink with red currant jelly.

STRAWBERRIES DIVAN • *Fraises Divan*

Marinate large fresh strawberries in kümmel. Arrange them in a pyramid in the center of a ring mold of MOLDED CARAMEL CUSTARD, made without the caramel. Decorate strawberries with whipped cream rosettes and sprinkle with chopped pistachios.

STRAWBERRIES MAGALI · *Fraises Magali*

1 cup grated blanched almonds	Strawberries
1½ cups sweet white wine	Confectioners' sugar
4 egg yolks	Whipped cream, tinted a delicate pink
½ cup granulated sugar	Red currant jelly

Heat almonds and white wine over simmering water.

In saucepan beat egg yolks and granulated sugar until sugar is dissolved.

Gradually whisk in wine and almonds.

Pour into a buttered and sugared 8-inch layer cake pan, set pan in larger pan containing about 1 inch hot water, and bake in a preheated 325° F. oven for about 45 minutes, or until silver knife blade comes out clean.

Cool and chill.

To serve: Unmold custard on chilled platter and arrange a pyramid of strawberries, rolled in confectioners' sugar, in center. Surround strawberries with a crown of pink whipped-cream rosettes. Keep cold until serving time and, just before serving, surround with a ribbon of red currant jelly, heated and thinned to sauce consistency with a little sweet white wine or water. *Serves 4.*

PEARS ALMINA · *Poires Almina*

3 fresh pears	1 cup milk
VANILLA SYRUP	Grated rind of ½ orange
3 egg yolks	Thin julienne rind of ½ orange
½ cup sugar	
1 teaspoon flour	1 cup heavy cream, whipped

Peel and halve pears. Poach in vanilla syrup and chill.

In saucepan combine egg yolks, sugar, flour, milk, and grated rind. Cook over low heat, stirring constantly, until custard coats the spoon. Do not let custard boil.

Chill.

Simmer julienne rind in water to cover for 5 minutes and drain. Fold julienne rind and half the whipped cream into the custard.

Arrange pears side by side on serving platter, hollow side up.

Pour custard over pears and garnish with remaining whipped cream in center of each pear. *Serves 6.*

BEAU RIVAGE CREAM • *Crème Beau Rivage*

1½ cups sugar	Pinch salt
½ cup water	2 cups hot milk
¼ teaspoon cream of tartar	Whipped cream
2 eggs	12 CORNETS filled with
4 egg yolks	whipped cream
1 teaspoon vanilla	

In a small saucepan combine sugar, water, and cream of tartar.
Bring to a boil and boil rapidly until syrup just begins to turn amber in color.
Remove from heat to cool a little.
Beat eggs and yolks until light.
Gradually beat in 1 cup of the amber syrup.
Stir in vanilla, salt, and hot milk.
Pour mixture into buttered and sugared 1-quart ring mold, place mold in pan containing about 1 inch hot water, and bake in a preheated 350° F. oven for 35 to 40 minutes, or until cream is set.
Cool and chill.
When ready to serve, unmold onto serving plate.
Fill center with whipped cream and arrange the cornets filled with whipped cream around edge of platter. *Serves 6.*

SNOW EGGS • *Oeufs à la Neige*

2 cups milk	4 egg whites
½ cup heavy cream	4 tablespoons fine granulated
2 tablespoons granulated	sugar
sugar	4 egg yolks, lightly beaten
1 one-inch piece vanilla bean	

In large saucepan combine milk, cream, the 2 tablespoons granulated sugar, and vanilla bean and bring to a simmer.
Beat egg whites until stiff and gradually beat in the fine granulated sugar to make a smooth meringue.
Drop meringue by spoonfuls into the simmering milk, turning each mound over two or three times as it poaches. Poach for about 3 minutes and remove meringues to a towel to drain.

Beat egg yolks and gradually pour hot milk mixture over them, stirring vigorously. Stir over low heat until custard thickens and coats the spoon.

Pour custard into serving dishes and chill.

When ready to serve, decorate custard with the meringue "eggs." *Serves 4.*

LEMON SNOW EGGS · *Oeufs à la Neige au Citron*

Omit vanilla bean. Add the grated rind of ½ lemon to the egg whites. Flavor custard with 1 tablespoon lemon juice.

SNOW EGGS WITH CHOCOLATE CUSTARD · *Oeufs à la Religieuse*

Prepare SNOW EGGS as in recipe above, adding along with the granulated sugar ½ cup PRALINE POWDER. To the hot milk mixture add 2 ounces (2 squares) bittersweet chocolate and stir until melted. Make custard using the chocolate milk. Cool and chill.

To serve: Put eggs in center of a serving plate and pour chilled custard over them. Sprinkle with toasted slivered almonds.

FLOATING ISLAND · *Ile Flottante Praline*

4 *egg whites*	ENGLISH CUSTARD
⅔ *cup sugar*	*Chopped pistachios or*
1 *teaspoon vanilla*	*almonds*
½ *cup* PRALINE POWDER	

Beat egg whites until stiff and gradually beat in sugar, 1 tablespoon at a time.

Fold in vanilla and praline powder.

Turn meringue into a buttered and sugared 2-quart mold. Place mold in a deep pan containing 2 inches hot water. Cover and bake in a preheated 350° F. oven for about 20 minutes, or until firm. Cool.

When ready to serve, unmold meringue into center of a deep serving dish, surround it with the English custard, and sprinkle the "island" with finely chopped pistachio nuts or almonds. *Serves 6.*

SCOTTISH TRIFLE

½ plain layer cake (or equivalent in slices of sponge cake)
¼ cup peach preserves
1 can (8 ounces) pears
⅓ cup sherry
2 medium bananas, peeled and sliced

1½ cups ENGLISH CUSTARD
1½ cups heavy cream, whipped
¼ cup slivered toasted almonds
Candied cherries

Split cake in half and sandwich together with peach preserves between.

Cut cake into squares and arrange in large shallow serving dish.

Drain pears; reserve ¼ cup syrup.

Combine the ¼ cup syrup and the sherry and pour over cake.

Arrange pears and bananas on cake.

Pour over the custard.

Pipe large rosettes of cream all over surface and garnish with almonds and cherries.

Chill until ready to serve. *Serves 8.*

APRICOTS REGENCE · *Abricots à la Régence*

2½ cups milk
1½ teaspoons vanilla
1 3½-ounce package ladyfingers (12 ladyfingers)
4 eggs
¼ cup sugar

6 fresh apricots (or 1-pound, 14-ounce can apricot halves)
¼ cup apricot preserves
¼ cup cherry preserves

Scald milk. Add vanilla and pour over ladyfingers. Let stand 5 minutes.

Press ladyfingers and milk through sieve or blend in blender until smooth.

Beat eggs lightly with sugar and add to milk mixture. Mix well.

Pour into buttered and sugared 8-inch layer cake pan. Place in larger pan containing 1 inch water.

Bake in a preheated 325° F. oven for 45 minutes, or until custard is set.

Let stand 5 minutes, then run knife blade around edge and unmold onto serving plate.

Meanwhile, if fresh apricots are used cut in half and remove pits. Poach in a light syrup of sugar and water. Drain and reserve syrup.

Boil syrup (either fresh or canned) until it is reduced to ¾ cup and stir in apricot preserves. Arrange apricot halves hollow side up around the cream and fill centers with cherry preserves. Serve with apricot syrup. *Serves 6.*

The two following creams are frequently used as cake and tart fillings:

FRANGIPANE CREAM · *Crème Frangipane*

4 tablespoons sugar	½ cup hot cream
2 tablespoons flour	1 teaspoon vanilla
3 egg yolks	2 tablespoons sweet butter
1 egg	1 tablespoon ALMOND PASTE
Pinch salt	1 tablespoon crushed
½ cup hot milk	macaroons

In top of double saucepan combine sugar, flour, egg yolks, and egg.

Add salt. Stir in hot milk and cream, and cook over simmering water, stirring constantly, until cream is smooth and thick.

Remove cream from heat and stir in vanilla, butter, almond paste, and crushed macaroons.

Pour into serving dish and serve hot. *Serves 3.*

BOURDALOUE CREAM · *Crème Bourdaloue*

⅓ pound almonds	2 egg yolks
1½ cups water	3 tablespoons rice flour
¾ cup sugar	2 tablespoons butter
1 egg	1 tablespoon kirsch

Make almond milk as follows:

Blanch almonds and dry in a slow oven (300° F.) for 30 minutes. Put them through a food chopper, adding the water gradually. Grind water and ground nuts in a mortar until liquid becomes milky and almond-flavored, and strain liquid through a sieve lined with cheesecloth. Or blend water and nuts on high speed in an electric blender and strain.

In saucepan combine sugar, egg, egg yolks, and rice flour.

Scald the almond milk and very gradually stir into egg mixture.

Cook over low heat, stirring constantly, until thickened and smooth. Do not let it boil.

Remove from heat and stir in butter and kirsch. *Serves 3.*

CHAPTER 3

Gelatin Desserts

F<small>RANCE</small>, the country that has given more finesse and subtleties to the art of cooking than any other country in the world, adopted the English "boiled" custard and gave England her just recognition by calling it *crème à l'Anglaise*, or English cream. But expert cooks, knowing the danger of cooking a custard over direct heat, soon changed the name to *crème au bain-marie*, cream cooked over steaming water, thereby emphasizing the fact that a mixture containing eggs must be cooked over hot water, and never boiled.

Then came the great Carême, who devised the scheme of adding a small amount of gelatin to the egg mixture, converting the English custard, the *crème à l'Anglaise*, to *crème Française*. Soon followed a succession of *crème vanille*, *crème au chocolat*, *crème praline*, and so on, according to the flavor added to *crème Française*.

The discovery of gelatin opened a whole new world of desserts —sparkling clear jellies made of sweetened fruit juice and gelatin, sponges and chiffons, clear or creamy mixtures into which are folded stiffly beaten egg whites, and Spanish or Bavarian creams, made rich and luscious by the addition of whipped cream.

Gelatin desserts, for the most part, are simple to make. The right amount of gelatin must be added to make the dessert keep its shape, but never to make it stiff and hard. It's not so long since gelatin could be purchased in bulk and was measured by the tablespoon, but now it comes in little packets, each equivalent in jellying strength to one tablespoon, and the average amount needed to make a quart of liquid into jelly is the contents of two envelopes.

Gelatin should be softened in a little cold water, then thoroughly dissolved to a clear, smooth liquid over simmering water. It can be added directly to a quantity of cold liquid or sauce that is about to be cooked over moderate heat, since the length of time it takes to heat the mixture gives the gelatin a chance to soften and swell before it melts into the hot liquid. Either way that gelatin is used, it must be thoroughly and evenly incorporated into the other ingredients or the finished jelly or cream will be lumpy.

Gelatin desserts are most attractive when allowed to set in a decorative mold. A ring mold is particularly pleasant with the center filled with fruit or berries, whipped cream or ice cream, or when served with a fruit or custard sauce.

To prepare a mold, dip it in cold water and shake to remove loose drops, or rub it lightly with salad oil.

To unmold a gelatin dessert, run a thin knife around the edge of the mold to loosen it. Dip the mold slowly in and out of water that is very hot to the hand, but not uncomfortable, three times. The water should come almost to the top, but not over the top of the mold. Place a chilled serving plate on top of the mold and invert both plate and mold. If the dessert still does not come out, tip the mold a little to one side so that the weight of the dessert will pull it away from the side.

A gelatin dessert should be so delicate that it cannot be moved after it is unmolded without breaking, so be sure to turn it out into the exact center of the serving dish.

English custard to which a little gelatin is added is the basis of the delicious Bavarian creams.

ENGLISH CUSTARD WITH GELATIN · Crème à l'Anglaise Collée

1 envelope gelatin	½ cup sugar
2 tablespoons cold water	1 cup hot milk
4 egg yolks	1 one-inch piece vanilla bean

Soften gelatin in cold water.

Combine egg yolks and sugar in a saucepan and work with a wooden spoon until smooth and creamy.

Gradually add hot milk, stirring rapidly.

Add vanilla bean and cook over simmering water, stirring constantly, until cream is thick and smooth.

Discard vanilla bean.

Add softened gelatin and stir until gelatin is thoroughly dissolved.

Cool the cream, stirring from time to time to prevent a crust from forming. *Serves 2.*

VANILLA BAVARIAN CREAM • *Crème Bavaroise à la Vanille*

Make ENGLISH CUSTARD WITH GELATIN and, when cold, fold in 1 cup heavy cream, whipped. *Serves 4.*

COFFEE BAVARIAN CREAM • *Crème Bavaroise au Café*

Make ENGLISH CUSTARD WITH GELATIN omitting vanilla bean. Add 1½ tablespoons coffee extract with the gelatin and, when cream is cold, fold in 1 cup heavy cream, whipped. *Serves 4.*

CHOCOLATE BAVARIAN CREAM • *Crème Bavaroise au Chocolat*

Make ENGLISH CUSTARD WITH GELATIN. Add 2 ounces (squares) bitter chocolate, melted, with the gelatin and, when cream is cold, fold in 1 cup heavy cream, whipped. *Serves 4.*

PEACH BAVARIAN CREAM • *Crème Bavaroise aux Pêches*

Make ENGLISH CUSTARD WITH GELATIN and, when cool, fold in 1 cup peach purée along with 1 cup heavy cream, whipped. *Serves 6.*

PRALINE BAVARIAN CREAM • *Crème Bavaroise Praline*

Make ENGLISH CUSTARD WITH GELATIN and, when cool, fold in 1 cup heavy cream, whipped, and ½ cup PRALINE POWDER. *Serves 4.*

PISTACHIO BAVARIAN CREAM · *Crème Bavaroise aux Pistaches*

Make ENGLISH CUSTARD WITH GELATIN, adding a few drops green food coloring. When cool fold in ½ cup finely ground pistachio nuts and 1 cup heavy cream, whipped. *Serves 4.*

LIQUEUR BAVARIAN CREAM · *Crème Bavaroise au Liqueur*

Make ENGLISH CUSTARD WITH GELATIN, omitting vanilla bean. When cream is cool, fold in 1 cup heavy cream, whipped, and ¼ cup of any favorite spirit or liqueur such as chartreuse, Cointreau, crème de menthe, maraschino, cognac, Benedictine, kirsch, curaçao, mirabelle, eau-de-vie de framboise, or apricot, cherry, or peach brandy. *Serves 4.*

ALMOND BAVARIAN CREAM · *Crème Bavaroise aux Amandes*

1 envelope gelatin	4 egg yolks, beaten
½ cup water	1 teaspoon vanilla
1 cup ALMOND PASTE	2 cups heavy cream, whipped
2 cups milk	

Soften gelatin in water.

Heat almond paste and milk over low heat, stirring until smooth.

Pour almond milk over egg yolks and cook over simmering water, stirring constantly, until cream is hot and slightly thickened.

Stir in gelatin.

Add vanilla.

Place saucepan in bowl of cracked ice and stir until cool and beginning to set.

Fold in whipped cream.

Pour into serving dish and chill. *Serves 6.*

STRAWBERRY BAVARIAN CREAM · *Crème Bavaroise aux Fraises*

4 cups strawberries, washed and hulled	2 envelopes gelatin
1 tablespoon lemon juice	¼ cup water
¾ cup sugar	2 cups heavy cream, whipped

Mash berries and press through fine sieve to make purée.

Add lemon juice and sugar to the strawberry purée and stir until sugar is completely dissolved.

Soften gelatin in water, then stir over hot water until dissolved.

Fold dissolved gelatin into strawberry purée.

Stir purée over cracked ice until mixture begins to thicken.

Fold in whipped cream.

Pour into serving dish and chill. *Serves 6.*

RUM BAVARIAN CREAM · *Crème Bavaroise au Rhum*

1 envelope gelatin	4 egg yolks, beaten
¼ cup water	⅛ cup dark rum
2 cups hot milk	1 cup heavy cream, whipped
¾ cup sugar	

Soften gelatin in water for 5 minutes.

Stir in hot milk and sugar and stir over low heat until mixture is very hot but not boiling.

Pour hot mixture slowly over egg yolks, stirring vigorously.

Add rum.

Stir over cracked ice until mixture begins to thicken.

Fold in whipped cream.

Pour into serving dish and chill. *Serves 6.*

NOTE: If you wish to mold this dessert, increase gelatin to 2 envelopes.

CHOCOLATE BAVARIAN MOUSSE · *Mousse Bavaroise au Chocolat*

3 ounces semi-sweet chocolate	1 cup hot milk
2 tablespoons strong coffee	1 cup heavy cream, whipped
1 envelope gelatin	2 egg whites, stiffly beaten
¼ cup water	Additional whipped cream,
3 egg yolks	optional
¼ cup sugar	

Combine chocolate and coffee and stir over low heat until smooth.

Soften gelatin in water for 5 minutes.

Beat together egg yolks and sugar and gradually stir in hot milk.

Cook over simmering water, stirring constantly, until custard begins to thicken.

Add gelatin and stir until thoroughly dissolved.

Add melted chocolate.

Stir over cracked ice until mixture begins to thicken.

Fold in whipped cream and egg whites.

Pour into serving dish and chill.

Serve with additional whipped cream if desired. *Serves 4.*

RUM BAVARIAN MOUSSE • *Mousse Bavaroise au Rhum*

1 envelope gelatin	3 egg whites, stiffly beaten
¼ cup water	½ cup heavy cream, whipped
1½ cups hot milk	1 tablespoon dark rum
5 egg yolks	Ladyfingers
4 tablespoons sugar	Chopped nuts or fresh fruit

Soften gelatin in water for 5 minutes, add to hot milk, and stir until dissolved.

In saucepan beat egg yolks and sugar until thick and pale in color.

Gradually stir in hot milk.

Cook over low heat, stirring constantly, until thickened. Do not let it boil.

Stir over cracked ice until mixture begins to set.

Fold in egg whites and whipped cream.

Stir in rum and pour into serving dish.

Serve with ladyfingers and decorate with chopped nuts or fresh fruit. *Serves 4.*

SAVOY TRIFLE

Make a JELLY ROLL. When jelly roll is cool, cut it into thin slices. Line bottom and sides of a glass dish with the slices and sprinkle with a little sherry or rum. Fill bowl with RUM BAVARIAN MOUSSE. Decorate top with more slices of jelly roll and garnish with large rosettes of whipped cream.

STRAWBERRIES MARGOT • *Fraises Margot*

Make STRAWBERRY BAVARIAN CREAM using half the amount of gelatin. Pour into a crystal coupe dish and chill until set. When set, arrange on top some large strawberries and between each strawberry press out a rosette of whipped cream. Sprinkle with chopped pistachio nuts.

PEARS CARMEN • *Poires à la Carmen*

Peel and halve 6 large pears. Poach pears in VANILLA SYRUP until just tender. Drain and chill. Make STRAWBERRY BAVARIAN CREAM, using half the gelatin. Pour into a crystal coupe dish and chill. When set, arrange pears on top and cover with ENGLISH CUSTARD. Sprinkle with chopped pistachio nuts.

MOLD OF CHESTNUT CREAM • *Sultane de Marrons à la Chantilly*

Make ENGLISH CUSTARD WITH GELATIN flavored with vanilla. When cold, fold in 1 cup CHESTNUT PUREE. Pour into a small 3-cup mold and chill. When set, unmold and fill center with a pyramid of whipped cream flavored with vanilla. Garnish with preserved chestnuts.

MOLDED BAVARIAN CREAMS

Any of the Bavarian creams may be molded: Rinse a mold in ice water, pour in cream, and chill for about 2 hours, or until set. When ready to serve, unmold on large serving platter and garnish with cherries, glacéed chestnuts, or sliced fruits.

TRI-COLORED BAVARIAN CREAM • *Bavaroise Rubané*

2 *cups* VANILLA BAVARIAN CREAM	2 *cups* STRAWBERRY BAVARIAN CREAM
2 *cups* CHOCOLATE BAVARIAN CREAM	*Whipped cream*
	Fresh strawberries

Rinse a 1½-quart timbale mold in ice water.

Pour vanilla Bavarian cream into mold and chill for 30 minutes, or until cream is set.

Add chocolate Bavarian cream and let this set.

Add strawberry Bavarian cream and chill for at least 2 hours.

When ready to serve, unmold on cold serving plate, decorate top and sides with whipped cream pressed through a fluted pastry tube, and garnish with a circle of whole fresh strawberries. *Serves 6.*

MARQUISE ALICE

Mold CHOCOLATE or STRAWBERRY BAVARIAN CREAM in an 8-inch layer cake pan 2 inches deep. On top arrange a layer of ladyfingers moistened with kirsch. Chill. When set, unmold on round serving plate and cover with whipped cream flavored with vanilla and sweetened to taste. Surround by a ribbon of red currant jelly melted with a little hot water to sauce consistency and flavored with kirsch.

STRAWBERRIES FEMINA • *Fraises à la Femina*

Mold a PEACH BAVARIAN CREAM in a ring mold. Chill. When set unmold on chilled serving plate. Fill center with strawberries marinated with sugar and kirsch and well chilled. Coat strawberries with a purée of strawberries sweetened and bound with red currant jelly to make a sauce consistency. Chill until serving time.

BAVARIAN SURPRISE • *Bavaroise Fontages*

Make 2 different Bavarian creams of contrasting colors that complement each other in flavor. Select a large mold, such as a timbale mold, that allows you to set a second smaller mold inside. Set the large mold in ice and in it pour one of the Bavarian creams. Fill the smaller mold with ice and water and press it into the cream in such a way as to force the cream up the sides of the large mold to make a coating about 1 inch thick. When this cream is set, fill small mold with a little warm water, and it can be removed easily, leaving a hole in the center. Fill the hole with the second Bavarian cream and chill until set.

NESSELRODE PUDDING • *Pouding Nesselrode*

Make VANILLA BAVARIAN CREAM. Fold in 1 cup CHESTNUT PURÉE and ½ cup chopped preserved chestnuts. Mold and chill. When ready to serve, unmold and garnish with rosettes of whipped cream.

DIPLOMAT PUDDING • *Pouding Diplomate*

Pour a layer of VANILLA BAVARIAN CREAM in bottom of a timbale mold and chill until set. Cover with a layer of ladyfingers soaked in kirsch. Sprinkle with preserved chopped fruits. Cover with more cream, another layer of ladyfingers and fruit, and finally fill mold with remaining cream. Chill. When ready to serve unmold and serve with either an APRICOT SAUCE flavored with kirsch or a RED CURRANT SAUCE flavored with Cointreau.

QUEENLY EGGS • *Oeufs à la Reine*

Prepare SNOW EGGS and chill. Make ENGLISH CUSTARD WITH GELATIN and cool until beginning to set. Line bottom of a timbale mold with the cream and chill until set. Then arrange the SNOW EGGS in the mold in layers alternately with the cream. Chill. Unmold on cold serving plate and serve with RED CURRANT or RASPBERRY SAUCE.

CHARLOTTE RUSSE

Line a buttered charlotte or timbale mold with ladyfingers: Place a small round of a ladyfinger in center of bottom of mold and cover bottom closely with triangles of ladyfingers radiating from center. Place uncut ladyfingers upright and close together all around inside wall. Fill mold with VANILLA BAVARIAN CREAM and chill for at least 2 hours. When ready to serve, unmold on chilled serving platter. *Serves 6.*

CHARLOTTE MONTREUIL

Line a charlotte mold with ladyfingers. Fill with PEACH BAVARIAN CREAM into which is folded 1 cup ripe peaches, chopped and sweetened to taste.

CHARLOTTE NESSELRODE

Line charlotte mold with rectangles of GENOISE or ladyfingers. Fill with VANILLA BAVARIAN CREAM into which is folded chopped preserved chestnuts and seeded Malaga raisins and currants, washed and plumped in syrup flavored with maraschino.

CHARLOTTE OPERA

Line charlotte mold with ladyfingers and fill with VANILLA BAVARIAN CREAM into which is folded ½ cup sweet CHESTNUT PUREE and ½ cup preserved fruits, chopped and marinated in maraschino.

RASPBERRY CREAM • *Crème aux Framboises*

2 envelopes gelatin	2 packages (10 ounces each)
½ cup water	raspberries, defrosted
2 tablespoons sugar	1 cup heavy cream
1 tablespoon lemon juice	Whipped cream, optional

Soften gelatin in water, then stir over hot water until gelatin is dissolved.

Stir in sugar and lemon juice.

Press raspberries through a fine sieve and stir the resulting purée into the gelatin mixture. Chill until purée begins to thicken.

Whip the cream and fold into the purée.

Turn into a 1-quart ring mold and chill until set.

Unmold and, if desired, decorate with rosettes of whipped cream. *Serves 6.*

GENOISE CREAM • *Crème de Génoise*

4 macaroons	4 egg yolks
¼ cup brandy	2 tablespoons chopped
1 cup rich milk	candied fruits
¼ cup sugar	½ cup heavy cream, whipped
Finely cut orange rind of ½	Crushed, sweetened straw-
small orange	berries flavored with brandy
1 envelope gelatin	or kirsch
¼ cup water	

Crush macaroons and soak in the brandy.

In saucepan combine milk, sugar, and orange rind. Bring to a boil and simmer for 10 minutes.

Add gelatin, soaked in water, and stir until gelatin is completely dissolved.

Beat egg yolks lightly and gradually stir in hot milk mixture.

Cook over low heat for 3 minutes, stirring constantly.

Pour or strain custard over the macaroons and brandy.

Add chopped candied fruit and mix well. Cool.

When custard is cool, fold in whipped cream.

Turn into a 3-cup melon mold, rinsed in cold water, and chill until firm.

Unmold on chilled serving platter and surround with strawberries. *Serves 6.*

SPANISH CREAM

4 egg yolks
½ cup sugar
2 cups hot milk
1 envelope gelatin
¼ cup water

4 egg whites, stiffly beaten
½ teaspoon vanilla
Whipped cream or fresh or
  cooked fruit or berries

Beat egg yolks until light, add sugar, and beat until thick and pale.

Stir in hot milk and cook over low heat, stirring constantly, until cream is thick enough to coat a spoon.

Remove from heat and stir in gelatin, soaked in the water.

Stir over cracked ice until cool and thick. Fold in egg whites and vanilla.

Turn cream into a decorative quart mold and chill for 2 hours, or until set.

Unmold onto serving plate and serve with whipped cream or fresh or cooked fruit or berries. *Serves 6.*

BLANCMANGE · Le Blanc-Manger

2 cups ALMOND MILK
2 envelopes gelatin
¼ cup water
1 cup cream
½ cup sugar

1 drop almond extract
2 tablespoons kirsch
Fresh or cooked berries or
  sliced fruit, optional

Soften gelatin in water for 5 minutes.

Add the 2 cups almond milk, the cream, and sugar.

Bring mixture almost to a boil but do not boil, stirring constantly to thoroughly dissolve gelatin.

Cool and stir in almond extract and kirsch.

Pour into oiled quart ring mold and chill until blancmange is firm.

When ready to serve, loosen edges and unmold onto chilled serving plate. If desired fill center of mold and garnish with fresh or cooked berries or sliced fruit. *Serves 6.*

MOSCOVITE OF FRUITS • *Moscovite aux Fruits*

1 *cup fruit purée*	¼ *cup water*
1 *cup* SUGAR SYRUP	1 *cup heavy cream, whipped*
Juice of 1 lemon	*Fruit or berries*
2 *envelopes gelatin*	

Combine fruit purée, sugar syrup, and lemon juice.

Heat without boiling.

Stir in gelatin softened in water.

Cool and chill briefly until mixture begins to set.

Fold in whipped cream.

Pour into 1-quart ring mold and chill until set.

Unmold and fill center with the same fruits used in the purée, such as fresh strawberries, raspberries, blueberries, peaches, apricots, or poached pears or apples. If desired, the raw fruit may be mixed into the gelatin mixture along with the cream and molded in a cake pan or timbale mold. *Serves 4.*

CHERRIES VICTORIA • *Cerises Victoria*

½ *pound red currants*	1 *cup heavy cream, whipped*
⅔ *cup sugar*	1 *pound sweet cherries, pitted*
1 *envelope gelatin*	½ *cup red wine, sweetened to*
2 *tablespoons water*	*taste*

Press juice from red currants. Add sugar to juice and heat.

Stir in gelatin softened in water.

Cool, then chill briefly until jelly begins to set.

Fold in three-quarters of the whipped cream and fill 6 small china or ceramic cups about ¾ full of the red currant cream. Chill.

Poach cherries in sweetened red wine until tender. Drain and chill.

Cover the cream with the cherries and mask with remaining whipped cream. *Serves 6.*

The cold soufflé is really a mousse molded in a soufflé dish. The dish is collared with waxed paper to let the mousse mixture rise above the edge of the dish like a soufflé hot from the oven.

COLD CHOCOLATE SOUFFLE • *Soufflé au Chocolat Froid*

4 *eggs*	2 *envelopes gelatin*
3 *egg yolks*	¼ *cup water*
¼ *cup sugar*	1 *cup heavy cream, whipped*
3 *squares (ounces) sweet*	*Additional whipped cream,*
chocolate	*optional*
2 *tablespoons cold coffee*	

Beat eggs, egg yolks, and sugar with an electric beater until very thick and pale in color. If no electric beater is at hand, beat vigorously over hot water with a rotary beater.

Melt chocolate with the coffee over simmering water and cool, stirring occasionally.

Stir chocolate into egg mixture.

Soften gelatin in the cold water, then stir over simmering water until gelatin is thoroughly dissolved. Stir dissolved gelatin into egg mixture.

Fold in whipped cream.

Tie a double strip of waxed paper around the outside of a buttered 1-quart soufflé dish, letting the paper rise about 2 inches above edge of dish. Pour mousse mixture into the dish and chill until set.

When ready to serve, remove the paper band and, if desired, decorate with whipped cream rosettes. *Serves 6.*

COLD FRUIT SOUFFLE • *Soufflé aux Fruits Froid*

Follow directions for making the COLD CHOCOLATE SOUFFLE, but omit the chocolate-coffee mixture. Substitute 1 cup fresh fruit purée, such as strawberry, raspberry, peach, or apricot.

LEMON OR ORANGE COLD SOUFFLE • *Soufflé au Citron ou à l'Orange*

Follow directions for making the COLD CHOCOLATE SOUFFLÉ, but omit the chocolate. Substitute the grated rind of 1 large lemon or orange for the chocolate-coffee mixture. Soften and dissolve the gelatin in the juice of the lemon or orange.

COLD PRALINE SOUFFLE (Blender Method) • *Soufflé Praline Froid*

1 envelope plain gelatin	1 cup PRALINE POWDER
⅓ cup boiling water	1½ cups heavy cream,
1 tablespoon dark rum	whipped
2 eggs, separated	¼ cup chopped toasted
½ cup milk	almonds

Tie a double strip of waxed paper around the outside of a buttered 1-quart soufflé dish, letting the paper rise about 2 inches above edge of dish.

Into container of an electric blender put gelatin and boiling water.

Cover and blend on high speed for 40 seconds.

Add rum, egg yolks, milk, and praline powder.

Cover and blend for 10 seconds longer.

Chill for a few minutes until mixture begins to thicken.

Reserve one-third of the whipped cream for garnish.

Beat egg whites until stiff but not dry.

Fold gelatin mixture into egg whites and whipped cream.

Pour into prepared soufflé dish and chill until set.

To serve: Remove waxed paper band and press the toasted almonds into sides of soufflé where it rises above edge of dish. Decorate top with small rosettes of the reserved whipped cream. *Serves 6.*

COLD SOUFFLE MILANAISE • *Soufflé Froid Milanaise*

2 envelopes plain gelatin	1½ tablespoons grated lemon
½ cup water	rind
2 eggs, separated	1½ cups heavy cream
½ cup sugar	Whipped cream, optional
½ cup lemon juice	

Tie a double band of waxed paper around the outside of a buttered 1-quart soufflé dish, letting paper rise about 2 inches above edge of dish.

Soften gelatin in water, then stir over simmering water until gelatin is dissolved. Cool.

Beat egg yolks and sugar until mixture is thick and pale in color.

Stir in gelatin, lemon juice, and lemon rind and chill until mixture begins to thicken.

Beat egg whites until stiff but not dry.

Whip the cream.

Fold egg whites and cream into the lemon mixture with a few drops yellow food coloring if desired.

Spoon into soufflé dish and chill until set.

When ready to serve, remove paper band and, if desired, decorate with whipped cream rosettes. *Serves 6.*

CHOCOLATE SPONGE

1 envelope plain gelatin	½ cup sugar
¼ cup cold water	1 teaspoon vanilla
¾ cup boiling water or coffee	3 egg whites, stiffly beaten
3 squares (ounces) unsweet-	Cream, slightly whipped
ened chocolate	

Soften gelatin in the cold water, add boiling liquid, and stir until gelatin is dissolved.

Melt chocolate over simmering water.

Remove chocolate from heat and gradually stir in sugar, dissolved gelatin, and vanilla. Cool, then chill until it begins to set.

Beat the chocolate mixture with a rotary beater for 3 to 4 minutes.

Fold in beaten egg whites.

Put into a 1-quart mold and return to refrigerator until set.

Turn out onto a dessert plate and serve with slightly whipped cream. *Serves 6.*

ORANGE SPONGE

1 envelope plain gelatin	½ cup water
¼ cup sugar	1 tablespoon lemon juice
Rind and juice of 2 medium	2 egg whites, stiffly beaten
oranges	

In a small saucepan combine gelatin, sugar, thin orange rind from the oranges, and the water.

Let soak for 5 minutes, then stir over low heat until gelatin and sugar are dissolved.

Add orange juice. Cool and strain.

Add lemon juice and chill until mixture begins to thicken.

Fold in beaten egg whites.

Spoon into serving dish and chill until set. *Serves 6.*

LEMON SPONGE

1 envelope plain gelatin	1 tablespoon grated lemon
¼ cup cold water	rind
3 eggs, separated	¼ cup lemon juice
¾ cup sugar	Pinch salt

Soften gelatin in the cold water, then stir over hot water until gelatin is dissolved.

Beat egg yolks and sugar until mixture is thick and pale in color.

Stir in gelatin, lemon rind, and lemon juice.

Beat egg whites with salt until stiff, but not dry, and fold into the yolk mixture.

Spoon into serving dish and chill until set. *Serves 6.*

APRICOT JELLY

2 one-pound cans apricot	4 envelopes plain gelatin
halves	1 cup cold water
Juice of 4 oranges	2 cups boiling water
Juice of 2 lemons	Cream, optional
1 cup sugar	

Drain the apricots, saving the juice.

Press apricots through a fine sieve or purée in electric blender.

Combine apricot juice, orange juice, lemon juice, and sugar.

Soften the gelatin in the cold water. Add boiling water and stir until gelatin is dissolved.

Add sweetened fruit juice.

Stir in apricot purée and mix well.

Pour into a 2-quart mold and chill until set.

When ready to serve unmold, and, if desired, serve with cream. *Serves 8.*

STRAWBERRY-COATED ALMOND CREAM

For this dessert you must have a 1-quart mold and a 2-quart mold of the same shape so that one will fit inside the other, leaving a space of about 1 inch between.

STRAWBERRY JELLY

2 quarts fresh strawberries	3 envelopes gelatin
2 cups water	1 cup cold water
1 cup sugar	

Wash and hull the fresh strawberries. Mash well and add the 2 cups water and sugar. Bring to a boil and simmer for 1 minute. Skim and strain through a fine sieve. Soften the gelatin in the cold water, then stir into the hot strawberry juice. Cool, then chill until the jelly begins to set. Pour 2 cups of the jelly into the bottom of the 2-quart mold and chill until set. When firm, place the second mold into the large mold and fill with ice. Pour remaining strawberry jelly into the space between the molds and chill until very firm.

ALMOND CREAM

1 envelope plain gelatin	4 egg yolks, well beaten
¼ cup water	Pinch salt
½ cup ALMOND PASTE	1 teaspoon vanilla
1 cup milk	2 cups heavy cream

Soften gelatin in the water.

Combine almond paste and milk and heat to simmering, stirring until almond paste is melted and mixture is smooth.

Pour the almond milk gradually into egg yolks, beating briskly.

Cook, stirring, over low heat until custard thickens slightly.

Stir in gelatin and vanilla and cool.

When mixture begins to set, whip the cream until stiff and fold it in.

Put a little warm water into the small mold to loosen it.

Remove small mold from the strawberry jelly and fill space in the middle with the almond cream. Chill until thoroughly set.

When ready to serve, unmold and garnish with fresh strawberries. *Serves 12.*

CHAPTER 4

Cornstarch, Rice, Farina, and Other Creamy Desserts

W<small>HEN</small> the quantity of eggs needed to thicken a cup of liquid is reduced or completely omitted from a dessert, some other ingredient must be added to make the mixture creamy. Cornstarch and rice are the two most usual ingredients used, and both make a variety of delicious, nourishing desserts, which are included in this chapter.

In using cornstarch, care must be taken not to add too much to make the dessert too stiff, and the mixture must be cooked until any raw taste of starch disappears.

Rice provides a great number of delicious desserts, from the simple bowl of rice pudding, sprinkled with brown sugar and brimming with heavy cream, to the equally delicious but more masterful *Riz à l'Impératrice*, a cream of rice, bejeweled with bits of finely chopped candied fruits and flavored with kirsch. The basic cream of rice used in this dessert is the progenitor of many other fruit and rice combinations, all of which contribute to "the most sweet end" of a meal.

This dessert is the American version of the French *Blanc-Manger*.

AMERICAN WHITE PUDDING · *Pouding à l'Américaine*

2 cups milk	½ cup cold milk
1 cup cream	1 teaspoon vanilla
½ cup sugar	Fruit or fruit purée
6 tablespoons cornstarch	

In saucepan combine the 2 cups milk, cream, and sugar and bring to a boil.

Mix cornstarch and the ½ cup cold milk and stir into the hot milk. Cook, stirring, until mixture is thick. Remove from heat and stir in vanilla.

Pour into a 4-cup ring mold or into individual custard cups and chill until set.

Unmold and serve with fresh or poached fruit or with strawberry or raspberry purée. *Serves 6.*

GERMAN FRUIT PORRIDGE · *Rothe Grütze*

3 tablespoons cornstarch	Sugar to taste
2 cups mixed fruit juice such	Pinch salt
as red currant and raspberry	Cream

Mix cornstarch with ¼ cup of the fruit juice.
Bring remaining juice to a boil and sweeten to taste.
Add salt and stir in cornstarch.
Cook, stirring, until juice is clear and thickened.
Pour into a serving bowl and chill.
Serve with cream. *Serves 4.*

SEMOLINA PUDDING · *Flamri de Semoule*

2 cups milk	1 whole egg, beaten
1 one-inch piece vanilla bean	3 egg whites, stiffly beaten
½ cup sugar	RED CURRANT SAUCE, *flavored*
½ cup semolina (or wheat	*with kirsch*
farina)	

Heat milk with vanilla bean and sugar.
Stir in semolina and cook, stirring, until mixture is thick.
Remove from heat and discard vanilla bean.

Add egg and stir rapidly until well blended.

Fold in beaten egg whites.

Pour into buttered and sugared 8-inch layer cake pan, set pan into larger pan containing 1 inch hot water, and bake in a preheated 350° F. oven for 35 minutes.

Cool, then chill.

Unmold on cold serving plate and serve with red currant sauce. *Serves 4.*

PEARS RICHELIEU • *Poires Richelieu*

Bake SEMOLINA PUDDING in a buttered and sugared ring mold sprinkled with chopped preserved fruits. Chill. Unmold on serving plate and arrange in the center a pyramid of quartered pears cooked in VANILLA SYRUP. Mask with FRANGIPANE CREAM to which is added ¼ cup macaroon crumbs and 1 cup heavy cream, whipped.

FARINA CREAM • *Crème de Farine*

⅓ cup enriched farina	1 two-inch piece vanilla bean
1 envelope plain gelatin	1 cup heavy cream, whipped
Pinch salt	Fruit, fruit purée, or RED
⅓ cup sugar	CURRANT SAUCE
2 cups milk	

In saucepan combine farina, gelatin, salt, and sugar.

Gradually stir in milk. Add vanilla bean and cook over low heat, stirring, until mixture is smooth and thickened.

Cool. Remove vanilla bean and fold in whipped cream.

Spoon into an oiled 4-cup ring mold and chill until set.

Serve with fresh or cooked fruit, with strawberry or raspberry purée, or with a red currant sauce. *Serves 6.*

PEARS FLORETTA • *Poires à la Floretta*

FARINA CREAM	
¾ cup red wine	1 tablespoon cornstarch
⅓ cup sugar	2 tablespoons currant jelly
1 one-inch stick cinnamon	Whipped cream, optional
3 pears, peeled, cored, and quartered	

Make farina cream in ring mold.

In a saucepan combine wine, sugar, and cinnamon.

Bring to a boil and add pears. Cover and simmer for 10 minutes, or until pears are tender.

Cool pears in liquid. Discard cinnamon.

Drain liquid from pears into saucepan and bring to a boil.

Stir in cornstarch mixed with a small amount of water and the jelly.

Stir over low heat until sauce is clear and thickened.

Unmold the FARINA CREAM onto serving platter.

Pile pears in center, pour sauce over pears, and, if desired, garnish with rosettes of whipped cream. *Serves 6.*

PEACHES CHEVREUSE • *Pêches à la Chevreuse*

Prepare either a SEMOLINA PUDDING or a FARINA CREAM and pour into an 8-inch layer cake pan. Bake or chill according to the recipe. When set, unmold and arrange 8 peach halves, poached in VANILLA SYRUP, in a ring on top, rounded side up. Place a glacé cherry and a leaf of angelica between each peach. Chill. Just before serving fill center with whipped cream pressed out through a large fluted tube. Sprinkle cream with chopped pistachios. Coat peaches with APRICOT SAUCE tinted pink and flavored with curaçao.

RICE PUDDING • *Pouding de Riz*

¾ cup rice	1 teaspoon vanilla
3 cups water	1 quart hot milk
4 egg yolks	4 egg whites
¾ cup sugar	4 tablespoons sugar
Pinch salt	½ teaspoon vanilla

Rinse rice in cold water and drain.

Put rice in saucepan, add water, and bring to a boil. Simmer for 25 minutes, or until rice is very tender. Drain.

In mixing bowl beat egg yolks with the ¾ cup sugar and salt until pale in color. Stir in the 1 teaspoon vanilla.

Stir yolk mixture into the hot milk and cook, stirring, until custard coats the spoon, being careful not to let it boil.

Add rice, mix well, and turn into buttered baking dish.

Beat egg whites until stiff but not dry and beat in the 4 tablespoons sugar, one tablespoon at a time. Stir in the ½ teaspoon vanilla. Spread this meringue over the pudding and brown in a preheated 350° F. oven for 12 to 15 minutes. Serve hot or cold. *Serves 6.*

CREAM OF RICE • *Tôt-Fait*

½ cup sugar	½ cup melted butter
½ cup rice flour	3 egg whites, stiffly beaten
½ cup milk	Grated rind of 1 orange
4 eggs	

Mix sugar, rice flour, and milk in mixing bowl.

Beat in eggs.

Fold in melted butter, egg whites, and orange rind.

Pour into a buttered and sugared charlotte mold, and bake in a preheated 350° F. oven for 30 minutes.

Serve warm. *Serves 6.*

DESSERT RICE • *Pouding de Riz à la Crème*

¾ cup rice	¼ cup water
1 quart hot milk	1 teaspoon vanilla
½ teaspoon salt	1 cup cream, whipped
¾ cup sugar	Dessert sauce or cream
2 envelopes gelatin	

Wash rice, put into saucepan, and cover with water.

Bring rice and water just to a boil. Drain.

Add milk, salt, and sugar. Bring to a rapid boil, cover, reduce heat to very low, and cook for about 25 minutes, or until rice is very soft.

Force rice through a fine sieve or blend in an electric blender.

Soften gelatin in the water and stir into the hot rice.

Cool to lukewarm, stirring occasionally. Stir in vanilla.

Fold in whipped cream and turn mixture into a 6-cup ring mold. Chill for 2 hours, or until set.

Unmold and serve with a favorite dessert sauce or with cream. *Serves 8.*

STRAWBERRIES SINGAPORE • *Fraises à la Singapore*

Make DESSERT RICE and mold in a 6-cup ring mold. When set unmold on cold serving platter and fill center with 3 cups fresh strawberries marinated for half an hour in 2 ounces kirsch or Cointreau and ½ cup sugar.

STUFFED PEARS CARMELITA • *Poires Farcies à la Carmélite*

Make DESSERT RICE and mold in a 6-cup flat mold such as a layer cake pan. When set, unmold on cold serving plate. Meanwhile peel 8 large pears and cook them in lemon-flavored water until just tender. Drain, cut in half lengthwise, and remove center core. Fill center with a mixture of diced fruit bound with APRICOT PUREE. Put pear halves together again. Arrange pears on the layer of DESSERT RICE. Coat pears with red currant jelly diluted with hot water and thickened to sauce consistency with a little cornstarch.

ORIENTAL PEACHES • *Pêches à l'Orientale*

Peel and halve 4 large fresh peaches and poach in VANILLA SYRUP. Drain. Arrange peaches rounded side up on a ring of DESSERT RICE to which has been added, along with the whipped cream, some chopped pineapple marinated in kirsch. Brush peaches with melted apricot jelly and sprinkle with chopped toasted almonds. Fill center with a pyramid of small FRIED CREAMS. Decorate the fried creams with whipped cream rosettes and serve with a RED CURRANT SAUCE flavored with kirsch.

PEACHES CONDE • *Pêches à la Condé*

½ cup rice
2 cups milk
1 two-inch piece vanilla bean
Pinch salt
⅓ cup sugar
2 tablespoons butter
4 egg yolks, beaten

6 large peaches (or a one-pound, 14-ounce can peach halves)
2 tablespoons cornstarch
½ cup peach preserves
Kirsch to taste
Glacé cherries and angelica

Cook rice in boiling water for 2 minutes and drain.

Combine rice, milk, vanilla, and salt.

Cook over low heat for 25 minutes, or until rice is tender, stirring occasionally.

Discard vanilla bean. Stir in sugar, butter, and egg yolks, and cook, stirring rapidly, for 2 minutes longer.

Turn into a buttered 1-quart bowl and let stand for 5 minutes.

Meanwhile, for fresh peaches, peel peaches, cut in half, and remove pits. Poach peach halves in a syrup of sugar and water or heat canned peaches in the syrup. Drain, reserving syrup.

Blend cornstarch with a small amount of water and stir into syrup.

Add preserves and cook over low heat, stirring, until clear and thickened. Stir in kirsch.

Unmold rice cream onto serving plate and arrange peach halves over it.

Strain syrup over cream and peaches and decorate with cherries and angelica. *Serves 6.*

RICE PUDDING JOSEPHINE • *Pouding de Riz Josephine*

1½ *cups rice*	3 *tablespoons cream*
1 *quart hot milk*	1 *tablespoon kirsch or*
Pinch salt	*maraschino*
2 *tablespoons butter*	1 *pound or 1 quart fine*
1 *one-inch piece vanilla bean*	*strawberries*
¾ *cup sugar*	*Kirsch or maraschino*
3 *egg yolks*	1 *cup cream, whipped*

Wash rice and put into saucepan. Cover with cold water, bring to a boil, and drain.

To rice in saucepan add milk, salt, butter, and vanilla.

Cover and bring to a rapid boil. Turn heat to very low and cook for 12 minutes.

Stir in sugar and continue to cook for 12 minutes longer, or until all milk is absorbed and rice is tender.

Remove from heat and stir in egg yolks beaten with the cream.

Flavor with the 1 tablespoon kirsch or maraschino and pour into a crystal bowl. Chill.

Wash and stem strawberries.

Marinate two-thirds of the best strawberries in kirsch or maraschino with a little sugar.

Press remaining strawberries through a sieve to make a purée and add to the marinating strawberries.

To serve, arrange a crown of whole berries in a ring on top of the pudding and fill center with whipped cream. Serve remaining strawberries separately. *Serves 6.*

EMPRESS RICE • *Riz à l'Impératrice*

½ cup rice	¾ cup mixed candied fruits, finely chopped
1½ cups milk	
4 egg yolks	¼ cup kirsch
½ cup sugar	1 cup heavy cream, whipped
¾ cup hot milk	Candied cherries
1 one-inch piece vanilla bean	Citron or angelica
1 envelope gelatin	Red currant jelly flavored with kirsch
2 tablespoons cold water	

Wash rice in cold water, put in a saucepan, and cover with cold water.

Bring water to a boil and simmer for 2 minutes.

Drain and rinse in cold water.

To rice add the 1½ cups milk and cook for about 20 minutes, or until rice is very tender.

In top of double boiler combine egg yolks and sugar.

Stir in hot milk, add vanilla bean, and cook over simmering water, stirring constantly, until custard is smooth and thickened.

Stir in gelatin softened in the cold water and strain custard through a fine sieve.

Add rice, mix well, and chill until mixture begins to set.

Marinate candied fruits in kirsch for 30 minutes.

Fold marinated fruits and the whipped cream into the rice.

Turn mixture into an oiled decorative ring mold and chill for at least 2 hours.

When ready to serve, unmold rice onto a chilled serving plate and garnish with cherries and small diamonds of citron or angelica.

Serve with red currant jelly melted over low heat and flavored with kirsch. *Serves 6.*

EMPRESS PEARS • *Poires à l'Impératrice*

Chill EMPRESS RICE in a ring mold for at least 2 hours. When ready to serve, unmold onto chilled serving plate and pile center high with whipped cream. Poach 6 whole pears until just tender in a light syrup made by combining 2 cups water and 1 cup sugar. Arrange pears on the rice around the cream and decorate base of pears with a little more whipped cream pressed through a pastry bag fitted with a fluted tube. Surround by a ribbon of melted red currant jelly.

MANDARIN RICE • *Riz à la Mandarin*

Omit candied fruits from recipe for EMPRESS RICE and substitute the thin layer of orange peel from 3 tangerines, cut into very fine julienne strips, simmered in boiling water for 2 minutes, and drained. Add a drop of orange food coloring and chill rice mixture in a decorative mold for at least 2 hours. When ready to serve, unmold on serving platter and arrange around it a crown of peeled tangerine sections that have been steeped for 30 minutes in curaçao with a little sugar and a spoonful of apricot marmalade. Serve with TANGERINE SAUCE.

RUFFLED RICE WITH CHESTNUTS • *La Frou-Frou aux Marrons*

Chill EMPRESS RICE in a ring mold for at least 2 hours. Unmold onto chilled serving plate and fill center with slightly sweetened whipped cream, piling high into a dome. Fill small cooky CORNETS (*Petits Cornets*) with CHESTNUT CREAM and arrange them on top of the rice. Decorate sides of rice with a little whipped cream mixed with an equal amount of chestnut cream pressed through a pastry bag fitted with a fluted tube.

EMPRESS STRAWBERRIES • *Fraises à l'Impératrice*

Mold EMPRESS RICE in a crystal coupe dish. Cover with whipped cream pressed through a fluted pastry tube and piled high in center. Stud cream with large fresh strawberries and brush strawberries with melted red currant jelly.

PEARS MARIE ANNE • *Poires à la Marie Anne*

Mold EMPRESS RICE in a round layer cake pan. When set, unmold and arrange on top a circle of pears poached in VANILLA SYRUP. Decorate between pears with cherries and leaves of angelica. Fill center with whipped cream pressed out through a fluted tube and coat pears with APRICOT SAUCE flavored with kirsch.

TAPIOCA PUDDING · *Pouding au Tapioca à l'Anglaise*

3 tablespoons quick-cooking tapioca	2 egg whites
⅓ cup sugar	2 tablespoons sugar
Pinch salt	½ teaspoon vanilla or 1 teaspoon grated lemon rind
2 egg yolks	Fruit, fruit sauce, or purée
2 cups milk	

In top of double boiler combine tapioca, the ⅓ cup sugar, salt, and egg yolks.

Stir in milk and cook over simmering water for about 7 minutes. Stir and continue to cook for 5 minutes longer.

Remove from heat and cool.

Beat egg whites until stiff and gradually beat in the 2 tablespoons sugar. Fold into the pudding along with the vanilla or grated lemon rind.

Chill and serve with fresh or canned fruit, a fruit sauce, or purée. *Serves 4.*

Such ingredients as butter, chocolate, purée of chestnuts, and cream cheese solidify when chilled and are used to thicken molded desserts.

CHARLOTTE MALAKOFF

Ladyfingers	¼ cup kirsch
½ cup sweet butter	2 cups heavy cream, whipped
½ cup sugar	Additional whipped cream
½ cup grated blanched almonds	

Line bottom of a buttered charlotte or timbale mold with waxed paper and place a layer of ladyfingers vertically and close together all around the inside walls.

Cream butter until soft, gradually add sugar, and cream together until mixture is light and fluffy.

Beat in almonds and kirsch and gently fold this mixture into the whipped cream.

Turn mixture into the mold and chill for at least 2 hours.

When ready to serve, unmold onto serving dish and remove waxed paper. Decorate with a little whipped cream pressed through a pastry bag fitted with an open-star tube. *Serves 6.*

One of the most delicious desserts in the world is the *Mont Blanc,* or white mountain. In China this dessert is flavored with brandy and is known as Peiping Dust.

WHITE MOUNTAIN OF CHESTNUTS • *Mont Blanc aux Marrons*

2 *pounds chestnuts*	⅓ *cup water*
2 *cups hot milk*	4 *drops lemon juice*
2 *one-inch pieces of vanilla bean*	2 *tablespoons soft butter*
1 *cup sugar*	2 *cups cream, whipped*

CHESTNUT PUREE • *Purée aux Marrons*

With a sharp knife slit shells of chestnuts on the convex side. Put in a saucepan with water to cover, bring to a boil, and simmer for 5 minutes. Remove from heat and, without draining, take chestnuts from pan, one by one. Remove shells and inner skins while nuts are still hot and drop them into the hot milk. Add one of the pieces of vanilla bean, bring milk to a boil, and simmer nuts for about 20 minutes or until tender. Drain and rub chestnuts through a fine sieve to make chestnut purée.

CHESTNUT CREAM • *Crème de Marrons*

In a heavy saucepan combine sugar, water, lemon juice, and the other piece of vanilla bean. Bring to a boil and cook until syrup spins a light thread.

Discard vanilla bean and add syrup gradually to the chestnut purée, beating constantly. Let cream cool to lukewarm and beat in soft butter.

Fill a pastry bag fitted with a small round tube with the chestnut cream and press it into a buttered and sugared ring mold, letting it fall at random to form a nestlike effect. While chestnut cream is still warm, unmold the nest carefully onto a serving platter and chill for about 1 hour.

When ready to serve, fill center of the chestnut cream nest with whipped cream, sweetened and flavored to taste with vanilla, pressing it through a pastry bag or cone fitted with a large fluted tube and building it up high in the center. *Serves 6.*

LOAF OF TURIN · *Turinois*

1 *pound chestnuts*	*½ cup sugar*
½ cup sweet butter	1 *teaspoon vanilla*
½ cup grated chocolate	*Whipped cream*

With a sharp knife slit shells of the chestnuts on convex side. Put them in a saucepan with water to cover, bring to a boil, and simmer for 5 minutes. Remove pan from heat and, without draining, take each chestnut from the pan, one by one. Remove shells and inner skins while nuts are still hot. Cook peeled nuts in boiling water for about 20 minutes, or until tender. Drain and press through a fine sieve.

Mix the chestnut purée, while still hot, with the butter, grated chocolate, sugar, and vanilla.

Press mixture firmly into a buttered, paper-lined loaf pan and chill overnight.

Unmold the loaf onto a serving plate, cut it into thin slices, and serve with whipped cream. *Serves 6.*

NEGRITAS

3 *ounces bittersweet chocolate*	3 *egg whites, stiffly beaten*
3 *egg yolks*	*Whipped cream*
Pinch salt	*Chopped pistachios or toasted slivered almonds*
1 *teaspoon vanilla or* 1 *tablespoon rum or brandy*	

Melt chocolate over hot water. Remove from heat but leave over the hot water.

Beat egg yolks with salt and stir in.

Remove from hot water and stir in vanilla, rum, or brandy.

Fold in beaten egg whites.

Pour into serving dish or 6 individual glasses and chill for 4 to 6 hours.

Garnish with whipped cream and chopped nuts. *Serves 6.*

PAVE AU CHOCOLAT (Blender Method)

> 1 *package (6 ounces) semi-sweet chocolate pieces*
> ¼ *cup boiling water or strong coffee*
> 4 *egg yolks*
> ½ *cup (1 stick) soft butter*
>
> 4 *tablespoons cognac*
> ½ *cup cold water*
> 2 *packages (5 ounces) lady-fingers*
> *Whipped cream*

Into container of an electric blender put chocolate pieces and boiling liquid.

Cover and blend on high speed for about 10 seconds, or until sauce is smooth.

Remove cover and add egg yolks and butter and continue to blend until smooth, stopping to stir down if necessary.

Empty chocolate cream into a bowl.

Add half the cognac to the container, cover, and blend for a few seconds.

Add to chocolate cream and mix.

Combine remaining cognac and cold water.

Line bottom of a spring form pan with waxed paper. Dip ladyfingers, one at a time, into the diluted cognac and arrange a layer of ladyfingers in pan. Spread with a layer of chocolate cream, using about half the cream. Arrange another layer of ladyfingers and top with remaining chocolate cream. Cover with ladyfingers and chill for at least 2 hours.

To serve: Run knife around sides of pan and invert dessert on serving plate. Discard waxed paper and decorate with rosettes of whipped cream. *Serves 8.*

CHAPTER 5

Dessert Omelets and Soufflés

DESSERT OMELETS

Sweet omelets are too seldom served, yet they make a delicious dessert after a light luncheon or supper. The only drawback to omelets is that they are something that cannot be made in advance, served up from a hot oven or a cold refrigerator. They must be made and served the moment they are cooked, and individual omelets are by far the best. On the other hand, since it takes only 30 seconds to make an omelet, many can be turned out in a few minutes.

A good omelet is nothing more than an oval of creamy eggs enclosed in a soft blanket of lightly scrambled eggs. For dessert the eggs are slightly sweetened. The perfect omelet is golden, plump, and light and should be creamy or *baveuse* in the center.

Omelets are tricky to make and the only way to learn is to make one—make many in fact; perfect the technique on yourself and your family before trying your new art on guests. The motions of making an omelet must become automatic and this is purely a question of practice.

Two things are absolutely necessary: a thick pan and brisk heat. The pan should be heavy iron, aluminum, or stainless steel with sides curving into a bottom that is about 7 inches in diameter. This is the perfect size for a 2- or 3-egg omelet. The pan should be reserved for omelets alone and never used for anything else. A new pan or one that has been used for cooking must first be treated or seasoned: Scrub the pan with scouring powder, rinse, and dry. Then put a thin layer of cooking oil in bottom and set over low heat for half an hour. Remove from heat and let stand overnight. Before making the first omelet, discard the oil, sprinkle with a teaspoon of salt, heat for a moment, and rub vigorously with a paper towel. Then rub clean and it is ready to use. After making an omelet or omelets wipe clean with paper towel. Do not wash. If by mistake the pan is washed it should be treated again before use.

SWEET OMELET • *Omelette*

3 *eggs*	1 *tablespoon butter*
2 *teaspoons fine granulated* *sugar*	*Confectioners' sugar, optional*

Break eggs into mixing bowl. Add sugar and beat with a table fork until whites and yolks are just blended, about 40 strokes.

Put butter in omelet pan and set over high heat. As butter melts, tilt and swirl pan to coat bottom and sides evenly. When butter has stopped foaming and begins to brown, giving off a characteristic nutty aroma, it is time to pour in the eggs.

Pour eggs into pan. Hold pan with left hand and immediately start shaking pan back and forth over heat. At the same time, stir eggs briskly with table fork, then smooth out with back of fork and add desired filling. It's a little like rubbing your head and patting your tummy at the same time!

Lift handle of pan to tilt it at a 45 degree angle. Run fork all around edge of omelet and, with the aid of the fork, roll up to edge of pan.

Hold over heat for 1 or 2 seconds longer to brown bottom.

Turn omelet pan so handle is on the right.

Grasp handle with right hand, *thumb up*. Hold plate in left hand. Rest edge of pan slightly off center of plate and turn pan upside down over plate. The omelet will drop into position.

Garnish as desired or sprinkle with confectioners' sugar and serve. *Serves 1 to 3 for dessert.*

TO GLAZE AN OMELET

Sprinkle with fine granulated sugar and either run under broiler for a moment or make crisscross marks with a red-hot poker.

TO MAKE SEVERAL OMELETS

Beat the necessary number of eggs and the sugar in a large mixing bowl. Use a ladle to measure the amount of eggs into the pan, giving the eggs a few vigorous beats in between each omelet.

Three eggs, beaten, equals about ½ cup.

JAM OMELET • *Omelette au Confiture*

Make SWEET OMELET according to directions. Just before folding spread quickly with 1 tablespoon apricot, black currant, strawberry, or raspberry jam or orange marmalade. Fold, turn out on serving plate, and dust with fine granulated sugar.

APPLE OMELET • *Omelette aux Pommes*

Make SWEET OMELET according to directions. Just before folding, spread with applesauce, sweetened to taste and folded into an equal quantity of whipped cream.

RUM OMELET • *Omelette au Rhum*

Make SWEET OMELET according to directions. Fold and turn out on warm serving plate and sprinkle with fine sugar. Pour 1 ounce warm rum over the omelet and serve flaming. Pass unsweetened whipped cream separately.

OMELET JUBILEE • *Omelette Jubilée*

Make SWEET OMELET according to directions. Just before folding, put in a spoonful of dark sweet cherries heated in their own juice. Fold, turn out on warm serving plate, and sprinkle with fine sugar. Pour 1 ounce warm brandy over the omelet and serve flaming.

GINGER OMELET • *Omelette Gingembre*

Make SWEET OMELET according to directions. Just before folding, spread with whipped cream into which is folded chopped preserved ginger. Serve surrounded by a ribbon of ginger syrup.

FRUIT OMELET • *Omelette aux Fruits*

Make SWEET OMELET according to directions. Before folding, put a spoonful of fresh, frozen, or preserved fruits in the center. The fruits may be sliced strawberries, shredded pineapple, diced apricots, or fresh peaches. If fresh fruit is used, it should be mixed with a little sugar syrup. Turn omelet out on warm serving plate and surround by a ribbon of liqueur-flavored fruit syrup.

FROSTED OMELET • *Omelette Surprise*

Beat until stiff an extra egg white for each SWEET OMELET to be made. Beat in 2 tablespoons fine granulated sugar for each egg white used and continue to beat until the meringue is stiff and glossy. Make sweet omelet according to directions. Fill with jam, jelly, or preserved fruit. Fold and turn out on a flameproof platter. Spread meringue smoothly over the omelet, sprinkle with fine granulated sugar, and brown under broiler or in a hot oven.

BANANA OMELET • *Omelette aux Bananes*

Make SWEET OMELET according to directions. Fill with sliced bananas sweetened with sugar and sprinkled with a little lemon juice. Fold, turn out on flameproof serving dish, sprinkle with fine granulated sugar, and glaze under broiler.

CHRISTMAS OMELET • *Omelette de Noël*

Make SWEET OMELET according to directions, adding to the beaten eggs a little grated orange rind and a dash of rum. Just before folding place a spoonful of heated mincemeat in center. Turn out on warm serving plate, sprinkle with fine granulated sugar, and blaze with warm brandy.

THE SOUFFLE OR PUFF OMELET · *Omelette Soufflée*

In this type of omelet the eggs are separated, the yolks beaten with the sugar until they are thick and pale in color and the whites beaten until stiff. Often an extra white for every 2 yolks is used. The beaten whites are folded lightly into the yolks and sugar.

The soufflé omelet is frequently cooked over direct heat until the bottom is golden and set. It is then put into a hot oven (400° F.) to puff. I prefer to bake it in a very hot oven (450° F.) for 10 to 15 minutes. It will puff like a soufflé and must be rushed to the table.

A SOUFFLE OMELET

6 *egg whites*	1 *tablespoon fine granulated*
4 *egg yolks*	*sugar*
	1 *tablespoon butter*

Beat egg whites until stiff.
Beat egg yolks and sugar until yolks are thick and pale in color.
Fold half the beaten whites carefully and thoroughly into the yolks.
Fold remaining whites quickly and lightly into the mixture.
Pour mixture into a buttered frying pan or ovenproof dish and bake in a preheated 450° F. oven for 10 minutes. Serve immediately. *Serves* 2.

VANILLA PUFF OMELET FOR FOUR · *Omelette Soufflée au Vanille*

5 *eggs, separated*	3 *tablespoons butter*
⅓ *cup granulated sugar*	*Confectioners' sugar*
1 *teaspoon vanilla*	

Beat egg whites until stiff.
Beat egg yolks and sugar until very thick and pale in color.
Beat in vanilla.
Fold egg whites into yolk mixture.
Heat butter in a large frying pan with a heatproof handle.

Pour in eggs and cook over direct moderate heat without stirring until set on bottom.

Place pan in a preheated 400° F. oven and bake for 15 minutes, or until set.

Fold omelet in half and turn out on hot serving platter.

Sprinkle generously with confectioners' sugar and serve at once. *Serves 4.*

STRAWBERRY PUFF OMELET • *Omelette Soufflée aux Fraises*

Crush some fresh strawberries and flavor to taste with sugar, lemon juice, and kirsch. Chill for at least 1 hour to draw out juice. When ready to make the omelet, whip ½ cup cream. Drain juice from berries and set aside. Fold whipped cream into the berries. Make a SOUFFLE OMELET according to directions. When cooked, quickly fold cold fruit and cream into center and turn out on serving plate. Serve the reserved juice separately. The omelet should be very hot and puffed and the filling should be icy cold.

ORANGE PUFF OMELET • *Omelette à l'Orange*

Make a SOUFFLE OMELET, beating with the egg yolks and sugar 1 tablespoon orange juice. When cooked, cover half the omelet with orange segments and sprinkle with confectioners' sugar. Fold, turn out on serving plate, and garnish with more orange segments. Sprinkle with confectioners' sugar and serve at once.

OMELET SOUFFLE SURPRISE • *Omelette Soufflée en Surprise*

Prepare a SOUFFLE OMELET. Butter an ovenproof dish and cover the bottom with a 1-inch slice spongecake. On top arrange scoops of very hard vanilla ice cream, keeping them away from the sides of the dish by about 1 inch. Pour the soufflé mixture over ice cream and cake and bake in a preheated 450° F. oven for about 15 minutes. Garnish as desired with fruit. Half peaches poached in a light syrup make an excellent garnish. Place them on the soufflé hollow side up, and fill the hollows with red currant jelly or strawberry jam. *Serves 4.*

OMELET MOUSSELINE · *Omelette Mousseline*

This is a soufflé omelet, but it is cooked in omelet pan in the same way as a rolled omelet.

2 egg whites	2 tablespoons heavy cream
4 egg yolks	1 tablespoon butter
1 tablespoon fine granulated	Confectioners' sugar
sugar	Fresh fruit or berries

Beat egg whites until stiff.
Beat egg yolks and sugar until thick and pale in color. Gradually beat in cream.
Fold in egg whites.
Heat butter in an omelet pan until it starts to turn color. Pour in eggs and stir over high heat until they begin to set. Fold, turn out on warm serving plate, and sprinkle with confectioners' sugar. Garnish as desired with fresh fruit or berries, sweetened to taste. *Serves 2 to 3.*

CHOCOLATE OMELET · *Omelette au Chocolat*

Make a SOUFFLE OMELET according to directions, increasing the sugar to 2 tablespoons and beating 2 ounces melted bittersweet chocolate into the egg yolk mixture. Pour into buttered ovenproof pan and bake in a preheated 450° F. oven for 15 minutes. Fold over onto serving plate, sprinkle with fine granulated sugar, and serve with whipped cream or HOT CHOCOLATE SAUCE.

VANILLA OMELET SOUFFLE · *Omelette Soufflée au Vanille*

8 egg whites	2 teaspoons vanilla
6 egg yolks	Confectioners' sugar
⅓ cup sugar	

Beat egg whites until stiff.
Beat egg yolks until fluffy, add sugar, and continue to beat until mixture is thick and pale in color.
Stir in vanilla.
Fold in egg whites.
Turn mixture into a buttered and sugared soufflé dish, or put it on

a buttered and sugared oval ovenproof platter. Smooth it sleekly with a knife, shaping it high in the center. Part of the mixture may be reserved and pressed through a fluted pastry tube to make a decorative effect.

Bake in a preheated 450° F. oven for about 20 minutes.

Sprinkle with confectioners' sugar and run under broiler for 1 minute to glaze. Serve immediately. *Serves 6.*

COFFEE OMELET • *Omelette Soufflée au Café*

Make according to instructions for VANILLA OMELET, substituting coffee extract for the vanilla.

LEMON OR ORANGE SOUFFLE OMELET

Make according to instructions for VANILLA OMELET, substituting the juice and grated rind of 1 lemon or ½ orange for the vanilla.

MARASCHINO OMELET SOUFFLE • *Omelette Soufflée au Maraschino*

Make according to directions for VANILLA OMELET, substituting 2 tablespoons maraschino liqueur for the vanilla. If desired, fold in ¼ cup sieved macaroon crumbs.

DESSERT SOUFFLES

The basis of a sweet soufflé is a bland, smooth cream of flour, sugar, and milk. While still hot, egg yolks are beaten into it. This part of your sweet soufflé can be made well in advance of baking. After cooling, the flavoring, fruit purée, ground nuts, or melted chocolate is added, then the stiffly beaten egg whites.

The egg whites should be added the moment before the soufflé is put into the oven.

Light the oven ahead of time so the temperature will be even and constant. Set it for 400° F.

Have a soufflé dish buttered and dusted lightly with sugar. The soufflé dish may be high and large enough to hold the raised soufflé in its entirety, or a shallow 1-quart baking dish may be used if it is collared.

TO COLLAR A DISH FOR A SOUFFLE

Cut a piece of brown paper long enough to encircle the dish and about 4 inches wide. Butter it lightly and fold in half lengthwise. Wrap it around the top of the dish, letting it rise a good 2½ to 3 inches above the edge of the dish, and tie securely with string.

THE SECRET OF A SOUFFLE

The egg whites should be beaten until stiff but not dry, and there should be more egg whites than egg yolks, the correct proportion being 5 egg whites to every 4 yolks. Even large quantities of egg whites will do no harm, but the way the egg whites are beaten is important. Beat the egg whites with a pinch of salt until soft peaks are formed. Sprinkle over them 1 tablespoon fine granulated sugar and continue to beat until the peaks become stiff but not dry. The egg whites should increase in volume from 6 to 7 times.

TO FOLD IN EGG WHITES

Add about three-quarters of the egg whites to the cream and fold it in lightly but thoroughly. It is the air beaten into the egg whites that expands in the oven heat and raises the soufflé. So the egg whites must be evenly distributed throughout the cream to keep all particles in suspension or you are likely to find a layer of custard in the bottom of the soufflé dish. But the air within the egg whites must not be allowed to escape by beating or rapid stirring. So fold gently, quickly, and thoroughly. Then add the remaining whites and fold them in carelessly and quickly. A few patches of egg white throughout the mix do not matter, providing the first addition of the whites is complete.

TO BAKE A SOUFFLE

Turn the soufflé mixture into the prepared dish. Place the dish in the center of the oven preheated to 400° F. *Immediately*, turn oven heat down to 375° F. At the end of 25 minutes' baking time, the soufflé will be puffed and lightly browned. Quickly sprinkle the top with confectioners' sugar. Continue baking until the soufflé is done to taste, about 5 to 10 minutes longer. Serve immediately.

BAKING TIME: at 375° F.

A 3-cup dish	15 to 20 minutes
A 6-cup dish	30 to 35 minutes
An 8-cup dish	40 to 45 minutes

BASIC VANILLA SOUFFLE • Soufflé à la Vanille

3 tablespoons butter
3 tablespoons flour
¾ cup hot milk
¼ cup sugar
4 egg yolks, lightly beaten
1 tablespoon vanilla

Pinch salt
5 egg whites
1 tablespoon fine granulated sugar
Confectioners' sugar

In saucepan melt butter.

Remove pan from heat and stir in flour.

Return pan to heat and gradually stir in hot milk.

Stir in the ¼ cup sugar and continue to stir over low heat for 5 minutes, or until cream is smooth and thickened.

Remove from heat and gradually beat in egg yolks.

Let this mixture, which may be made well in advance of baking, cool.

Stir in vanilla.

Beat salt and egg whites until they stand in soft peaks. Sprinkle the 1 tablespoon sugar over egg whites and continue to beat until they stand in stiff peaks.

Fold egg whites into yolk mixture.

Turn mixture into a buttered and lightly sugared 6-cup soufflé dish.

Place dish in center of an oven preheated to 400° F. Immediately turn oven down to 375° F. and bake for 25 minutes.

Quickly dust top of soufflé with confectioners' sugar and continue to bake for 10 to 15 minutes longer. Serve immediately. *Serves 6.*

ALMOND SOUFFLE • Soufflé aux Amandes

Use 1 teaspoon almond extract in place of the vanilla in BASIC VANILLA SOUFFLE. Stir in ½ cup blanched ground almonds before folding in egg whites.

APPLE RUM SOUFFLE • *Soufflé aux Pommes*

Line buttered soufflé dish with apple slices cooked until soft in LIGHT SYRUP. Sprinkle with sugar and fill with BASIC VANILLA SOUFFLE. At the moment of serving pour 2 tablespoons warm rum over top and serve blazing.

APRICOT SOUFFLE • *Soufflé aux Abricots*

Stir 1 cup cooked apricot purée into BASIC VANILLA SOUFFLE before folding in egg whites.

BANANA SOUFFLE • *Soufflé aux Bananes*

Line a buttered soufflé dish with sliced bananas sautéed until tender in a little butter. Sprinkle with sugar and fill with BASIC VANILLA SOUFFLE. At moment of serving blaze with 2 tablespoons warm rum.

CAMARANGO SOUFFLE • *Soufflé Camarango*

Make BASIC VANILLA SOUFFLE egg yolk mixture and cool. Divide in half. To one half stir in 1 teaspoon grated orange rind and 2 tablespoons orange juice. To other half stir in ¼ cup grated pecans or hazelnuts. Divide and fold egg whites into each mixture. Put mixture into soufflé dish in layers, dividing each layer with a layer of ladyfingers soaked in curaçao or Cointreau.

CHOCOLATE SOUFFLE • *Soufflé au Chocolat*

Increase the sugar added to milk mixture in BASIC VANILLA SOUFFLE to ⅓ cup. Stir into the egg yolk mixture 2 ounces unsweetened chocolate melted with 2 tablespoons cold coffee, before folding in egg whites.

CHOCOLATE RUM SOUFFLE • *Soufflé au Chocolat au Rhum*

Melt 4 ounces sweet chocolate with 3 tablespoons water or cold coffee and 2 tablespoons rum. Stir into BASIC VANILLA SOUFFLE before folding in egg whites.

COFFEE SOUFFLE · *Soufflé au Café*

Use half very strong coffee and half milk in place of all milk in the BASIC VANILLA SOUFFLE. Add a few drops of coffee extract before folding in egg whites.

GINGER SOUFFLE · *Soufflé au Gingembre*

Substitute ½ teaspoon powdered ginger for the vanilla in the BASIC VANILLA SOUFFLE. Stir in 1 cup ground preserved or candied ginger before folding in egg whites.

LEMON SOUFFLE · *Soufflé au Citron*

Omit vanilla from BASIC VANILLA SOUFFLE. Stir in juice and grated rind of 1 lemon before folding in egg whites.

LIQUEUR SOUFFLE · *Soufflé au Liqueur*

Omit vanilla from BASIC VANILLA SOUFFLE. Stir in ¼ cup Grand Marnier, Benedictine, curaçao, Cointreau, or maraschino before folding in egg whites.

MARMALADE SOUFFLE · *Soufflé au Confiture*

Omit vanilla from BASIC VANILLA SOUFFLE and reduce sugar added to milk mixture to 1 tablespoon. Stir in grated rind of 1 lemon and 1 orange and 4 tablespoons orange marmalade before folding in egg whites.

CHESTNUT SOUFFLE · *Soufflé aux Marrons*

Press chestnuts preserved in VANILLA SYRUP through a fine sieve to make 1 cup purée. Stir the purée and 3 tablespoons Benedictine into BASIC VANILLA SOUFFLE before folding in egg whites.

NUT SOUFFLE · *Soufflé aux Noix*

Stir 1 cup ground nuts—hazelnuts, pecans, blanched almonds, black walnuts, or pistachio nuts—into BASIC VANILLA SOUFFLE before folding in egg whites.

ORANGE SOUFFLE · *Soufflé à l'Orange*

Omit vanilla from BASIC VANILLA SOUFFLE. Stir in grated rind of ½ orange and ¼ cup orange juice before folding in egg whites.

PANACHE SOUFFLE · *Soufflé Panaché*

Make BASIC VANILLA SOUFFLE but do not fold in egg whites. Divide yolk mixture in half and to one half stir in 2 ounces sweet chocolate melted with 2 tablespoons water or cold coffee and 1 tablespoon rum. Beat 6 egg whites until they stand in soft peaks. Gradually beat in 2 tablespoons sugar and continue to beat until mixture is stiff and glossy. Divide and fold half the egg whites into each soufflé mixture. Put vanilla soufflé into dish and top with the chocolate mixture. Bake as usual.

PEACH SOUFFLE · *Soufflé aux Pêches*

Omit vanilla from BASIC VANILLA SOUFFLE. Stir in 1 cup crushed fresh peaches and 1 teaspoon lemon juice before folding in egg whites. Or make the same as APRICOT SOUFFLE, using canned peaches.

PEACH MACAROON SOUFFLE

Make BASIC VANILLA SOUFFLE. Stir 1 cup peach purée and ½ cup macaroon crumbs soaked in brandy into egg yolk mixture before folding in egg whites. Serve with whipped cream flavored with brandy.

PRALINE SOUFFLE · *Soufflé Praliné*

Omit sugar from BASIC VANILLA SOUFFLE. Stir in ½ cup PRALINE POWDER before folding in egg whites.

PRUNE NUT SOUFFLE

Substitute prune juice for the milk in BASIC VANILLA SOUFFLE. Stir in 1 cup chopped cooked prunes and ½ cup chopped nuts before folding in egg whites.

SARAH BERNHARDT SOUFFLE • *Soufflé Sarah Bernhardt*

Line soufflé dish with a bed of macaroons soaked in curaçao. Add BASIC VANILLA SOUFFLE. Bake as usual and serve with whipped cream mixed with sugared sliced fresh strawberries flavored with curaçao.

STRAWBERRY SOUFFLE • *Soufflé aux Fraises*

Marinate 1½ cups sliced and sweetened strawberries in ½ cup orange juice and ¼ cup orange curaçao. Drain and reserve juice. Put berries into a buttered soufflé dish and top with BASIC VANILLA SOUFFLE mixture. Bake and serve with whipped cream flavored with the reserved juice.

STRAWBERRY ALMOND SOUFFLE

Omit vanilla from BASIC VANILLA SOUFFLE and increase sugar to ⅓ cup. Stir 1 cup crushed strawberries and ¾ cup blanched shredded almonds into yolk mixture before folding in egg whites.

CREAM CHEESE SOUFFLE

2 3-ounce packages cream
   cheese
¾ cup sour cream
5 teaspoons honey
Pinch salt
3 egg yolks, well beaten

4 egg whites
1 tablespoon sugar
Heavy cream and cream
   cheese or sliced sugared
   strawberries

Mash cream cheese and gradually stir in sour cream, beating until smooth.

Stir in honey, salt, and egg yolks.

Beat egg whites until they stand in soft peaks. Sprinkle with the sugar and continue to beat until stiff and glossy.

Fold egg whites into yolk mixture and bake in a preheated 375° F. oven for 30 to 35 minutes.

Serve with a sauce made by mixing together equal parts of heavy cream and cream cheese, or with sliced sugared strawberries. *Serves 4.*

Some soufflés eliminate the basic sauce and egg yolk mixture and simply fold a sweetened fruit purée into stiffly beaten egg whites.

EGG WHITE FRUIT SOUFFLE

1 cup fruit purée, fresh or
  canned
2 to 4 tablespoons sugar
2 tablespoons brandy or
  kirsch

5 egg whites
1 tablespoon sugar
Pinch salt
Confectioners' sugar

Make a fruit purée by pressing soft fruit or berries through a fine sieve.

To 1 cup fresh fruit purée add 4 tablespoons sugar or to taste. To 1 cup cooked or canned fruit purée add 2 tablespoons sugar or to taste.

Stir in brandy or kirsch.

Beat egg whites until they stand in soft peaks. Sprinkle with sugar and salt and continue to beat until stiff and glossy.

Fold beaten egg whites into fruit mixture.

Turn into a buttered and sugared 1-quart soufflé dish and bake in a preheated 350° F. oven for 30 to 35 minutes.

Sprinkle with confectioners' sugar and serve immediately. *Serves 4.*

Try the Following Combinations:

Fresh apricot or peach purée and kirsch.
Cooked prune purée and mirabelle.
Cooked black cherry purée and cherry brandy.
Cooked apple purée and Calvados.
Cooked or canned fig purée and cognac.

CHAPTER 6

Dessert Pancakes
and Crepes

P ANCAKES, or *crêpes*, have become traditional with the weeks of feasting before the austere forty days and nights of Lent.

When February comes to provincial towns in France, the smell of sweet thin *crêpes* drifts from long-handled black skillets heated over open fires. In many parts of England, too, the tolling of the bell on Shrove Tuesday summons cooks to their frying pans and is the signal for other work to cease. Everyone joins in feasting and merrymaking as gay as the festivities of the Christmas season.

Pancakes have progressed far since primeval man satisfied his hunger with cakes of meal and water baked on heated stones. Today we have *crêpes Suzette*, swimming in an orange sauce, blazed with liqueur, that are a perfect ending to a meal at any time of the year.

The *crêpe* differs greatly from the American pancake. The thin batter contains little flour and the cakes are delicate and fine in texture. They are extremely easy to make and may be made in advance and reheated in a sweet sauce.

BASIC RECIPE FOR CREPES

1⅛ cups sifted flour
4 tablespoons sugar
Pinch salt
3 eggs

1½ cups milk
1 tablespoon melted butter
1 tablespoon brandy or
cognac

Sift flour, sugar, and salt into a mixing bowl.

Beat eggs with a rotary beater and gradually beat in milk.

Stir the milk-egg mixture into the dry ingredients and continue to stir until batter is smooth. The batter should be just thick enough to coat a spoon.

Stir in melted butter and brandy or cognac and let batter stand for 1 to 2 hours before using it. This improves the texture of the cakes.

TO COOK THE CREPES:

Heat a small frying pan, from 5 to 6 inches in diameter, until very hot. The crepes must cook quickly or they will be tough.

Put ½ teaspoon butter in the pan and swirl pan to coat bottom and sides with butter.

As soon as butter stops foaming, pour in about 2 tablespoons of the crepe batter, and again tilt the pan in a circular motion to spread the batter evenly and thinly over bottom of the pan. This must be done quickly before the batter has a chance to set.

Cook crepe for about 1 minute, or until set and brown on one side; turn and brown the other side.

Turn crepe out onto a clean towel and roll or fold into quarters.

The first crepe will tell if the batter is right. If crepe is too thick, stir in a little milk; if too dry, stir in a little melted butter. If the crepe is so fragile it cannot be turned, sift in a little flour and stir it into the batter.

Serve the crepes warm with dessert sauce, honey, or jam, or simply sprinkled with confectioners' sugar and a wedge of lemon.

Or cover with waxed paper to reheat later in a sauce. *Makes 24.*

Crepes suzette were originated by a M. Jean Reboux and named for the Princesse de Carnignan, whose name was Suzette. They captivated the fancy of Louis XIV and have been intriguing palates ever since.

CREPES SUZETTE

Make crepes not larger than 5 or 6 inches in diameter and keep covered until ready to use.

THE SAUCE:

4 *lumps sugar*	¼ *cup curaçao or Cointreau*
Rind and juice of 1 orange	¼ *cup Benedictine or Grand*
5 *tablespoons sweet butter*	*Marnier*
1 *teaspoon lemon juice*	½ *cup warm brandy*

Rub the sugar lumps on the skin of the orange until they are covered with the aromatic oil, or zest.

Crush sugar lumps with 3 tablespoons of the butter and mix until creamy.

Put remaining butter in a flat skillet or in the blazer of a chafing dish and add orange and lemon juice and the liqueurs.

Bring liquid to a boil and stir in the creamed sugar-butter mixture.

Arrange crepes in the sauce one by one, spoon sauce over them so they are moistened on both sides, and fold them in quarters.

Pour the warm brandy over the crepes and blaze.

Serve with the sauce. *Serves 6.*

CREPES SIMON

Make crepes according to BASIC RECIPE FOR CREPES, but flavor batter with cherry brandy instead of cognac. Spread each crepe with FRANGI-PANE CREAM mixed with a little cherry jam. Fold in quarters, reheat in melted sweet butter, and blaze with warm cognac.

CREPES WITH CHARTREUSE • *Crêpes au Chartreuse*

Make crepes according to BASIC RECIPE, but flavor batter with chartreuse instead of cognac. Spread each crepe with a paste made by creaming together ½ cup butter, ¼ cup sugar, ¼ cup macaroon crumbs, and ¼ cup green chartreuse. Roll crepes, sprinkle with fine granulated sugar, and glaze in a hot oven or under broiler flame.

CREPES A L'ALSACIENNE

Make crepes according to BASIC RECIPE, but flavor batter with eau-de-vie de framboise instead of brandy or cognac. Spread each crepe with FRANGIPANE CREAM mixed with raspberries. Fold in quarters, reheat in melted sweet butter, and blaze with warm cognac.

CREPES WITH KIRSCH • *Crêpes au Kirsch*

Make crepes according to BASIC RECIPE, but flavor batter with kirsch instead of cognac. Spread with butter creamed with sugar and a little kirsch. Roll and arrange on a serving dish. Sprinkle with fine granulated sugar, pour over 2 ounces warm kirsch, and blaze.

CREPES A LA BONNE FEMME

Make crepes according to BASIC RECIPE, flavoring batter with a little grated orange rind and rum instead of cognac. Spread each crepe with applesauce and fold in quarters. Sprinkle lightly with finely chopped toasted almonds, pour over 2 ounces warm rum, and blaze.

CREPES LONGUEVILLE

Make crepes according to BASIC RECIPE, adding to the batter a little grated orange rind and ¼ cup finely chopped blanched almonds. Spread each crepe with 1 cup applesauce mixed with ⅓ cup PASTRY CREAM (*Crème Pâtissière*) and a pinch of cinnamon. Fold in quarters, sprinkle with fine granulated sugar, and glaze in a hot oven or under broiler flame.

CREPES WITH JAM • *Crêpes aux Confitures*

Make crepes according to BASIC RECIPE. Spread each crepe lightly with marmalade, jam, or jelly and roll. Arrange in a buttered heatproof serving dish, sprinkle with fine granulated sugar, and blaze in a hot oven for a few minutes.

PINEAPPLE CREPES • *Crêpes aux Ananas*

Make crepe batter according to BASIC RECIPE. Drain a can of pineapple slices and split each slice into 2 thin slices. Dry on a towel. Heat and butter a very small frying pan, the bottom of which is only slightly larger than the pineapple slices. Pour in a little batter to cover bottom, place a slice of pineapple on it, and pour another very thin layer of batter over it. When crepe is brown on one side, turn and brown on other side. Serve warm sprinkled with confectioners' sugar.

CREPES YVONNE

BASIC RECIPE FOR CREPES
2 squares (ounces) sweet
  chocolate, melted
1 cup FRANGIPANE CREAM
Fine granulated sugar

Make tiny crepes not more than 3 inches in diameter.

Stir melted chocolate into the frangipane cream.

Sandwich 2 crepes together with the chocolate cream and arrange in a buttered ovenproof serving dish.

Sprinkle with fine sugar and glaze in a hot oven or under broiler.

CREPES TRIOMPHANTE

1 cup (8 ounces) vanilla ice cream	2 tablespoons butter
¼ cup chopped pistachio nuts	Juice of 1 orange
	1 long strip orange peel
4 crepes made according to BASIC RECIPE	2 ounces cognac
	4 squares (ounces) bitter chocolate
3 tablespoons sugar	Whipped cream

Put 2 tablespoons ice cream and 1 tablespoon chopped pistachio nuts on each crepe and roll up. Use 2 serving plates, placing 2 crepes on each.

Sprinkle bottom of a chafing dish with the sugar and heat over a high flame.

Add butter and cook until butter and sugar caramelize.

Add orange juice and strip of peel and stir with the peel pricked with a fork until all is well carmelized.

Add cognac and flame.

Pour sauce into a saucepan containing the chocolate and stir over heat until chocolate is melted and sauce is smooth.

Pour sauce over the crepes and serve with whipped cream. *Serves 2.*

SWEDISH PANCAKES · Plättar

1 cup all-purpose flour	2 cups milk
2 teaspoons sugar	Lingonberries, canned or
Pinch salt	defrosted
3 eggs, beaten	Confectioners' sugar

Sift flour, sugar, and salt into a mixing bowl.

Add eggs and milk gradually, stirring until batter is well blended. Let batter stand for 2 hours.

Fry thin pancakes on a hot greased griddle.

Roll pancakes and arrange on hot serving platter.

Sprinkle with confectioners' sugar and serve with lingonberries. *Makes 36.*

HUNGARIAN BERRY PANCAKES

2 cups sour cream	2 cups sliced strawberries,
1 egg, beaten	sweetened to taste
¼ teaspoon salt	¾ cup blanched shredded
½ teaspoon ground ginger	and toasted almonds
2 cups sifted all-purpose flour	

Combine sour cream, egg, salt, and ginger.

Stir in flour and beat until batter is blended. It should be the consistency of thick cream. Adjust consistency by adding a little milk or more flour.

Heat a small frying pan, brush with butter, and pour in a spoonful of batter. Tip pan so batter will flow evenly over bottom, and cook for 1 minute. Turn and brown other side lightly.

Slide baked pancakes onto a floured board and continue to bake cakes until all batter is used.

When ready to serve, put a spoonful of strawberries in center of each pancake and roll up. Place in buttered ovenproof shallow pan. Sprinkle with almonds and glaze in a hot oven or under broiler until pancakes blister, but be careful they do not burn. *Makes 24.*

BLINTZES

1 cup all-purpose flour	2 eggs, beaten
1 cup water	½ teaspoon salt

Combine all ingredients in a mixing bowl to make a thin batter. Pour batter into a large measuring cup or jug and stir occasionally.

Heat a small frying pan about 6 inches in diameter and brush lightly with butter.

Pour into it about 2 tablespoons of batter and tip pan over the bowl, rotating it so that the bottom will be covered by a thin layer of batter and any excess batter will drain out.

Hold pan over the heat for about 30 seconds, or until the cake is dry. Bake on one side only.

Shake the cake onto a damp towel and repeat, first heating the pan again thoroughly, as it is the heat of the pan that almost cooks the pancakes.

When all batter has been used, roll the cakes in the damp towel until ready to fill and sauté. *Makes 12 to 16.*

FILLING

½ pound cottage cheese	¼ cup light raisins
Sugar to taste	¼ cup shredded almonds
Pinch cinnamon	Vanilla, sherry, lemon juice,
1 egg	or lemon rind, optional

Mash cheese with sugar and cinnamon.

Beat in egg and stir in raisins and almonds.

If desired flavor with vanilla, sherry, lemon juice, or a little grated lemon rind.

Put a spoonful of filling in center of each blintz and roll up, folding in sides to make little "packages."

Sauté the blintzes until golden brown in hot melted butter, turning in order to brown on all sides.

Serve with sour cream and a little jelly or jam. *Serves 4.*

PANTYCAKES

½ cup sifted all-purpose flour	4 eggs, well beaten
¾ cup sugar	1 cup sour cream
½ teaspoon baking soda	About 3 tablespoons water
1 teaspoon double-acting baking powder	Butter and syrup or confectioners' sugar and jam
1 teaspoon salt	
1 cup coarsely crushed graham crackers	

Stir flour, sugar, baking soda, baking powder, and salt into a bowl. Add graham crackers and stir in eggs, sour cream, and water. The batter should be just thin enough so that the cakes will run a little at the edges when dropped onto a hot griddle.

Pour batter in small cakes onto a hot greased griddle and cook until dark brown on both sides. The cakes should have a crisp lacy surface and uneven edges. If they are almost impossible to turn, your batter is the right consistency.

Serve hot with butter and syrup or with confectioners' sugar and jam. *Makes 24.*

CHAPTER 7

Dessert Fritters, Fried Cakes, and Croquettes

DEEP-FRIED DESSERTS

F<small>RIED</small> cakes are of ancient origin, and almost every country has its popular variation. The Saracen version of what later became known in France as *le beignet*, and to us as the "fritter," was a fruit-filled batter fried in sweet oil and served with honey.

Our English word "fritter" is derived from the French verb *frire* —to fry—and there is a mistaken notion regarding the meaning of this culinary term. Frying is *not* cooking in a little fat in a frying pan. It means completely or almost completely immersing the food in hot fat or oil.

The first requirement for successful frying is a deep, straight-sided pan and a wire frying basket. The second is a quantity of fat or oil that may inhibit a frugal housewife. Yet, after the initial investment, this same fat may be used time and time again, providing it is restricted exclusively to sweet foods and is never allowed proximity to meat, fish or vegetables.

The last, and possibly the most important, safeguard to perfect deep-fried foods is a thermometer, for there should be little fluctuation above or below the temperature of the fat—365° to 370° F. Fat that is not hot enough will soak into the fritters, making them soggy and indigestible. Too-hot fat means overbrowned crusts and undercooked centers.

If you lack a thermometer, there are various ways to test the temperature of the fat, but these are uncertain at best. The browning of a chunk of bread in 1 minute is influenced by the freshness of the bread: stale bread browns faster than fresh. Of some merit as an indication of the temperature of the fat is the fritter itself. It should be golden brown in 3 to 5 minutes. If it browns more quickly, the fat is too hot; conversely, if it takes longer, the fat is too cool. But a thermometer is a good investment and eliminates the guesswork.

And now that we are equipped, let's get on with the fritters.

FRUIT FRITTERS

The surface of fruit, especially canned fruits, must be dried before it is dipped into batter, otherwise a pocket of steam forms between the batter and the fruit. Brandy or rum will not react like water, for the alcohol in the liquor is rapidly dispersed by the heat of the fat.

The fritter batter should be handled delicately. Beating makes it elastic, and it will not cling to the fruit. When a batter is prepared in advance, more vigorous stirring is permissible, since the elasticity disappears on standing. Beaten egg whites should be folded into the batter just before they are used.

Sometimes fruit, such as a raw apple, is not completely cooked in 5 minutes. The temperature of the fat should not be lowered from 370° F. in order to increase the frying time. Instead, brown the fritters and drain them as usual. Sprinkle them with a little sugar and put them in a moderate oven (350° F.) for a few minutes to glaze and to complete the cooking.

WINE BATTER FOR FRITTERS

½ cup all-purpose flour
Pinch salt
1 tablespoon sugar

White wine
1 tablespoon melted butter
2 egg whites, stiffly beaten

In mixing bowl combine flour, salt, and sugar.

Stir in enough wine to make a batter the consistency of heavy cream.

Stir in butter and let batter rest for 1 hour.

Fold in egg whites.

BEER BATTER FOR FRITTERS

½ cup flour
Pinch salt
1 tablespoon melted butter

1 egg, beaten
½ cup beer
1 egg white, stiffly beaten

In mixing bowl combine flour and salt.

Stir in butter and egg.

Add beer gradually, stirring only until mixture is smooth.

Let batter rest for 1 hour, then fold in egg white.

BRANDY BATTER FOR FRITTERS

¾ cup all-purpose flour
1 tablespoon sugar
½ cup warm water
1 tablespoon melted butter

2 tablespoons brandy
Pinch salt
1 egg, separated

In mixing bowl combine flour and sugar.

Gradually stir in warm water and melted butter.

Stir in brandy, salt, and egg yolk, beaten. Add a little more warm water if necessary to make the batter the consistency of thick cream.

Fold in stiffly beaten egg white.

LARGE CANNED FRUIT, SUCH AS PEACHES, PEARS, AND APRICOTS

Drain canned fruit and dry surface on paper towels. Dip each piece in fritter batter, making sure it is completely covered. Drop a few at a time into hot fat (370° F.) and cook from 3 to 5 minutes, or until golden brown. Drain on absorbent paper; arrange in a shallow pan, sprinkle with sugar, and put under broiler until sugar is glazed, being very careful not to let sugar burn.

FRESH FRUIT

Peel, pit, and cut large fresh fruit in half or into slices. Sprinkle sections with sugar and a little lemon juice and let stand for about 1 hour. Dry on absorbent paper, dip in fritter batter, and fry as above.

SMALL FRUIT AND BERRIES

Wash and pick over berries or other small fruit, sprinkle with sugar, and let stand for about 1 hour. Drain thoroughly. Add 2 cups to 1 cup fritter batter. Drop batter by spoonfuls into hot deep fat (370° F.) and cook until fritters are golden brown, or from 3 to 5 minutes. Drain on absorbent paper and serve hot with confectioners' sugar.

APPLE FRITTERS A LA PRINCESSE • *Beignets de Pommes à la Princesse*

Pare and core large apples, allowing ½ apple per serving. Cut into thin slices, sprinkle with sugar, cinnamon, and a few drops of rum or kirsch. Cover and let slices stand for about 1 hour. Drain well, adding any juice to a fritter batter. Dip slices into batter and fry a few at a time in hot deep fat (370° F.) until golden. Drain and arrange fritters in a shallow pan. Sprinkle with sugar and glaze in a hot oven (450° F.). Serve sprinkled with chopped pistachio nuts.

BANANA FRITTERS • *Beignets de Bananes*

Peel bananas, split them in half lengthwise, and cut each piece in half. Put in a shallow dish and sprinkle with confectioners' sugar, lemon juice, and sherry, rum, or brandy to taste. Cover dish and let bananas stand for 30 minutes, turning them several times. Drain well, adding any juice to a fritter batter. Dip each piece in batter and fry a few at a time in hot deep fat (370° F.) until golden. Drain on absorbent paper. Serve hot with sugar and whipped cream or with a dessert sauce flavored with sherry, rum, or brandy.

ORANGE FRITTERS • *Beignets d'Oranges*

Peel oranges and separate into segments. Prepare a sugar syrup by boiling together 2 cups water, 1 cup sugar, and 4 tablespoons brandy for 5 minutes. Add orange segments and simmer for 5 minutes. Remove sections from the syrup to cool. Dip in BRANDY BATTER and fry a few at a time in hot deep fat (370° F.) until delicately browned, turning over once with a wooden spoon. Drain on absorbent paper and serve hot. Serve with the syrup boiled down to a sauce consistency and flavored with orange juice and grated orange rind.

PINEAPPLE FRITTERS • *Beignets d'Ananas*

Peel and cut a fresh pineapple into slices ½ inch thick. Cut each slice in half, sprinkle with sugar and kirsch, and let stand for 30 minutes. Drain well, adding any juice to a fritter batter. Dip pieces in fritter batter and fry in hot deep fat (370° F.) until lightly browned. Drain, sprinkle with sugar, and glaze under broiler.

BLUEBERRY FRITTERS

1 cup all-purpose flour	2 eggs, separated
1 teaspoon double-acting baking powder	2–3 tablespoons water
½ teaspoon salt	¾ cup blueberries
2 tablespoons sugar	Confectioners' sugar or dessert sauce

In mixing bowl combine dry ingredients.

Beat egg yolks lightly with the water and stir into the dry ingredients, mixing only until smooth.

Fold in stiffly beaten egg whites.

Fold in blueberries.

Drop by spoonfuls into hot deep fat (370° F.) and cook until lightly browned.

Drain and serve hot sprinkled with confectioners' sugar or serve with a dessert sauce. *Makes 12.*

CHERRY FRITTERS • *Beignets de Cerises*

Pit 1 quart large sweet cherries and sprinkle with sugar and a little kirsch or maraschino liqueur. Stir into a fritter batter and drop by the spoonful into hot deep fat (370° F.). Fry until fritters are lightly browned. Drain and serve sprinkled with confectioners' sugar.

DOUGHNUTS

AMERICAN DOUGHNUTS

¼ cup butter	1 teaspoon salt
1 cup sugar	¾ cup milk
2 eggs	1 teaspoon vanilla
4 cups sifted enriched flour	
4 teaspoons double-acting baking powder	

Cream butter and sugar until well blended.
Stir in eggs.
Combine dry ingredients and add alternately with milk and vanilla, stirring after each addition until blended. The dough should be soft and a little sticky. Divide dough into 3 parts. Wrap each part in waxed paper and chill for 1 hour.
Roll out ⅓ of the dough at a time ¼ inch thick on a lightly floured board and cut with a floured doughnut cutter.
Fry a few doughnuts at a time in hot deep fat (365° F.) for 3 minutes. As soon as a doughnut rises to surface and shows color, turn it over. Turn again as soon as underside is browned. When completely brown, remove with slotted spoon to absorbent paper to drain. *Makes 3 dozen 3-inch doughnuts.*

SOUR-MILK DOUGHNUTS

Use buttermilk or sour milk in place of sweet milk in AMERICAN DOUGHNUTS recipe. Use only 2 teaspoons baking powder and add ½ teaspoon soda to dry ingredients.

MOLASSES DOUGHNUTS

Follow recipe above, adding ½ cup molasses and 1½ teaspoons ginger.

ORANGE DOUGHNUTS

Follow recipe above, using ¼ cup orange juice in place of ¼ cup of the milk. Add grated rind of 1 orange.

CHOCOLATE DOUGHNUTS

Follow recipe above, adding 1½ ounces chocolate, melted, to the butter-sugar mixture. Flavor with 1½ teaspoons vanilla.

NUT DOUGHNUTS

Follow recipe above, adding ½ cup broken nutmeats to dough.

SPICED DOUGHNUTS

Follow recipe above, adding to the dry ingredients ¼ teaspoon each cinnamon and nutmeg.

QUICK CRULLERS

⅔ cup sugar
4 eggs, lightly beaten
¾ teaspoon grated lemon rind
⅓ cup melted butter
⅓ cup milk

3½ cups sifted enriched flour
½ teaspoon cream of tartar
½ teaspoon soda
¼ teaspoon salt
Confectioners' sugar

Beat sugar gradually into eggs and beat until mixture is thick and pale in color.

Stir in lemon rind, butter, and milk.

Sift dry ingredients and stir into the egg mixture to make a soft dough.

Roll out dough ¼ inch thick on lightly floured board and cut into strips with a crimped pastry cutter.

Fry a few at a time in hot deep fat (365° F.) for about 3 minutes, or until brown.

Drain on absorbent paper and sprinkle with confectioners' sugar. *Makes 3 dozen.*

SWEET YEAST DOUGHNUTS

1 *package active dry yeast*	¼ *cup butter*
¼ *cup lukewarm water*	½ *cup hot milk*
¼ *cup sugar*	2–2½ *cups enriched flour*
½ *teaspoon salt*	1 *egg, lightly beaten*

Soften yeast in the lukewarm water for 5 minutes, then stir until blended.

Measure sugar, salt, and butter into mixing bowl.

Add hot milk and stir, mashing butter against sides of bowl until melted. Cool to lukewarm.

Stir in 1 cup of the flour to make a thick batter and beat until batter is smooth and elastic, about 100 strokes.

Add yeast and egg and stir until blended.

Stir in another cup flour and work in enough additional flour to make a dough that does not stick to fingers.

Turn dough onto lightly floured board and knead for 2 minutes, about 100 kneading strokes, until dough is springy and elastic. Shape into a ball and put into oiled bowl. Spread surface lightly with oil, cover, and let rise until double in bulk, about 1½ hours.

Punch dough down and turn onto floured board. Roll out ½ inch thick.

Cut with floured doughnut cutter.

Let rise, uncovered so that a light crust will form on surface, until double in bulk, about 30 minutes.

Fry a few doughnuts at a time for about 3 minutes in hot deep fat (365° F.). As soon as a doughnut rises to surface and begins to show color, turn it over. Turn again as soon as underside is brown. When brown, drain on absorbent paper. *Makes 1½ dozen.*

FRIED TWISTS

Follow SWEET YEAST DOUGHNUTS recipe. When dough is double in bulk, punch down and roll out ½ inch thick on lightly floured board. Cut into strips ½ inch wide and 10 inches long. Double a strip and pinch ends together firmly. Twist once to make a figure eight or twist twice for a double twist. Let rise and fry as above. Drain and coat with sugar. *Makes 16.*

DUTCH FRUIT-FILLED DOUGHNUTS • *Olykoek*

Follow SWEET YEAST DOUGHNUTS recipe. When dough is double in bulk, punch down and shape into 1½-inch balls, enclosing in center of each ½ teaspoon seedless raisins or mixed chopped candied fruits. Let balls rise until double in bulk, about 40 minutes, and fry as above. Drain. *Makes 2 dozen 1½-inch balls.*

FRENCH FRITTER DOUGHNUTS • *Les Beignets Soufflés*

1 *cup water*	*Vanilla, lemon extract,*
¼ *cup butter*	*brandy, or rum*
½ *teaspoon salt*	2 *egg whites, stiffly beaten*
1 *teaspoon sugar*	*Confectioners' sugar or*
1 *cup sifted enriched flour*	*custard or fruit sauce*
4 *eggs*	

In a small saucepan bring to a boil the water, butter, salt, and sugar. When butter is melted and water is boiling rapidly, remove from heat and add flour all at once. Hold saucepan over heat and stir briskly until batter comes away from sides of pan and forms a smooth ball in the center.

Beat in eggs, one at a time, beating after each addition until batter is smooth and glossy.

Add a teaspoon of any desired flavoring.

Fold in egg whites.

Fill a tablespoon with the paste and using a knife slip half of it off into hot deep fat (365° F.). Then slip off the other half, making 2 *beignets* from each spoonful. Fry for about 5 minutes, or until golden.

Drain on absorbent paper and serve immediately, sprinkled with confectioners' sugar or sauced with a custard or fruit sauce. *Makes 3 dozen.*

FRENCH CRULLERS

Make the same paste as for FRENCH FRITTER DOUGHNUTS. Put the paste into a pastry bag fitted with a large open-star (or fluted) tube.

Press out rings onto buttered heavy paper a few at a time. Invert paper over pan containing hot deep fat (365° F.) and the rings will slip from the paper into the fat. Fry for about 5 minutes or until nicely brown. Drain on absorbent paper and serve hot, sprinkled with confectioners' sugar.

SPANISH DOUGHNUTS • *Churros*

⅔ cup water	2 large eggs
1½ tablespoons sugar	1 tablespoon orange-flower
Pinch salt	water or rum
¼ cup butter	⅛ teaspoon mace
⅞ cup sifted all-purpose flour	Confectioners' sugar

In a saucepan combine water, sugar, salt, and butter.

Stir with wooden spoon over low heat until butter is melted and mixture is boiling rapidly.

Remove pan from fire and stir in flour. Stir rapidly until batter comes away cleanly from sides of pan and forms a smooth ball in center.

Beat in eggs vigorously, one at a time, beating until paste is smooth and shiny.

Beat in flavoring and mace.

Chill paste for 1 hour.

Put paste into a pastry bag fitted with a large fluted tube and press out strips of paste about 8 inches long and ¾ inch wide onto waxed paper.

Invert paper over a pot of hot deep fat (365° F.) and let the strips of dough drop off into the fat a few at a time. When golden on both sides drain on absorbent paper and keep in a warm oven until ready to serve.

Sprinkle generously with confectioners' sugar before serving. *Makes about 2 dozen.*

SNOW BALLS • *Sneeuwballen* (from the Netherlands)

½ cup water	2 tablespoons currants
Pinch salt	2 tablespoons finely shredded
½ cup butter	citron
10 tablespoons sifted all-purpose flour	1 tablespoon rose water
3 large eggs	Confectioners' sugar

In a saucepan combine water, salt, and butter. Stir with a wooden spoon over low heat until butter is melted and mixture is boiling rapidly. Remove pan from fire and stir in the flour. Continue to stir rapidly until batter comes cleanly away from sides of the pan and forms a smooth ball.

Beat in eggs, one at a time, and beat vigorously, until paste is smooth and shiny.

Beat in currants, citron, and rose water.

Dip a metal spoon into hot deep fat (365° F.) and fry spoonfuls of the batter until golden brown and puffed, dipping spoon into the hot fat between each spoonful of batter.

Drain on absorbent paper and sprinkle heavily with confectioners' sugar to give appearance of snowballs. *Makes 24.*

ROMANIAN FRIED TWISTS • *Minciunele*

4 egg yolks, beaten	2 tablespoons whiskey
5 tablespoons heavy cream	2¼ cups all-purpose flour
1 egg white, stiffly beaten	Confectioners' sugar
Pinch salt	

Mix eggs yolks and cream.

Fold in egg white.

Add salt and whiskey.

Add 1 cup flour and stir well. Add as much of the remaining flour as necessary to make a dough that is stiff enough to knead.

Turn dough out onto floured board and knead until smooth and not sticky.

Roll out dough thinly and cut into rectangles about 5 inches long and 2 inches wide. Make a 2-inch slit in center of each rectangle and slip one end of the rectangle through the slit.

Drop cakes a few at a time into hot deep fat (365° F.) and fry until golden brown on both sides.

Drain on absorbent paper.

Sprinkle with confectioners' sugar. *Makes about 3 dozen.*

DANISH DEERHORNS

½ cup butter	2 cups sifted all-purpose flour
½ cup sugar	Confectioners' sugar
4 eggs, beaten	

Cream butter and sugar.

Add eggs and mix well.

Add flour gradually, mixing to a soft dough.

Chill dough for 1 hour, then roll out thinly, using a little more flour if necessary.

Cut into triangles and roll as for horns or crescents.

Fry in hot deep fat (365° F.) until lightly browned.

Drain on absorbent paper.

Serve hot sprinkled with confectioners' sugar. *Makes about 3 dozen.*

NORWEGIAN KNOTS • *Fattigmands Bakkelse*

8 egg yolks	1 egg white
½ cup sugar	2⅜ cups sifted all-purpose
½ cup heavy cream	flour
¼ cup cognac	Confectioners' sugar
½ teaspoon ground carda-	
mom seeds	

Beat egg yolks with half the sugar until thick and pale in color.

Whip cream lightly and fold in remaining sugar and cognac.

Combine cream and egg yolk mixture and stir in cardamom.

Beat egg white until stiff and fold into the mixture.

Gradually work in flour, stirring after each addition until batter is smooth. Chill overnight.

Next day roll out dough very thinly on lightly floured board and cut into strips about 1½ inches wide and 4 or 5 inches long. Make a gash in the center of each and pull one end of the dough through the gash. Or take 2 strips and tie together into a loose knot.

Fry the knots in hot deep fat (365° F.) for about 3 minutes, or until golden. Drain on absorbent paper and sprinkle with confectioners' sugar. *Makes about 3 dozen.*

SWEDISH CHRISTMAS CRULLERS • *Klenater*

4 egg yolks	1 tablespoon brandy
¼ cup confectioners' sugar	1 tablespoon lemon rind,
3 tablespoons butter	grated
1½ cups sifted all-purpose	Jam
flour	

Mix all ingredients except jam and stir until well blended. Chill.

Turn dough onto floured board and roll out thinly.

With a pastry wheel or knife, cut strips ¾ inch wide and 3 inches long. Cut a gash in the center of each strip and twist one end through the gash.

Fry in hot deep fat (365° F.) until lightly browned.

Drain on absorbent paper and serve with jam. *Makes about 2 dozen.*

SWISS FRIED CAKES

1 cup light cream	2 cups sifted all-purpose flour
2 eggs, lightly beaten	½ cup butter
1 teaspoon salt	Sugar

Combine cream, eggs, and salt and mix well.

Add flour to make a soft dough.

Turn dough onto floured board. Dot with butter and, with the hands, work butter into dough. The butter should be firm but not hard.

Chill dough for 1 hour.

Roll out ⅛ inch thick on lightly floured board.

Cut into any desired shape, making a ½-inch gash through center of each.

Fry in hot deep fat (365° F.) until golden.

Drain on absorbent paper and roll in sugar while still hot. *Makes 3 dozen.*

GERMAN YEAST CAKES • *Krapfen*

1 package active dry yeast	Grated rind of 1 lemon
¼ cup lukewarm water	1 egg, well beaten
1 tablespoon sugar	4–5 cups all-purpose flour
¼ cup butter	Jam, marmalade, or jelly
⅜ cup sugar	Melted butter
½ teaspoon salt	Confectioners' sugar
1 cup milk, scalded and cooled to lukewarm	

Soak yeast in lukewarm water with the 1 tablespoon sugar for 5 minutes.

Cream together butter and the ⅜ cup sugar.

Add salt, the softened yeast, milk, lemon rind, egg, and enough of the flour to make a dough that is soft but not sticky.

Let dough rise, covered, in a warm place until double in bulk.

Knead dough on a lightly floured board and roll out 1/16 inch thick. Cut into rounds 3 inches in diameter. Spread edges with a little beaten egg to keep filling from running out and spread center of every other round with 1 teaspoon jam, marmalade, or jelly. Place a plain round on top of each filled round, pinch edges together securely, and spread with melted butter.

Let rise in a warm place for 1 hour.

Fry in hot deep fat (365° F.), frying unbuttered side first.

Drain on absorbent paper and dust with confectioners' sugar. *Makes 4 dozen.*

FAST NIGHT CAKES · *Fastnachtskuchen*

These German favorite fried cakes, eaten on Shrove Tuesday, the day before the beginning of Lent, are made the same way as the YEAST CAKES above, except the dough is rolled out ¼ inch thick and cut into squares.

SYRIAN HONEY CURLS

4 eggs
½ teaspoon double-acting
   baking powder
½ teaspoon salt
2½ cups sifted enriched flour
¼ cup butter
Honey and chopped nuts

Beat eggs with rotary beater until well beaten.

Beat in baking powder and salt and 2 cups flour.

Work in remaining flour and a little more if necessary to make a soft dough that does not stick to fingers.

Turn dough out on lightly floured board and knead in butter, one tablespoon at a time. Continue to knead until dough is smooth and soft.

Cut dough into 4 parts and roll out one part at a time paper-thin on a heavily floured board. Cut into rectangles 4×6 inches.

Drop, one at a time, into hot deep fat (365° F.). Using two forks, turn dough over immediately, and before it has a chance to brown roll it as you would a piece of paper. When brown, drain on absorbent paper.

Dribble honey over the curls and sprinkle with chopped nuts. *Makes 20.*

SWEDISH ROSETTES • *Sockerstruvor*

2 eggs	2 tablespoons sugar
1 cup milk	Pinch salt
1 cup sifted all-purpose flour	Confectioners' sugar

Beat eggs and milk.

Gradually stir in flour, sugar, and salt and stir until batter is well blended. Chill for 1 hour.

Dip a rosette iron into deep fat heated to 370° F. Remove iron, drain on absorbent paper, and dip into the batter up to but not over the edge of the iron. Lower iron into the fat and fry the fritter for 1½ minutes, or until golden brown.

Slip rosette carefully from the iron to absorbent paper to drain. Heat iron again in the fat and repeat.

Store rosettes in a tight container in a dry place, where they will keep crisp and fresh for many weeks.

Dust generously with confectioners' sugar before serving. *Makes 30.*

VIENNESE RUFFLES • *Zuckerstrauben*

⅔ cup sifted all-purpose flour	6 egg whites
½ teaspoon salt	Sugar
4 tablespoons sugar	SABAYON SAUCE
White wine	

Mix together flour, salt, and sugar.

Stir in enough white wine to make a medium-thick batter.

Beat egg whites until stiff and fold into batter.

Press batter through a pastry bag fitted with a plain or fluted tube into hot deep fat (370° F.) and fry until delicately browned.

Drain "ruffles" on absorbent paper.

Sprinkle with sugar and serve with sabayon sauce. *Makes about 30.*

DESSERT CROQUETTES

CHESTNUT CROQUETTES • *Croquettes de Marrons*

1 *pound chestnuts*	1 *egg beaten with ¼ cup*
Milk	*milk and 1 tablespoon*
1 *one-inch piece vanilla bean*	*cooking oil*
½ *cup sugar*	*Fine dry bread crumbs*
3 *tablespoons butter*	*Confectioners' sugar*
3 *egg yolks, lightly beaten*	APRICOT RUM SAUCE
Flour	

Slit shells of the chestnuts on the convex side. Put in pan with water to cover, bring to a boil, and simmer for 5 minutes. Take chestnuts from hot water, one by one, and remove shells and inner skins.

Put shelled nuts in a saucepan with enough milk to cover, add vanilla bean, and cook until soft.

Rub chestnuts and milk through a fine sieve (or purée in an electric blender), return the purée to the heat, and cook, stirring constantly, until thick and dry.

Into the purée stir the sugar, butter, and beaten egg yolks. Stir rapidly over heat for a few minutes until well blended.

Spread mixture in a shallow oiled pan and chill.

When cold, shape into small balls the size of walnuts.

Roll balls in flour, then in the egg mixture, and finally in bread crumbs.

Place a few croquettes in a wire frying basket and fry in hot deep fat (370° F.) until crisply browned.

Drain on absorbent paper, sprinkle with confectioners' sugar, and serve with apricot rum sauce. *Serves 6.*

FRIED CREAM • *Crème Frite*

3 *egg yolks, beaten*	3 *tablespoons milk*
1 *tablespoon dark rum*	2 *cups heavy cream*
Pinch salt	½ *cup fine dry bread crumbs*
¼ *cup sugar*	*Beaten egg*
1 *half-inch stick cinnamon*	¼ *cup ground almonds*
3 *tablespoons cornstarch*	*Warm rum*

Combine egg yolks, rum, salt, and sugar.

Add cinnamon stick.

Moisten cornstarch with the milk and stir into the egg yolk mixture.

Scald cream and stir gradually into the egg yolk mixture.

Cook over simmering water, stirring constantly, until cream is smooth and thick.

Pour cream into an oiled shallow pan ¾ inch thick and cool.

Cut into squares, roll in bread crumbs, dip in beaten egg, and roll in ground almonds.

Fry in hot deep fat (370° F.) for about 2 minutes, or until lightly browned.

Drain on absorbent paper and arrange on serving dish.

Pour a jigger of warm rum over the fried cream and serve blazing. *Serves 6.*

CHAPTER 8

Meringue
and
Meringue Desserts and
Baked Alaskas

In 1720 a Swiss baker who lived in a tiny village in Switzerland called Meiringen discovered the delicate confection that resulted from the baking of beaten egg whites and sugar. It was not long before meringues became a favorite pastry of the courts and Marie Antoinette made them with her own royal hands in the kitchen at the court of Trianon.

Probably she dropped the meringue from the tip of a teaspoon onto a baking sheet in the form of dainty "kisses" or shells. It would have been easier if she could have used a pastry bag fitted with a fancy tube to press out decorative nests or *barquettes*—boat shapes—to make fragile containers for rich creams or sugared fruits. But pastry bags came later. Perhaps she tinted the meringue pale yellow with saffron or rose-pink with cochineal, flavored them with rose water, or dredged them with colored sugars before "drying" them in a slow oven. At any rate, we know they are no less delicious today than they were then.

The basic recipes for meringue require nothing more than the correct proportion of fine granulated sugar to each egg white and a copious amount of beating. So use an electric beater if you are fortunate enough to have one—at medium speed, and remember that egg whites beat to greater volume if they are at room temperature.

There are three basic types of meringues and, while ORDINARY MERINGUE is used for most meringue desserts, it seems appropriate to include the others in this chapter.

Meringues are baked in a very slow oven and much depends on the constancy of the oven for perfect results, for they should not be allowed to color in the least and often do not need an oven at all. They can be dried at room temperature providing the kitchen is warm and dry or in a warming oven, or over the heat of a radiator. And once dry they may be stored in a tightly closed container where they will keep fresh and crisp for many weeks.

Never try to make meringues on a hot, humid day. But here's a trick. Perhaps you have made a cake and have a couple of egg whites left over. Make meringues while the cake is baking. Remove cake from oven and place meringues in center of the oven. Immediately turn off oven heat and let the meringues dry in the cooling oven. After 1 hour, remove and continue to dry in a warm, dry place.

Should your meringues take on color, don't throw them away. They taste like spun taffy!

ORDINARY MERINGUE • *Meringue Ordinaire*

4 egg whites (½ cup)	1 cup fine granulated sugar
Pinch salt	1 teaspoon flavoring
¼ teaspoon cream of tartar or ½ teaspoon lemon juice or vinegar	

Beat egg whites with salt until stiff but not dry.

Beat in cream of tartar or lemon juice or vinegar.

Begin adding the sugar gradually, about 1 tablespoon at a time, beating constantly, until ¾ cup has been added and the resulting meringue is as thick and smooth as marshmallow. No grains of sugar should be felt when a small amount is rubbed between the fingers.

Stir or fold in the remaining sugar and flavoring.

ITALIAN MERINGUE • *Meringue Italienne*

1 cup sugar	4 egg whites
¼ teaspoon cream of tartar	1 teaspoon vanilla
⅓ cup water	

In a saucepan combine sugar, cream of tartar, and water.

Bring slowly to a boil, and boil rapidly (236° F.) until syrup spins a long thread when a little is dropped from the end of a spoon or fork.

With a rotary or electric beater, beat egg whites until stiff.

Continue beating and very slowly pour in syrup.

Add vanilla or other flavoring and continue to beat until meringue is glossy and holds its shape.

Use for cake frostings or pie toppings.

COOKED MERINGUE • *Meringue sur le Feu*

4 egg whites	1 cup fine granulated sugar
Pinch salt	1 teaspoon flavoring
¼ teaspoon cream of tartar	

Put all ingredients into top of a double boiler.

With a rotary or electric hand beater, beat over simmering water for about 7 minutes, or until meringue becomes stiff enough to hold its shape.

Use for cake frosting, for meringue mushrooms, and pie toppings.

When baked in a hot oven meringue remains creamy within.

MERINGUE SHELLS

Make ORDINARY MERINGUE and flavor with vanilla or almond extract.

Moisten a baking sheet and cover it with heavy unglazed paper.

With a tablespoon drop meringue onto the paper in the shape of half an egg. Or spoon meringue into a pastry bag fitted with a No. 7 plain tube. Press out shells to desired length and width. By pushing the bag gently away from you as you press out the meringue, an attractive wavy effect is made. Sprinkle the meringues with fine granulated sugar. Bake in a slow oven (250° F.) for about 30 minutes. Watch carefully as they bake and if they begin to take on color, turn off oven and let the meringues remain until dry. With the aid of a spatula remove shells from paper and scoop out a little of the soft part in the center of the underside. Should they stick, place the paper over a damp towel for a few minutes. Put shells upside down on the baking sheet and return them to the still-warm oven (heat off) to dry thoroughly. When ready to serve, fill the shells with sliced and sweetened fruit or berries or with a favorite PASTRY CREAM and top with whipped cream.

MERINGUES GLACEES

Put 2 meringue shells together with ice cream bulging between them. Decorate edge of shells with whipped cream pressed through a pastry bag fitted with a small fluted tube.

MERINGUE NESTS

Spoon ORDINARY MERINGUE into a pastry bag fitted with a No. 18 or 20 open-star tube. Line a baking sheet with waxed paper and on it outline the base of the nests the desired size. The shape of the base may be circular, heart-shaped, or boat-shaped (*barquettes*). Fill in the base with meringue, then build up a rim around the edge of the base from 1 to 2 inches high and about 1 inch thick. Sprinkle with fine granulated sugar and bake in a slow oven (250° F.) for 30 minutes, watching carefully. Remove nests from paper to a cake rack with the help of a spatula while they are still a little moist in the center and before they have had a chance to color. Let them dry and cool. Just before serving fill with PASTRY CREAM, ice cream, or with sugared fruits or berries and top with a rosette of whipped cream or with a meringue "kiss."

MERINGUE RING

Spoon ORDINARY MERINGUE into a pastry bag fitted with a No. 7 round tube. Cover a baking sheet with waxed paper and trace a circle of any desired diameter from 6 to 9 inches. Press out a ring of meringue, going round and round and building up a crown about 2 inches high and 1 inch thick. Decorate top of the crown with small kisses, using a No. 18 open-star tube. Bake in a slow (250° F.) oven for about 30 minutes. Loosen from paper with help of a spatula and return to the warm oven (heat off) to cool and dry.

MERINGUE TIMBALE • *Vacherin Meringué*

Make ORDINARY MERINGUE. Press out 4 MERINGUE RINGS about 6 inches in diameter and 1 inch high on baking sheets lined with waxed paper, using about half the meringue. Bake in a slow oven (250° F.) for 30 minutes. Remove rings from paper before they are completely dry and mount them, one upon the other, with a little unbaked meringue between. Frost sides smoothly with unbaked meringue and decorate top and sides with scrolls and "kisses," pressing the meringue from a pastry bag fitted with a small open-star or fluted tube. Return the decorated crown to the oven (heat off) for about 1 hour to dry.

An 8-inch crown will need double quantity of ordinary meringue.

APRICOT MERINGUE TORTE

1 *pound dried apricots*	1 *tablespoon lemon juice*
2½ *cups water*	1½ *cups heavy cream*
Pinch salt	1 8-*inch* MERINGUE RING
½ *cup sugar*	1 *can apricot halves*

In saucepan put apricots, water, and salt. Bring water slowly to a boil, cover, and simmer for 15 minutes, or until apricots are tender.

Stir in sugar and lemon juice and press apricots and juice through a fine sieve or purée in an electric blender.

If purée is too thin, stir over low heat until liquid is evaporated and purée is thick. Cool.

Whip cream until stiff.

Fold in apricot purée.

Fill meringue ring with the apricot cream and decorate with canned apricots, rounded side up. *Serves 6.*

MERINGUE CIRCLES

Make ORDINARY MERINGUE. Line 2 baking sheets with waxed paper and trace 2 circles on each, 8 inches in diameter and at least 1 inch apart. With a spatula, spread the circles thinly with the meringue and bake in a slow oven (250° F.) for about 20 minutes. Watch carefully so they do not brown. Remove from oven and loosen circles with a spatula while still pliable. They will crisp quickly as they cool.

Two entirely different types of desserts are made from baked meringue circles. The first is assembled just before serving so the meringue stays crisp. The other is allowed to ripen for 24 hours so that meringue and filling will blend.

PEACH MERINGUE CAKE

Whip 2 cups heavy cream until stiff. Reserve ¼ for the frosting. Into the rest fold 2 cups sliced and sugared peaches. Just before serving, sandwich 4 baked MERINGUE CIRCLES together with the peach-cream mixture between. Spread top and sides of cake with the reserved whipped cream and decorate with slices of peaches or with a grating of sweet chocolate.

BERRY MERINGUE CAKE

Substitute strawberries or raspberries for the peaches in the above recipe.

CHOCOLATE CREAM MERINGUE TORTE • *Crème de Chocolat Torte*

In top of double boiler over simmering but not boiling water beat 2 egg whites until foamy. Gradually beat in ½ cup sugar, 1 cup softened sweet butter, and 6 ounces semi-sweet chocolate, melted. Beat until smooth. Remove from heat and cool. When filling is cool and thick, spread it over 3 baked MERINGUE CIRCLES and put a fourth on top. Sprinkle top generously with sifted confectioners' sugar and chill for 24 hours before serving.

CHOCOLATE ANGEL PIE

Make half the quantity of ORDINARY MERINGUE flavored with vanilla. Make a nestlike shell with the meringue in a 9-inch pie plate, building up sides of shell a good inch above the edge of the plate. Bake in a slow oven (250° F.) for 30 minutes. Turn off heat and let the shell remain in the cooling oven for 15 to 30 minutes longer, watching carefully that it does not brown. Remove from oven and cool. Fill shell with CHOCOLATE PASTRY CREAM. Spread top of cream with 1 cup cream, whipped and sweetened with 1 tablespoon sugar. Sprinkle with grated semi-sweet chocolate.

VIENNESE SCHAUM TORTE

Make twice the quantity of ORDINARY MERINGUE, flavoring both batches with vanilla. Cover 2 baking sheets with waxed paper and trace 2 circles on each, 8 inches in diameter and at least 1 inch apart. Using a pastry bag fitted with an open-star tubé, make a ring around two of the circles about 1 inch high and 1 inch thick. Press out a wreath of large kisses around the third circle. With a spatula spread the fourth circle thinly with meringue to make the base of the torte.

Bake in a slow oven (250° F.) for about 30 minutes without letting the meringues take on color. While still moist and pliable loosen from sheets with a spatula and let them crisp and cool.

Just before serving, put the circle on a cake plate and set the two rings on top. Fill the container with sweetened whipped cream mixed with slices of fruit or berries or chopped candied fruits, or with ice cream, or with LIME CUSTARD. Top the torte with the wreath of kisses.

MERINGUE CAKE SYLVIA • Gâteau Sylvia

3 egg whites
¼ teaspoon almond extract
Pinch salt
¾ cup sugar
1 cup blanched ground
   almonds
VANILLA BUTTER CREAM

1 tablespoon instant coffee
   moistened with water to
   make a paste
1 ounce (1 square) semi-
   sweet chocolate, melted
⅓ cup toasted slivered
   almonds

Beat egg whites, almond extract, and salt until thick. Gradually beat in sugar, 1 tablespoon at a time, and continue to beat until meringue is stiff and glossy.

Fold in ground almonds.

Line baking sheets with waxed paper and trace 3 circles 8 inches in diameter. Spread meringue evenly over the circles.

Bake in a preheated 300° F. oven for 30 minutes.

Turn circles upside down and peel off paper. Cool on cake racks.

Flavor ⅔ of the butter cream with the coffee and spread between the 3 layers, sandwich-fashion.

Flavor remaining butter cream with the melted chocolate and spread around sides of the cake.

Pipe a wreath of the remaining chocolate frosting around top edge. Press slivered almonds on the sides of the cake and chill. *Serves 8.*

PROGRESS CAKE · *Progrès*

4 egg whites
Pinch salt
¼ teaspoon cream of tartar
1 cup sugar
½ cup grated blanched almonds
½ cup toasted ground hazelnuts

CHOCOLATE PRALINE BUTTER CREAM
½ cup chopped toasted almonds
Confectioners' sugar

Beat egg whites with pinch of salt and cream of tartar until stiff. Gradually beat in sugar, one tablespoon at a time, and continue to beat until meringue is stiff and glossy.

Fold in grated almonds and hazelnuts.

Grease and flour 2 baking sheets and trace 2 circles on each about 6 inches in diameter. Spread circles thinly with the meringue mixture and bake in a moderate (350° F.) oven for 10 minutes.

Remove from oven and immediately loosen circles from sheets. Let cool and crisp.

Put the layers together and frost top and sides with the chocolate praline butter cream.

Press toasted almonds around sides and sprinkle top with confectioners' sugar. *Serves 6.*

CHESTNUT CAKE · *Bibesco*

4 egg whites
Pinch salt
½ teaspoon lemon juice
1 cup sugar
1 cup ground filberts

2 cups CHESTNUT PUREE
2 cups heavy cream, whipped and sweetened and flavored to taste
Candied chestnuts

Beat egg whites, salt, and lemon juice until stiff. Gradually beat in sugar, 1 tablespoon at a time, and continue to beat until meringue is stiff and glossy.

Fold in filberts.

With a pastry bag fitted with a large round tube, press out rings of the meringue on greased and floured baking sheets about 6 inches in diameter.

Bake in a preheated 350° F. oven for 10 to 15 minutes, or until lightly browned.

Loosen rings immediately from sheets and let cool and crisp.

Superimpose the rings, one on top of the other, with chestnut purée between.

With a pastry bag fitted with a fluted tube, press out rosettes of the chestnut purée all around sides and top.

Fill center with whipped cream.

Top with candied chestnuts. *Serves 8.*

CHAMBORD CAKE • *Gâteau Chambord*

Make as CHESTNUT CAKE above, substituting ground dry almonds for the filberts. Use PRALINE BUTTER CREAM in place of the chestnut purée.

Miniature meringues in the form of drops or "kisses" make attractive additions to the tea table. They also contribute decorative touches to an otherwise plain dessert. Sandwich two together with frosting between. Perch them atop a cream or custard or circle them around a frosted birthday cake with a tiny candle inserted in the center of each.

KISSES • *Biscuits de Meringue*

Make ORDINARY MERINGUE flavored with vanilla, rose water, or orange-flower water. Moisten a baking sheet and cover it with heavy unglazed paper. Drop the meringue by the teaspoon, an inch apart, onto the baking sheet. Or press it through a pastry bag fitted with an open-star or fluted tube in the form of "kisses." To do this, hold the tube vertically over and close to the paper. Squeeze out the meringue, raising the tube slowly. Release pressure on the bag and draw the tube up and away. The greater the pressure, the larger the kiss will be. Sprinkle with fine granulated sugar and bake in a slow oven (250° F.) for about 25 minutes. Remove immediately from the paper to a cake rack to dry. They will crisp as they cool. *Recipe for ordinary meringue makes 2 dozen large or 4 dozen small kisses.*

CHERRY NUT KISSES • *Biscuits de Meringue aux Cerises*

Fold ½ cup chopped candied cherries and ½ cup chopped pecans, walnuts, or toasted almonds, and 1 extra teaspoon vanilla into ORDINARY MERINGUE. Drop by the teaspoonful, 1 inch apart, onto greased and floured baking sheets. Bake in a slow (250° F.) oven for about 30 minutes. Remove kisses immediately to a cake rack to dry.

COCONUT KISSES

Fold 1 cup shredded coconut and 2 teaspoons vanilla into ORDINARY MERINGUE before shaping and baking.

DATE KISSES

Put 1 cup pitted dates through the fine blade of a food chopper. Fold them into ORDINARY MERINGUE. Flavor with 2 teaspoons extract before shaping and baking.

MARGUERITES

Fold 1 cup finely chopped nuts and 2 teaspoons vanilla into ORDINARY MERINGUE and drop the mixture by the teaspoonful onto small round chocolate or vanilla wafers. Sprinkle with granulated sugar and bake in a slow oven (250° F.) for about 30 minutes. *Recipe for ordinary meringue will make 4 dozen marguerites.*

CHOCOLATE MERINGUES • *Meringuettes au Chocolat*

Make a COOKED MERINGUE. Stir in 3 tablespoons unsweetened cocoa and 1 teaspoon vanilla. Press out small sticks through a pastry bag fitted with a small round tube on greased and floured baking sheet.

Bake in a moderate (350° F.) oven for 10 minutes, or long enough to crust the tops. Remove from baking sheets to cake racks to cool and crisp.

MOCHA MERINGUES • *Meringuettes au Mocha*

Make the above recipe omitting the vanilla. Stir in 1 teaspoon instant coffee dissolved in 2 teaspoons hot water.

CHOCOLATE MERINGUE BISCUITS • *Biscuits Chocolat*

Make ITALIAN MERINGUE. Stir in 6 ounces semi-sweet chocolate pieces melted with ¼ cup water or coffee and 2 tablespoons confectioners' sugar. Press from pastry bag with plain round tube onto baking sheet lined with waxed paper. Bake in a slow oven (250° F.) for 30 minutes. Remove immediately from baking sheets to cake racks to cool and crisp. *Recipe for Italian meringue makes 4 dozen.*

ALMOND ROCKS • *Rochers d'Amandes*

3 egg whites	1 teaspoon vanilla
1¼ cups confectioners' sugar	½ cup dry shredded almonds

Beat egg whites, sugar, and vanilla over simmering water until meringue is thick enough to hold its shape.

Remove from heat and beat until cool.

Fold in almonds.

Drop from a teaspoon onto greased and floured baking sheets in irregular droplets, keeping them 1 inch apart.

Bake in a slow oven (250° F.) for 30 minutes, or until dry but not brown. *Makes 3 dozen.*

COCONUT ROCKS • *Rochers à la Noix de Coco*

½ cup shredded coconut	4 egg whites
⅓ cup dry grated almonds	1 teaspoon vanilla
12 tablespoons sugar	

In a mixing bowl beat thoroughly the coconut, almonds, 9 tablespoons of the sugar, and 2 of the egg whites.

Beat the remaining 2 egg whites until stiff and gradually beat in remaining 3 tablespoons sugar. Stir in vanilla.

Fold the meringue into the nut paste.

Drop from a teaspoon onto greased and floured baking sheets, keeping the mounds well apart.

Bake in a moderate (350° F.) oven for 15 to 20 minutes, or until lightly browned.

Remove immediately from baking sheets to cake racks to cool. *Makes 3 dozen.*

Since meringue is such an integral part of the Baked Alaska it seems appropriate to include these popular desserts in this chapter. The meringue, instead of being dried out in a slow oven, is toasted for just a few minutes in a very hot oven.

BAKED ALASKA • *Omelette en Surprise*

Preheat oven to 450° F. Make ORDINARY MERINGUE flavored to taste. Cover a thick wooden board with heavy unglazed paper and put in the center a layer of spongecake or GENOISE from 1 to 1½ inches thick. The cake should be cut the same shape as a quart of ice cream, whether brick or molded, but it should extend from ¾ to 1 inch beyond the ice cream.

Put ice cream on top of the cake (it should be very hard-frozen). Cover both ice cream and cake with a thick layer of meringue. Dust the meringue with fine granulated sugar and bake the Alaska in the hot oven for about 5 minutes, or until the meringue is delicately browned. The board, paper, cake, and meringue are all poor conductors of heat, and prevent the cream from melting. Slip the Baked Alaska quickly onto a chilled platter and serve immediately. *Serves 6.*

FLAMING ALASKA • *Omelette en Surprise Flambée*

Press 3 or 4 eggshell halves cup-fashion, into the meringue on top of the BAKED ALASKA. Bake. Slip the Alaska onto a chilled platter. Pour a little heated rum into each shell, set the rum aflame, and serve blazing.

NORWEGIAN SURPRISE • *Omelette en Surprise Norvégienne*

Follow recipe for BAKED ALASKA. Spread cake with a layer of fruit jelly, or sprinkle with kirsch, curaçao, maraschino, or any other desired liqueur before topping with ice cream and meringue.

ORANGE ALASKA • *Omelette en Surprise à l'Orange*

Follow recipe for BAKED ALASKA. Sustitute orange ice for the ice cream. Before serving, surround the Alaska with orange sections cooked in a LIGHT SYRUP until glazed.

FRUIT ALASKA • *Omelette en Surprise aux Fruits*

Follow recipe for BAKED ALASKA. Cover cake base with a layer of fresh or stewed fruit before topping with ice cream and meringue.

STRAWBERRY ALASKA • *Omelette en Surprise aux Fraises*

Follow recipe for BAKED ALASKA. Put a pint brick of vanilla ice cream on cake base, cover with a 1-inch layer of sliced chilled strawberries, and top with another pint brick of vanilla ice cream. Cover with ORDINARY MERINGUE and bake as usual.

CHERRY ALASKA • *Omelette en Surprise aux Cerises*

Follow recipe for BAKED ALASKA. Cover cake base with sweet black cherries, pitted and halved, lightly sugared, steeped in kirsch, and chilled. Substitute raspberry ice for the ice cream. Just before serving, surround the Alaska with more cherries, sprinkle with heated kirsch, and set aflame. Brandy may be used in place of kirsch.

PEACH ALASKA • *Omelette en Surprise aux Pêches*

Simmer 6 fresh peaches, peeled, halved, and pitted, in 2 cups water with ¾ cup sugar and 1 teaspoon vanilla for 15 minutes. Drain and chill. Follow recipe for BAKED ALASKA. Substitute raspberry ice for the ice cream and put poached peaches, rounded side up, in a circle on top of ice cream. Cover with ORDINARY MERINGUE and bake.

NEAPOLITAN SURPRISE • *Omelette en Surprise Napolitain*

Follow recipe for BAKED ALASKA. Put a pint brick of vanilla ice cream on the cake base and cover with a layer of chopped preserved chestnuts. Top with a pint brick of strawberry ice cream. Cover with ORDINARY MERINGUE. Press a baked MERINGUE NEST into top of meringue. When ready to serve fill the meringue with brandied cherries and blaze at table.

BAKED ALASKA PIE • *Omelette Surprise en Flan*

Bake a rich pastry shell. Fill shell with very hard-frozen ice cream and cover with a thick layer of ORDINARY MERINGUE. Sprinkle meringue with fine granulated sugar, put pie cn a thick wooden board, and bake in a very hot preheated oven (450° F.) for about 5 minutes, or until meringue is golden. Serve immediately.

MELON ALASKA • *Melon Glacé*

Discard seeds from half a honeydew or cantaloupe for each person and chill. Fill cavities with very hard-frozen ice cream, piling it high in center. Cover both cut surface of melon and ice cream with a thick topping of ORDINARY MERINGUE. Put melons in a shallow pan filled with crushed ice and bake in a very hot preheated oven (475° F.) for 3 minutes, or until meringue is delicately browned.

CHAPTER 9

Cream Puff Pastries

Fragile pastry puffs of French origin can be the basis of many delicious desserts—the most famous of which are represented in this chapter. Filled with whipped cream, ice cream, or pastry cream, the puffs are always a delectable treat.

Contrary to appearance, cream puffs and desserts made from cream puff paste are relatively simple to make. Once the basic principles of making and baking the paste, or *le pâte à chou*, have been mastered, cream puffs, éclairs, and other glamorous desserts can be quickly made to mark you as a pastry cook of distinction.

Puffs fashioned into swans, with wings outspread, the "bodies" billowing with a mound of whipped cream, are always a delight to children. More sophisticated, but no less attractive, is a crown of puff pastry filled with pastry cream and topped with toasted almonds. Even the sensational pyramid of tiny cream-filled puffs known as *le croquembouche* is possible for anyone to make in the home kitchen, but the success of all of these desserts is based on knowing how to make a simple cream puff.

CREAM PUFF PASTE · *Pâte à Chou*

1 cup hot water	1 teaspoon sugar
¼ cup butter	1 cup enriched flour
Pinch salt	4 large eggs

Pour hot water over butter in a saucepan and stir until butter is melted.

Add salt and sugar and bring mixture to a rapid boil.

Add flour all at once, raise saucepan over heat, and stir vigorously with a wooden spoon until mixture comes away cleanly from sides of pan and forms a ball in the center.

Remove from heat and add eggs, one at a time, beating vigorously with a wooden spoon or a rotary electric beater after each addition until batter is smooth and glossy. The batter must be thick enough to hold its shape, and if the eggs are very large it may be necessary to add all but the last one. On the other hand, if the eggs are small it may be necessary to add an additional yolk or white.

This amount of paste makes 10 large cream puffs or 12 éclairs or 2 crowns or 32 tiny puffs known as profiteroles.

CREAM PUFFS • *Choux*

Drop CREAM PUFF PASTE from tablespoon or teaspoon, depending on size of puff desired, onto an oiled baking sheet. Bake in a preheated hot oven (425° F.) for 15 minutes. Lower temperature to 350° F. and bake until puffs are free from beads of moisture. The time required will depend on the size of the puffs, but if they are underbaked they will collapse when removed from the oven. Large puffs will need 40 to 45 minutes' baking time; small puffs about 30. When the puffs are cool, split and fill with whipped cream, sweetened and flavored to taste, ice cream, CHOCOLATE BAVARIAN CREAM, or PASTRY CREAM.

CREAM PUFF SWANS

Drop 4 large tablespoons of CREAM PUFF PASTE in mounds on an oiled baking sheet, keeping the mounds 3 inches apart. Press one part of each mound of paste with the spoon to flatten and elongate it slightly (this makes the tail of the swan). Put remaining paste into a pastry bag fitted with a plain round tube about the size of a dime. Press out S-shaped pieces onto an oiled pie plate to simulate swans' necks. Bake puffs in a preheated hot over (425° F.) for 10 minutes. Put in S-shaped pieces and bake for 10 minutes longer. Reduce oven temperature to 350° F. and bake until puffs and "necks" are dry. The necks will have to be removed sooner than the puffs.

To fashion the swans, cut one-third from top of each large puff.

Fill puffs with whipped cream, sweetened and flavored to taste. Cut top into halves and press into the filling on either side to make the wings. Insert neck into the filling.

ECLAIRS · *Eclairs*

Shape CREAM PUFF PASTE on an oiled baking sheet with a pastry bag fitted with a ½-inch flat tube, making strips 1×4 inches. Bake as for CREAM PUFFS. Cool, split, and fill as desired.

RINGS

Shape CREAM PUFF PASTE on an oiled baking sheet into rings about 3 inches in diameter, pressing the paste through a pastry bag fitted with a plain round tube about the size of a dime. Bake as for CREAM PUFFS. Cool, split, and fill with whipped cream. Spread with melted chocolate and sprinkle with shredded blanched almonds.

CROWN

With floured finger, trace a circle about 8 inches in diameter on an oiled baking sheet. Drop CREAM PUFF PASTE from a tablespoon in mounds around the circle, keeping the mounds close together to form a large ring. Brush surface with beaten egg and sprinkle with slivered blanched almonds. Bake as for CREAM PUFFS. When cool, split and fill with large rosettes of CHOCOLATE PASTRY CREAM alternated with rosettes of whipped cream. Dust generously with confectioners' sugar.

TRIPLETS

Drop three tiny mounds of CREAM PUFF PASTE close together on an oiled baking sheet so they will bake as one puff. Bake as for CREAM PUFFS. When cool, cut and lift the upper part of each small puff and fill each with a different colored and flavored PASTRY CREAM or ice cream. Dust tops with confectioners' sugar.

TINY CHOCOLATE PUFFS • *Profiteroles au Chocolat*

With a pastry bag fitted with a small plain tube, shape CREAM PUFF PASTE into small mounds on an oiled baking sheet (or drop paste from tip of a teaspoon). Brush tops with beaten egg and bake in preheated hot oven (425° F.) for 15 minutes, or until puffed to twice their size. Reduce oven temperature to 350° F. and bake for 15 to 20 minutes longer, or until dry and browned. Cool. Make a small hole in bottom of each and fill with sweetened whipped cream flavored with vanilla. To do this, use a pastry bag fitted with a small plain tube. Pyramid the *profiteroles* on a serving plate and serve with HOT CHOCOLATE SAUCE.

TINY STRAWBERRY PUFFS • *Profiteroles aux Fraises*

Make very small CREAM PUFFS and bake as for TINY CHOCOLATE PUFFS. Cool and fill with whipped cream mixed with STRAWBERRY PUREE. Prepare SABAYON SAUCE, flavored with a little strawberry syrup, and pour into a serving dish. Arrange the puffs on top.

NARCISSUS • *Narcisses*

Make CREAM PUFF PASTE. Press it out onto an oiled baking sheet through a pastry bag fitted with a large plain tube into the shape of large commas. Brush with beaten egg and sprinkle with shredded almonds. Bake as for CREAM PUFFS and cool. When cool, split on one side and fill with PASTRY CREAM or SAINT-HONORE CREAM.

MECCAS • *Pains de la Mecque*

Make CREAM PUFF PASTE and press out oblongs onto an oiled baking sheet through a pastry bag fitted with a large flat tube. Sprinkle with granulated sugar and lightly dent the center section of each oblong. Bake as for CREAM PUFFS. Cool and fill with jam.

SALAMBOS • *Salambôs*

Press out oblongs of CREAM PUFF PASTE on oiled baking sheet. Bake as for CREAM PUFFS. When cool fill with VANILLA PASTRY CREAM and dip in SYRUP cooked to the hard-crack stage. Sprinkle with chopped pistachios before the syrup hardens.

SELIKAS • *Selikas*

Make oblongs of CREAM PUFF PASTE on oiled baking sheet and bake as for CREAM PUFFS. Cool and fill with VANILLA BUTTER CREAM. Frost with CHOCOLATE FONDANT. Place half a grilled almond on top of each.

PARIS-BREST

Oil and flour a baking sheet and trace on it a circle 8 or 9 inches in diameter. Press out a circle of CREAM PUFF PASTE about 1 inch high and 1½ inches thick through a pastry bag fitted with a large plain tube. Brush paste with beaten egg and sprinkle generously with blanched shredded almonds. Bake in a preheated hot oven (425° F.) for 20 minutes, or until paste has puffed to twice its original size. Reduce oven temperature to 350° F. and continue to bake for 35 to 40 minutes, or until crown is dry and golden brown. Remove from oven to cool. Split carefully crosswise and put the halves together with PRALINE CREAM between. Decorate around sides with rosettes of whipped cream, sweetened and flavored to taste.

PEARS BRISTOL • *Poires à la Bristol*

Make some CREAM PUFFS. When cool, slice off tops and fill shells with PASTRY CREAM flavored with maraschino liqueur. Place a whole poached pear on top and mask with melted red currant jelly. Decorate around the base with preserved fruits and rosettes of whipped cream.

NUNS • *Les Religieuses*

Bake a small tart shell about 3 inches in diameter for each person to be served, and cool. Fill with PASTRY CREAM flavored with a little coffee extract.

For each tart shell you will need to make 3 small ECLAIRS, not larger than your first finger, and 1 tiny CREAM PUFF. Fill éclairs and cream puffs with whipped cream. Fit the ends of the three éclairs into the cream-filled tart shell and bring them together at the top to form a triangle. Dip the bottom of a cream puff in HOT CARAMEL SYRUP and place it on top of the éclair triangle. Decorate between the éclairs with MOCHA BUTTER CREAM forced through a pastry bag fitted with an open-star tube, and top the puff with a tiny rosette of the same cream.

SAINT CHRISTOPHER · Saint-Christophe

Roll out a thin round of SWEET PASTE or FLAKY PIE PASTE about the size of a large pancake. Prick with tines of a fork and bake in a preheated 450° F. oven for 12 to 15 minutes, or until lightly browned.

Meanwhile, using a pastry bag fitted with a large round pastry tube, shape some RINGS OF CREAM PUFF PASTE on an oiled baking sheet. Make 5 rings of graduating sizes, the largest being slightly smaller than the pastry crust and the others diminishing in size, with the smallest having at least a 2-inch-wide opening in the center. Brush with beaten egg and bake in a preheated hot oven (450° F.) for 15 minutes. Reduce oven temperature to 350° F. and bake for 20 to 30 minutes longer, or until rings are dry and golden. Cool. Frost rings with COFFEE FONDANT flavored with kirsch and arrange them in a pyramid on top of the pastry round. When 3 have been put in place, fill center with whipped cream mixed with sliced strawberries or candied chestnuts. Put last 2 rings in position and finish filling with cream, piling the cream high in the center. Garnish top with either a large whole strawberry or a candied chestnut.

GATEAU SAINT-HONORE

Roll out FLAKY PASTRY about ¼ inch thick and cut it into a circle 9 inches in diameter. Prick with tines of a fork and transfer to baking sheet. With a pastry bag fitted with a large plain tube, form an edge about ¾ inch thick around the circle with CREAM PUFF PASTE. Brush with egg yolk beaten with a little milk and bake in a preheated hot oven (425° F.) for 15 minutes. Reduce temperature to 350° F. and continue to bake for 20 to 30 minutes longer, or until the puffed edge is dry and golden brown.

Meanwhile, make some small CREAM PUFFS, brush with beaten egg yolk and milk, and bake as for cream puffs. Cool and fill with PASTRY CREAM or whipped cream, sweetened and flavored to taste. Dip the small filled puffs in hot CARAMEL SYRUP and arrange them around the edge of the pastry. Fill center with SAINT-HONORE CREAM and top with whipped cream.

CROQUEMBOUCHE · *Le Croquembouche*

Roll out FLAKY PASTRY ¼ inch thick and cut it into a circle 9 inches in diameter, or the size you wish the base of the croquembouche to be. Prick with tines of a fork and bake on a baking sheet in a preheated hot oven (400° F.) for 10 to 12 minutes, or until lightly browned. Cool.

Bake small CREAM PUFFS, about the size of walnuts, using twice the recipe for CREAM PUFF PASTE. Cool and fill with Bavarian cream or ENGLISH CUSTARD WITH GELATIN.

Make CARAMEL SYRUP and keep it hot over simmering water. Place the pastry base on a doily on a large serving plate. Dip bottoms of the little puffs in the hot caramel syrup and arrange a row of them around the outside edge of the base. Place a second row of puffs on top of the first row over the spaces between the first row of puffs. Continue to build the pyramid in this way until it is topped with one last little puff. If desired, garnish the croquembouche with rosettes of whipped cream or CHOCOLATE BUTTER CREAM, or sprinkle generously with confectioners' sugar and top with a real live rose. *Serves 12.*

CHAPTER 10

Puff Paste Desserts

Puff paste, or *Pâte feuilletée*, is the pride of every pastry chef and its uses are many. It is the basis for patty shells, fruit turnovers, flaky tarts, cream horns, palm leaves, napoleons, and many other delectable pastries.

It is not only the aristocrat of all fine pastries, but the most difficult to make. It's a challenge to dedicated cooks who are not discouraged by first-effort failure. Several tries may be necessary to get the "feel" of the paste and to master the art. However, with frozen patty shells now available to the homemaker, which need nothing but a hot oven to puff and brown them, it may not be long before some enterprising company will package frozen sheets of the paste so that all one has to do is to cut it into rounds, squares, or rectangles to make any one of the pastries in this chapter.

PUFF PASTE · *Pâte Feuilletée*

1 pound sweet butter or
 margarine
Ice water
4 cups (1 pound) enriched
 flour, unsifted

½ teaspoon salt
1½ cups ice water

Put butter into a bowl containing ice water and knead until it is the consistency of putty and is free of lumps. Form it into a ball and squeeze firmly to extract any pockets of water that may have been trapped in it.

Roll the washed butter in a little of the flour, wrap in waxed paper, and chill. It must be firm when it is used, but not hard. In warm weather the butter should be kneaded well in advance of making the paste. Chill the rolling pin as well, as the paste must be kept cold at all times.

Wash a table top with ice water, dry it thoroughly, and sift flour and salt on it in a mound.

Work the 1½ cups ice water gradually into the flour, adding a little more, if needed, to make a very firm dough, never soft or sticky. Work quickly and lightly, for the dough must not be handled or kneaded too much. Kneading gives the dough an elasticity that must be avoided in this particular paste.

The dough thus formed is called the *détrempe*, and in France, where the ingredients are weighed rather than measured, the rule is that the weight of the kneaded butter should be equal to half the weight of the *détrempe*, or about 1 pound. It is most important that both butter and *détrempe* be of the same firmness.

Form the dough into a rough ball and chill for 30 minutes.

Put dough on a floured board and roll it out away from you in a long rectangle ½ inch thick. Turn dough so it is horizontally in front of you. Press the butter into a flat cake about ½ inch thick and put it in the center of the dough. Fold the flap of dough on the left to cover the butter, then fold the flap of dough on the right over the left flap. The butter is now completely covered with two layers of dough. Press edges of dough firmly together to entrap as much air as possible and chill for 20 minutes.

The dough and butter must be cold, but never so cold that it is difficult to manipulate.

Put dough on the floured board *in the same position as it was before it was chilled* and again roll it out into a rectangle about ½ inch thick and 20 inches long. Roll to within ½ inch of either end, and be careful not to let the enclosed butter break through the layers of dough. If the butter breaks through, it means the air trapped between the layers of dough will be lost, and it is this enclosed air that is going to puff the pastry. If the *détrempe* is firm enough, and both *détrempe* and butter are of the same firmness, the butter will not break through.

MAKING TURNS

When dough is rolled out into a rectangle, turn it so it is horizontal and fold as before. Fold left-hand third of dough over the center, then fold right-hand third of dough over the two layers, making three layers of dough. *This rolling, turning, and folding is called a "turn."* Make another turn and chill dough for 20 minutes. Make two more turns, always making sure to place dough on table in same position as before the chilling. Two more turns are needed to complete the paste. If it is going to be used immediately, make these turns, chill again, then roll, cut, and bake. The first four turns, however, may be made a day or two before the paste is actually required. Store dough in a bowl in the refrigerator, covered with a cloth wrung in cold water, and save the last two turns until the paste is to be used. Chill dough for 20 minutes before rolling and cutting. Chill dough again before baking.

This amount of paste will make 12 PUFF PASTE PATTY SHELLS, 1 large *gâteau*, or 24 small cakes.

LEFTOVER SCRAPS OF PUFF PASTE

These cannot be rerolled and made into perfect pastries, for the butter and enclosed air would drain from the layers through the cut edges, and the paste would only partially puff. There are, however, several recipes in this chapter where the scraps can be used.

PUFF PASTE PATTY SHELLS • *Bouchées Feuilletées*

Roll out PUFF PASTE ⅛ inch thick on lightly floured board and cut into rounds with fluted pastry cutter about 2¼ inches in diameter. Press a smaller plain cutter, about 1¼ inches in diameter, into half the rounds without cutting all the way through. Place an uncut round on a moistened baking sheet and brush with beaten egg. Invert one of the cut rounds on top. Prick with tines of fork and brush with beaten egg. Chill. Bake in a preheated 450° F. oven for 10 minutes. Reduce oven temperature to 350° F. and continue to bake for about 20 minutes longer, or until shells are dry and golden. Remove indented center of upper round of paste with a sharp knife and return shells to the oven to dry. Serve with fruit and PASTRY CREAM or whipped cream, covering filling with the removed centers.

LARGE SHELL • *Vol-au-Vent*

Roll out PUFF PASTE ¼ inch thick on lightly floured board. Following lines of a round cutout of paper the size of the shell desired, cut out 2 rounds with point of a knife. Remove center from one of the rounds making a ring 1¼ inches wide. Place plain round on lightly moistened baking sheet, brush with beaten egg, and invert circle on top. Score sides with a knife, making slashes about ¼ inch deep, and brush top with beaten egg. Bake in a preheated (450° F.) oven for 20 minutes. Reduce temperature to 350° F. and continue to bake for about 30 minutes longer, or until dry and golden. Serve filled with ice cream or PASTRY CREAM and fruit.

CAKE OF ONE THOUSAND LEAVES • *Gâteau Mille-feuille*

Roll out PUFF PASTE ⅛ inch thick on lightly floured board and cut into 4 rounds each about 8 inches in diameter. Remove a circle 4 inches in diameter from center of two of the rounds. Put rounds on moistened baking sheets, sprinkle with fine granulated sugar, and prick with tines of a fork. Bake in a preheated 450° F. oven for 15 minutes, reduce temperature to 350° F., and bake for another 10 minutes. Reduce temperature to 300° F. and continue to bake for 10 to 15 minutes, or until rounds are golden and dry. Mount rounds with apricot marmalade or red currant jelly between, using the plain circles for top and bottom of the cake. Spread sides with marmalade and cover with finely chopped grilled almonds. Top cake with 20 fluted rings of puff paste 2 inches in diameter, baked in a hot oven (450° F.) for about 15 minutes until well puffed but not brown. Sprinkle heavily with confectioners' sugar.

ALMOND CREAM CAKE • *Gâteau de Pithiviers*

Roll out PUFF PASTE ⅛ inch thick on lightly floured board and cut into 3 circles, each 8 inches in diameter. Spread ALMOND CREAM ½ inch thick over one of the circles, leaving a ½-inch border around edge free of cream. Cut out center 7½ inches in diameter from second circle, making a ring ½ inch wide. Moisten edge of the first circle and place the ring of puff paste on top. Moisten the ring and cover ring and cream with the third circle. Seal the three layers of puff paste by pressing firmly all around with thumb. Brush top with an egg beaten with a little milk and score with a sharp-pointed knife to make a design. Place on a baking sheet lined with heavy paper and chill for 30 minutes. Bake in a preheated 450° F. oven for 15 minutes, or until paste is puffed. Reduce temperature to 350° F. and bake for about 25 minutes longer, or until golden. Sprinkle with confectioners' sugar and continue to bake for 5 minutes longer, or until sugar is caramelized.

CHAMPIGNY CAKE • *Gâteau Champigny*

Make in same way as ALMOND CREAM CAKE, but cut the PUFF PASTE into squares instead of circles and fill with apricot marmalade instead of the almond cream. Do not glaze with sugar but sprinkle heavily with confectioners' sugar after it is removed from oven.

DARTOIS • *Gâteau Dartois*

Roll out PUFF PASTE ¼ inch thick on lightly floured board and cut into a band 20 inches long and 8 inches wide. Put band on baking sheet lined with heavy paper and spread it ½ inch thick with PASTRY CREAM or apple marmalade, leaving a ½-inch border free of filling. Moisten border with water and press another band of paste, the same length and width as the first but ⅓ inch thick, on top. Brush with beaten egg and score with a sharp knife. Bake in the same way as for ALMOND CREAM CAKE and serve whole or sliced into small cakes about 1 inch wide.

Many countries celebrate the twelfth night after the birth of Christ. Sweden and England have their fruit-filled Twelfth Night Cakes, but the French version is made of scraps of puff paste and is called "the Cake of the Kings," in honor of the Three Kings of the Orient. A tiny doll known as *un baigneur*, or a pea or a bean, is hidden within the paste, and the person lucky enough to get this token is king or queen of the evening.

THE CAKE OF KINGS · *Galette des Rois*

Press scraps of PUFF PASTE gently into a ball and roll out on a lightly floured board into a round cake about ¾ inch thick. Make a small incision on one side and in it insert the token of royalty described above. Invert cake on a baking sheet lined with heavy paper, in such a way that the token will be at the bottom; brush top with beaten egg and mark it into diamond shapes with the point of a sharp knife. Bake cake in a hot oven (450° F.) for 20 to 25 minutes.

NORMAN CAKE · *Gâteau Normande*

Roll out PUFF PASTE ¼ inch thick and cut into two 8-inch squares. Place squares on moistened baking sheet and prick with tines of a fork. Bake in hot oven (450° F.) for 20 to 25 minutes. Remove from oven and spread one layer with ROYAL GLAZE. When cool, put the two layers together with a filling of applesauce between and sprinkle with chopped grilled almonds.

Many delicious small cakes are made from puff paste, the unanimous favorite being *les petits mille-feuilles*, called "napoleons" in this country.

"NAPOLEONS" · *Petits Mille-feuilles*

Roll out PUFF PASTE on lightly floured board into a rectangle ⅛ inch thick and cut into strips 2½ inches wide. Put strips on a baking sheet lined with several layers of heavy brown paper, prick surfaces with a fork, and chill. Bake in a hot oven (450° F.) for 10 minutes. Reduce temperature to 350° F. and bake for another 10 minutes. Place another cold baking sheet under the pastry, reduce oven temperature to 300° F., and bake for another 20 minutes, or until the strips are dry and golden brown.

Cool and put 3 strips together, one on top of the other, with cream between. The cream may be PASTRY CREAM, ALMOND CREAM, or sweetened whipped cream flavored with strawberries. Dust top with confectioners' sugar and cut crosswise with a serrated knife into slice 2 inches wide.

PEACH HEARTS · *Coeurs de Pêche*

Roll out PUFF PASTE ⅛ inch thick on lightly floured board and cut into heart shapes with a floured cooky cutter. Put hearts on a moistened baking sheet, prick with tines of a fork, and bake in a hot oven (450° F.) for about 15 minutes. When cool, put a spoonful of peach jam in the center of each and pipe a fluted edge of whipped cream around the heart.

BANANA JALOUSIES

Roll out PUFF PASTE 1/16 inch thick on lightly floured board, cut into rounds, and press rounds over the back of small oval or round buttered tart tins. Prick surfaces with tines of a fork, chill, and bake in a hot oven (450° F.) for about 15 minutes. Remove tart shells from tins and cool. When ready to serve, spread a thin layer of pineapple jam inside the shells, cover with overlapping layers of banana slices, and glaze the bananas with pineapple jam melted with a little hot water. Pipe a fluted edge of sweetened whipped cream all around.

Puff paste tart shells may be filled with other sliced fruits or berries, fresh, canned, or frozen.

CHESTNUT STARS

Roll out PUFF PASTE ⅛ inch thick on lightly floured board and cut into small star shapes with a floured cooky cutter. Put stars on a baking sheet moistened with water, prick with tines of a fork, and chill. Bake in a hot oven (450° F.) for about 15 minutes. When cool, put a glacéed chestnut in center of each star and surround it with tiny rosettes of whipped cream or BUTTER CREAM FROSTING.

COW TONGUES · *Langues de Boeuf*

Roll out PUFF PASTE ¼ inch thick on lightly floured board and cut into small rounds. Sprinkle with fine granulated sugar. Put each round on waxed paper sprinkled with sugar and roll each gently with a rolling pin to give it an oval contour. Reverse the "tongues" on a baking sheet, sugar side up, and bake in a hot oven (450° F.) for 7 or 8 minutes. Serve warm, sprinkled with a little confectioners' sugar.

LITTLE SLIPPERS · *Petits Chaussons*

Roll out PUFF PASTE ⅛ inch thick on lightly floured board and cut into rounds about 3 inches in diameter. Put a teaspoon of PASTRY CREAM or marmalade on one side, moisten the edges of the rounds, and fold in half over the filling. Pinch edges together securely, prick with tines of a fork, and brush with beaten egg. Bake in a hot oven (450° F.) for about 15 minutes.

FRENCH NAPOLEONS · *Les Napoléons*

Roll out PUFF PASTE ⅛ inch thick on lightly floured board and cut into rounds 2 inches in diameter. Put a dab of ALMOND CREAM in center of a round, moisten edge with water, and invert a second round on top. Put the napoleons on a baking sheet lined with a double thickness of heavy paper. Brush tops with a little of the same cream used as filling, thinned to spreading consistency with egg white, sprinkle with confectioners' sugar, and bake in a hot oven (450° F.) for about 15 minutes.

CREAM TART · *Jalousie à la Crème*

Roll out PUFF PASTE ⅛ inch thick on lightly floured board, cut into a rectangle 6 inches wide, and put on a baking sheet moistened with water. Garnish center of the rectangle with PASTRY CREAM, marmalade, or jam, leaving a ½-inch border all around. Roll out and cut a second rectangle the same dimensions as the first but ¼ inch thick. Fold band in half lengthwise and slash it along the fold every inch. The slashes should be 2 inches long, so that when the band is opened they will be 4 inches long. Moisten edge of first band and cover it with the decorative band, brush top with beaten egg, and bake in a hot oven (450° F.) for 20 minutes. When cool, cut it crosswise into small cakes 1 inch wide.

GODCAKES

Roll out PUFF PASTE ⅛ inch thick on lightly floured board and cut into 3-inch squares. Put a teaspoon of marmalade or CURRANT FILLING on a corner of each square. Moisten edges of the paste, fold over from corner to corner to make small triangles, and seal edges securely with the floured tines of a fork. Place turnovers on a baking sheet lined with several layers of brown paper, prick with tines of a fork, and chill thoroughly. Bake in a hot oven (450° F.) for 10 minutes. Reduce oven temperature to 350° F. and bake for another 15 minutes, or until golden brown.

WELLS OF LOVE • *Puits d'Amour*

Roll out PUFF PASTE ⅛ inch thick on lightly floured board. Cut out a round 2 inches in diameter and place on lightly moistened baking sheet. Moisten the round with water. Cut another round slightly smaller than the first and from this cut out the center, leaving a ring ½ inch wide. Invert this on the plain round. Brush with beaten egg and bake in a hot oven (450° F.) for 10 minutes. Reduce oven temperature to 350° F. and continue to bake for 20 minutes longer, or until golden. Cool and fill well in center with red currant jelly.

MARS

Roll out PUFF PASTE ⅛ inch thick on lightly floured board and cut into a long strip. Turn up edges ¼ inch all around and fill center with PASTRY CREAM. Bake in a 450° F. oven for 15 minutes. Remove and let cool a little. Cover with a 1-inch-thick layer of ITALIAN MERINGUE. Sprinkle heavily with confectioners' sugar and mark into 1-inch squares with back of a knife. Decorate each section with 2 almond halves and 3 raisins. Reduce oven temperature to 350° F. and bake for 10 to 15 minutes longer. Cool and cut into the marked squares.

PUFF PASTE CAKES • *Gâteaux Feuilletées*

Roll out PUFF PASTE 1/16 inch thick on lightly floured board and cut into diamonds, squares, or small rounds. Place on lightly moistened baking sheet, brush with egg, and score with a knife. Bake in a hot oven (450° F.) for 6 to 8 minutes, or until golden. Sprinkle generously with confectioners' sugar and continue to bake for 2 minutes longer, or until sugar is shiny and caramelized.

Several delicious French pastries are made from the leftover scraps of puff paste. An apple turnover is one of the best.

APPLE TURNOVER • *Chausson aux Pommes*

Peel, core, and grate or finely chop 5 tart apples. Melt 4 tablespoons butter in a skillet and in it sauté apples for about 5 minutes, or until partially cooked. Remove from heat and stir in sugar to taste, 1 teaspoon vanilla, 1 tablespoon rum or cognac, and a dash of freshly ground pepper. Let mixture cool.

Press leftover scraps of PUFF PASTE into a smooth ball and roll out on a lightly floured board into a large circle ¼ inch thick. Moisten edge with a little water and garnish the center with the fried apples. Fold circle of paste in half, enclosing the filling. Press the edges securely together and turn up ½ inch of the edge, forming a raised border, to keep the turnover from opening during the baking. Brush surface with beaten egg and prick deeply with a fork in 4 or 5 places. Bake in a hot oven (450° F.) for about 30 minutes, or until brown, and serve warm.

ALMOND TARTS • *Fonchonnettes*

Roll out scraps of PUFF PASTE thinly, cut into rounds, and line small tart pans.

Beat 6 tablespoons sugar with 2 egg yolks and 1 whole egg, 3 tablespoons finely grated almonds, ¼ cup flour, 2 tablespoons butter, and a pinch of salt. Fill lined tart pans ⅔ full. Bake in 450° F. oven for 10 minutes. Remove from oven and cover top with ITALIAN MERINGUE. Sprinkle with granulated sugar. Reduce oven temperature to 350° F. and continue to bake the tarts for 15 to 20 minutes, or until meringue is lightly toasted. Cool and top with a spoonful of red currant jelly.

CORKSCREWS • *Sacristains*

Press scraps of PUFF PASTE gently into a ball and roll out on a lightly floured board into a long band ¼ inch thick. Brush surface with beaten egg and sprinkle with finely chopped blanched almonds and confectioners' sugar. Cut band crosswise into strips ½ inch wide.

Twist each strip several times to give it the form of a corkscrew, put "corkscrews" on a moistened baking sheet 1 inch apart, and bake in a hot oven (450° F.) for 8 minutes. Turn with a spatula so they do not burn on the bottom, reduce oven temperature to 350° F., and continue to bake for another 8 minutes.

PALM LEAVES • *Palmiers Glacés*

Press scraps of PUFF PASTE gently into a ball and roll out on a lightly floured board into a long band. Give the paste 2 turns (see puff paste recipe), sprinkling the rolled-out paste heavily with sugar between each turn. Roll out the paste into a square ⅛ inch thick. Fold two sides of the square over to the middle, making a rectangle. Then fold the rectangle in half lengthwise, making 4 layers of paste. Slice across the layers at 1-inch intervals, put the slices on a moistened baking sheet 1 inch apart, and bake in a hot oven (450° F.) for 8 minutes. Turn with a spatula so they do not burn on the bottom, reduce oven temperature to 350° F., and continue to bake for another 8 minutes.

LADY LOCKS • *Cornets à la Crème*

Press scraps of PUFF PASTE into a ball and roll out ⅛ inch thick on a lightly floured board. Cut into strips 1 inch wide and 10 inches long. Wind each strip around a buttered metal tube, or "lady lock" form, overlapping the edges tightly. Start at the wide part of the tubes but do not roll quite to the end. Fasten the end securely. Put the paste-wrapped tubes 1 inch apart on a baking sheet lined with a double layer of heavy paper and bake in a hot oven (450° F.) for about 15 minutes. Slip the lady locks off the tubes, cool, and fill with PASTRY CREAM or whipped cream, sweetened and flavored to taste. Sprinkle with confectioners' sugar.

CHAPTER 11

Strudels and Baklava

I⊤ was Hungary, the land of the Dobos torte, that contributed the flaky fruit- or cheese-filled roll of paper-thin noodle paste to the culinary world. Austria and Germany were quick to embrace it, and it was not long before the rest of Europe became aware of this rich, butter-bathed dessert.

Today the strudel, originally known as the *rétes*, has been stripped of the mystery surrounding it, and its technique can be mastered by the ambitious cook.

Stretching and rolling strudel paste is as easy as apple pie, and infinitely more fun. Four hands are not essential to stretching the paste to a great thin sheet—it can be done alone. The strudel can be filled with fruits in season—strawberries, sweet cherries, peaches, or apples—flavored with nuts and spices, or with cheese, raisins and dates, or poppy seeds, if preferred.

The strudel is perfection served warm from the oven with a dusting of confectioners' sugar and a spoonful of whipped cream. It may be made a day before it is baked and served, or sections, cut to serve 4, 6, or 8, may be wrapped in aluminum foil and stored in the freezer for as long as three months. Reheat before serving.

Frozen sheets of strudel paste may be purchased in specialty stores in many large cities. Four sheets, each 17×23 inches, are packaged in a cellophane bag, then frozen. The sheets should be kept in the freezer. Remove from freezer and leave at room temperature for at least 3 hours, or overnight, before using, but do not open the cellophane bag until the filling is prepared, as the dough dries rapidly. Two sheets are sufficient for one strudel; however, for an especially delicious and flaky strudel, use 3 or all 4 sheets.

TO USE FROZEN STRUDEL SHEETS

Unfold sheets and place one sheet on a damp napkin. Brush with melted butter and sprinkle with sugar and crumbs. Place second sheet directly over first and again brush with butter and sprinkle with sugar and crumbs. Place filling along one end in a 3-inch strip. Roll loosely with the aid of the napkin, like a jelly roll. Place on buttered baking sheet and bake in a preheated hot oven (375° F.) for 30 to 40 minutes, basting frequently with melted butter.

STRUDEL PASTE

2½ cups sifted enriched flour
1 egg, lightly beaten
½ teaspoon salt

3 tablespoons olive or peanut
    oil or melted butter
⅔ cup warm water

Sift flour onto a pastry board and make a well in the center.

In the well put the egg, salt, and oil.

Gradually work in the flour, adding as much of the warm water as needed to make a very soft dough or paste. This paste will be sticky at first and must be worked vigorously to make it elastic. The most effective way of doing this is to lift up the dough in one hand and smack it down hard on the table. Repeat this lifting and smacking of the paste about 100 times, or until it no longer sticks to either the hand or the board.

Form the paste into a small ball, brush top with oil, and cover it with a warm bowl. Let dough rest for 30 minutes to 1 hour.

Stretching the Paste: Spread a clean tablecloth over a table about 3 feet wide and 5 feet long and spread the cloth lightly with flour. Put the paste in the center, sprinkle it lightly with flour, and roll it out into a large circle, turning it several times to prevent its sticking to the cloth and rolling the outer edges as thinly as possible. Now flour both hands and reach under the dough. Tuck in the thumbs and start stretching the dough from the center to the outer edge with the backs of the hands. Work cautiously, using a hand-over-hand motion and being careful not to tear the dough, for it cannot be mended.

Walk around the table while stretching the dough until it is as thin as tissue paper and hangs over the edges of the table. The edges of the overhanging dough will be thick. Cut them off with kitchen scissors, and let the sheet of dough dry for 10 minutes to lose its stickiness, but do not let it become brittle.

Filling and Rolling the Paste: Brush the entire surface of the stretched dough with melted butter. About 1 cup melted butter will be needed for filling and baking a strudel. Cover from half to two thirds of the length with filling (see recipes following), fold the flaps of dough hanging over the ends and sides of the table neatly over the filling, and brush these turned-up edges with butter. Start to roll the dough, jelly-roll fashion, from the end covered with filling. Pick up the tablecloth and turn the end of the dough over onto itself. Pull the cloth and dough toward you as you roll the strudel, and roll it rather loosely to give room for expansion during the baking. The last flip of the dough should deposit the strudel on a well-buttered baking sheet.

Baking the Strudel: Brush the strudel generously with melted butter and bake in a moderate oven (375° F) for 45 to 50 minutes, or until well browned, basting several times during the baking with the remaining melted butter. Sprinkle with confectioners' sugar and serve warm with unsweetened whipped cream.

APPLE STRUDEL • *Apfelstrudel*

STRUDEL PASTE	1 *cup sugar*
1 *cup melted butter*	1 *teaspoon cinnamon*
½ *cup fine bread crumbs*	1 *cup raisins*
6 *tart apples, peeled, cored,*	1 *cup chopped walnuts or*
*and finely sliced**	*almonds*

Make and stretch strudel paste according to instructions.

Brush paste with melted butter.

Sprinkle two-thirds of the length with bread crumbs and apples. Sprinkle sugar, cinnamon, raisins, and nuts over the apples.

Roll, brush with butter, and bake in a preheated 375° F. oven for 45 to 50 minutes, or until brown, basting frequently with butter. *Serves 10.*

* Other fruits, such as peaches or sweet cherries, may be used instead of the apples.

PINEAPPLE STRUDEL

STRUDEL PASTE
1 cup melted butter
½ cup dry bread crumbs
1½ cups sugar
1 teaspoon cinnamon

4 cups diced fresh pineapple
½ cup chopped maraschino cherries
1 cup seeded raisins
1 cup ground walnuts

Make and stretch strudel paste according to instructions.
Brush paste with melted butter.
Sprinkle with crumbs, sugar, and cinnamon.
Spread fruit and nuts over three-quarters of the paste.
Sprinkle filling with melted butter and roll.
Brush strudel with melted butter and bake in a preheated 375° F. oven for about 45 minutes, or until brown, basting frequently with melted butter. *Serves 10.*

LEMON STRUDEL

6 eggs, separated
1 cup sugar
Juice of 3 lemons
3 teaspoons cornstarch

⅓ cup water
Grated rind of 1 lemon
STRUDEL PASTE
½ cup melted butter

Beat egg yolks with sugar and lemon juice until thick and pale in color.
Dissolve cornstarch in water and stir into egg yolks.
Cook over simmering water, stirring, until cream is smooth and thickened.
Add lemon rind and cool.
Beat egg whites until stiff and fold into the cream mixture.
Make and stretch strudel paste according to instructions.
Brush paste with melted butter.
Spread filling over one-third of the dough and roll.
Brush strudel with melted butter and bake in a preheated 375° F. oven for 45 minutes, or until golden, basting with butter several times. *Serves 10.*

CHOCOLATE STRUDEL

STRUDEL PASTE
6 eggs, separated
6 tablespoons sugar
4 ounces semi-sweet
   chocolate, grated

1 cup walnuts, finely ground
1 teaspoon vanilla
½ cup melted butter
½ cup fine white bread
   crumbs

Make and stretch strudel paste according to instructions.

Beat egg yolks with sugar until thick and pale in color.

Add chocolate, nuts, and vanilla.

Beat egg whites until stiff and fold into egg yolk mixture.

Brush paste with melted butter and sprinkle with bread crumbs.

Spread chocolate filling over one-third of the paste, not too close to edge.

Roll, brush with butter, and bake in a preheated 350° F. oven for 45 minutes, or until golden, basting several times with melted butter. *Serves 10.*

ALMOND STRUDEL

STRUDEL PASTE
6 eggs, separated
6 tablespoons sugar
1 cup ground blanched
   almonds
1 cup fine bread crumbs

Juice and grated rind of 1
   lemon
½ cup melted butter
1 cup raisins
SABAYON SAUCE

Make and stretch strudel paste according to instructions.

Beat egg yolks and sugar until thick and pale in color.

Stir in half the almonds, half the bread crumbs, and the juice and rind of the lemon.

Beat egg whites until stiff and fold in.

Brush paste with melted butter and sprinkle with remaining almonds, bread crumbs, and raisins.

Spread filling over one-third of the dough, not too close to the edge.

Roll, brush with butter, and bake in a preheated 375° F. oven for 45 minutes, or until brown, basting several times with butter.

Serve hot with sabayon sauce. *Serves 10.*

TYROLESE STRUDEL

STRUDEL PASTE
⅔ cup butter
½ cup sugar
6 eggs, separated
⅔ cup chopped nuts
¼ cup sliced dates

¼ cup sliced figs
1 cup chopped raisins
Grated rind of 1 lemon
½ teaspoon cinnamon
½ cup melted butter

Make and stretch strudel paste according to instructions.
Cream butter until fluffy.

Gradually add sugar and cream together until light and fluffy.

Stir in beaten egg yolks, nuts, dates, figs, raisins, lemon rind, and cinnamon.

Beat egg whites until stiff and fold in.

Brush strudel paste with melted butter.

Spread filling over half the surface and roll.

Brush with melted butter and bake in a preheated 375° F. oven for 45 minutes, or until golden, basting several times with butter during the baking. *Serves 10.*

POPPY SEED STRUDEL

STRUDEL PASTE
1 cup ground poppy seeds
1½ cups sugar
1 teaspoon cinnamon
1 cup raisins

½ cup melted butter
½ cup heavy cream
1 large apple, peeled
Rind of 1 lemon

Make and stretch strudel paste according to instructions.

Mix poppy seeds with 1 cup of the sugar.

Add cinnamon and raisins.

Brush paste with melted butter and sprinkle with remaining sugar. Spread poppy seed filling over one-third of the dough and sprinkle with cream.

Grate apple and lemon rind over entire surface.

Roll, brush with melted butter, and bake in a preheated 375° F. oven for 45 minutes, or until brown, basting several times with butter. *Serves 10.*

CREAM CHEESE STRUDEL

STRUDEL PASTE
⅔ cup butter
⅔ cup sugar
8 eggs, separated
Pinch salt

Grated rind of 1 lemon
1⅔ cups sour cream
1 pound cream cheese
½ cup melted butter
1 cup sultana raisins

Make and stretch strudel paste according to instructions.

Cream butter, add sugar gradually, and cream together until light and fluffy.

Beat egg yolks and stir into butter-sugar mixture with salt, lemon rind, and sour cream.

Cream the cream cheese until soft and press through a fine sieve to remove any lumps.

Combine cheese with egg yolk mixture and press all through a sieve again.

Beat egg whites until stiff and fold in.

Brush paste with melted butter.

Spread filling about 1 inch thick over two-thirds of the paste.

Sprinkle with raisins and roll strudel very loosely.

Brush generously with butter and bake in a preheated 375° F. oven for 45 minutes, or until golden, basting frequently with melted butter. *Serves 10.*

COTTAGE CHEESE STRUDEL

STRUDEL PASTE
1 tablespoon butter
½ cup sugar
6 eggs, separated
1 pound cottage cheese

1 cup sour cream
½ cup melted butter
½ teaspoon cinnamon
Grated rind of 1 lemon

Make and stretch strudel paste according to instructions.

Cream butter with half the sugar and stir in egg yolks, lightly beaten.

Press cottage cheese through a fine sieve and stir into egg yolk mixture.

Stir in sour cream.

Fold in egg whites, stiffly beaten.

Brush paste with melted butter and sprinkle with remaining sugar mixed with cinnamon and grated lemon rind.

Spread cheese mixture over one-third of the paste and roll.

Brush with melted butter and bake in a preheated 375° F. oven for 45 minutes, or until golden, basting several times with melted butter. *Serves 10.*

SOUR CREAM STRUDEL

STRUDEL PASTE	
1 tablespoon butter	*Grated rind of 1 lemon*
½ cup sugar	½ *cup melted butter*
5 eggs, separated	½ *cup bread crumbs*
1 cup sour cream	½ *cup chopped nuts*
	1 *cup raisins*

Make and stretch strudel paste according to instructions.

Cream butter and sugar together until light and fluffy.

Add egg yolks, lightly beaten, sour cream, and lemon rind.

Fold in egg whites, stiffly beaten.

Brush paste with melted butter and sprinkle evenly with crumbs, nuts, and raisins.

Spread filling on one-third of the paste, not too close to edge.

Roll, brush with butter, and bake in a preheated 375° F. oven for 45 minutes, or until golden, basting with melted butter occasionally. *Serves 10.*

The layer strudel is an ideal pastry to make from frozen phylo pastry sheets (see below).

LAYER STRUDEL

Prepare twice the amount of STRUDEL PASTE as in the basic recipe at the beginning of this chapter; cut it in half and stretch one half at a time. Cut paste into sheets the size of a large baking pan. Butter baking pan and put three or four layers of paste in it, one on top of the other, buttering each layer generously. Butter the top layer, sprinkle with sugar and cinnamon, chopped nuts, and a few raisins. Continue until half the sheets have been used. Spread with any desired strudel filling and continue piling sheets of paste on top in the same way as on the bottom. Butter the top generously and bake in a moderate oven (375° F.) for 45 minutes, or until brown. Cut into serving squares, dust with powdered sugar, and serve with unsweetened whipped cream.

Armenian and Greek baklava and other Near Eastern pastries are made from the thin pastry sheets, or phylo, mentioned at the beginning of this chapter. They are similar to strudel sheets, but contain no egg. They are available in frozen form at many Greek stores throughout the country. They defrost rapidly and, while you work with them, they should be kept covered with a damp towel to keep them from drying out. Leftover sheets may be rolled in the damp towel, tightly enclosed in aluminum foil, and refrozen.

BAKLAVA

20 *sheets frozen phylo pastry*	1 *cup honey*
2 *cups melted butter*	1 *cup water*
2 *cups finely chopped*	
walnuts	

Spread out five sheets of pastry, one on top of the other.

Place a large square pan in center of these and cut dough around it.

Place layers in the pan, one at a time, brushing each layer generously with melted butter. Sprinkle with all the cuttings and brush cuttings with butter.

Repeat with five more sheets of pastry.

Spread walnuts evenly in pan and continue adding layers of pastry until all sheets have been used, adding last cuttings beneath the last sheet.

With a sharp knife, score top pastry diagonally into 5 sections in both directions, outlining 25 diamond-shaped cakes.

Let rest for 2 hours.

Heat oven to 450° F., then reduce to 350° F.

Pour one-third of remaining butter over pastry and bake for 7 minutes.

Pour over another third of remaining butter, reduce oven temperature to 325° F., and bake for 20 minutes longer.

Remove baklava from oven. Drain off all excess butter and return to oven to bake and crisp for 5 minutes.

Again drain off any excess butter and bake for 5 minutes longer.

In saucepan combine honey and water and boil to a thick syrup.

Pour hot syrup around edge of pan and over the pastry. Let cool and cut into diamonds so the pieces can absorb the syrup before serving. *Makes 25 small cakes.*

ALMOND BAKLAVA

Follow BAKLAVA recipe, using 2 cups ground blanched almonds in place of the walnuts.

In Persia, the same type of pastry is made this way:

PERSIAN PIE • *Baglava*

Grate 8 ounces mixed toasted almonds and pistachio nuts and combine with 1 cup sugar. Or blend ½ cup sugar and half the nuts in an electric blender until nuts are finely ground. Empty into bowl and repeat with another ½ cup sugar and the remaining nuts. Unroll 4 phylo pastry sheets on waxed paper and cut in half, making 8 pieces each 18 inches long and 9 inches wide. Melt 1 cup (2 sticks) butter in a small saucepan. Brush an 8-inch square cake pan with melted butter. Brush each piece of paste, one at a time, with melted butter and sprinkle generously with the nut-sugar mixture. Roll loosely from one 9-inch edge of end, like a little fat cigar, and place in pan. Keep remaining sheets of phylo covered with a damp towel as you work. Repeat until all pieces of pastry are rolled and packed tightly together in pan. Trim any ends of pastry overhanging pan edge. With a sharp knife, cut through rolls at intervals, making 1½-inch squares or diamonds. Pour remaining butter over top and around sides of pastry. Bake in a preheated 350° F. oven for 30 minutes.

While baglava is baking, combine ½ cup sugar, 3 tablespoons water, and 1 teaspoon lemon juice in a small saucepan. Bring to a boil and boil rapidly until syrup spins a long thread. Remove baglava from oven and pour hot syrup over it. Cool and sprinkle with chopped pistachio nuts. If desired serve with unsweetened whipped cream. *Serves 16.*

HORSESHOE PASTRIES • *Boorma*

Cut 4 phylo sheets in half, making strips 9 inches wide by 18 inches long. Brush each strip with melted butter and sprinkle with chopped nuts mixed with fine granulated sugar and a pinch each of nutmeg, cinnamon, and cloves. Roll strips into tubes and bend each tube into a horseshoe. Arrange on baking sheet, brush with melted butter, and bake in a preheated 350° F. oven for 12 minutes, or until golden. Remove from oven and sprinkle with a little honey. *Makes 8.*

CREAM PIE · *Galato Boureko*

1 quart milk	10 phylo sheets
2 cups sugar	½ cup melted butter
¾ cup farina	1 cup water
3 eggs	

In saucepan heat milk.

Add 1 cup sugar.

When nearly boiling, gradually stir in farina and cook, stirring, until thick and smooth.

Remove from heat and stir occasionally to prevent a crust from forming.

When lukewarm beat in eggs, one at a time.

Line a buttered baking pan with a sheet of pastry, letting it fall over edges of pan. Brush with melted butter. Continue adding pastry sheets and brushing with butter until half of them are used to form the bottom crust.

Spread filling evenly over the pastry and cover with remaining sheets, brushing each with butter. Trim pastry from edges and place the leftover scraps beneath the top sheet.

Baste surface with melted butter and brush edges all around with a little cold water to seal pastry ends.

With a pointed knife, score top sheets into diamonds about 3 inches wide.

Bake in a preheated 375° F. oven for 40 to 45 minutes, or until golden.

Meanwhile boil remaining sugar with water to make a thick syrup.

When pie is still hot from oven, baste it with the syrup, a little at a time, until all syrup is absorbed.

Cool and cut into diamond pieces. *Serves 16.*

NUT PASTIES · *Flogheres*

1 cup ground almonds or walnuts	1 cup melted butter
½ cup dry cracker meal	1 cup sugar
1 egg	½ cup water
5 phylo sheets	½ teaspoon cinnamon

Combine walnuts, cracker meal, and egg, and mix to a paste.

Cut phylo sheets into 4 strips and pile one on top of the other on a damp towel to keep them from drying out.

Take one strip at a time. Brush with melted butter and place a teaspoon of filling on one end. Roll up like a tiny jelly roll or "cigar."

Line a buttered baking pan with the rolls.

Sprinkle with remaining butter and bake in a preheated 350° F. oven for about 25 minutes, or until golden.

Meanwhile boil sugar, water, and cinnamon to a light syrup. Pour syrup over the pasties while still hot from oven.

Cool. *Makes 20.*

CHAPTER 12

Large Cakes

A MERICA is a cake-conscious country and there are more cakes baked in a week than there are soups brewed, roasts roasted, or beans baked. There are birthday cakes, wedding cakes, engagement cakes, Christmas cakes—cakes for all events and every occasion.

Modern cookbooks teem with recipes for every kind of cake conceivable, so I am not going to try to cover the gamut in a book devoted to desserts in which there is only room for one chapter on cakes. Instead I am going to try to tell you how to make a good cake, give some favorite tested recipes of my own, and explain how to decorate cakes. If you do not want to take the time to make your own cake from scratch, there are many good cake mixes on the market. To these add, if you wish, a little extra flavoring, some grated orange or lemon rind, a handful of nuts or raisins, but, in general, follow the directions on the package. In this way you can be sure of a good cake every time. Then give it your own special touch of frosting, creamy or fluffy, or take the time you have saved in using a packaged mix to decorate it for a special treat.

There are two basic types of cakes:

1. Butter-type cakes, which include shortening.
2. Sponge-type cakes made without any kind of shortening, or chiffon-type where liquid shortening is folded into the batter.

UNDERSTAND YOUR INGREDIENTS

FLOUR is the foundation of your cake. Always use the flour specified in the recipe, whether it is all-purpose, enriched, or cake flour.

BAKING POWDER produces lightness in cakes. With double-acting baking powder the leavening action begins when the dry ingredients are mixed with the liquid, but most action takes place when the batter begins to be affected by the oven's heat. All recipes in this book call for double-acting baking powder.

EGGS provide richness in a cake. Eggs, as you know, vary in size. Two medium eggs equal ⅓ cup. Three medium eggs or 2 large eggs equal ½ cup. Always use medium eggs unless the recipe specifies large. If the recipe specifies large and you have only medium use an extra medium egg for each 2 large eggs specified in the recipe.

LIQUIDS provide moisture and make the blending together of the dry ingredients possible. Use the liquid specified in the recipe. Sour milk and buttermilk are interchangeable.

SUGAR provides sweetness and regulates the tenderness of the cake. If a cake calls for sugar, it means granulated sugar and not confectioners' or brown sugar. Use the particular sugar specified and do not try to substitute one for the other.

SHORTENING produces tenderness and richness. Use butter or margarine when butter is called for. If using hydrogenated shortening, use not more than half; make the other half butter or margarine.

FOR CAKE SUCCESS

1. Read and follow recipe.
2. Assemble ingredients and utensils. Use standard measuring cups and spoons.
3. Choose correct-size pan. Too large a pan makes a cake pale, flat, and shrunken. Too small a pan makes cakes overflow and gives them a coarse texture. When using heatproof glass pans, always

reduce oven temperature by 25° F., but use the same baking time as called for in the recipe.

4. Prepare pans. Unless recipe specifies to line pans with paper, grease or oil bottom and sides well, then sprinkle with flour. Tap the flour around in the pan to give it an even coating, then tap bottom lightly to remove any excess. Or mix equal parts flour and shortening to a smooth paste and brush onto bottom and sides of pan with a pastry brush.

5. Turn batter into prepared pans and spread batter to edge. When layer pans are used, divide the batter evenly. Tap pans on table several times to remove air bubbles from batter.

6. Arrange pans in oven so that they do not touch sides or back of oven on rack placed a little below center of oven. If using 2 pans, stagger them in opposite corners. When baking 3 pans, place the third layer on another rack about 2 inches above the first, but do not place one pan directly over another.

7. Test for doneness. Check doneness by inserting a wooden pick in center. If the pick comes out dry and clean, your cake is done. Test the cake always after minimum baking time. If pick is moist, continue to bake for 5 to 10 minutes longer.

8. Remove cake from oven and place on wire rack to permit air to circulate all around it and insure even cooling. Allow cake to stand in pan for 10 minutes unless recipe specifies that you should remove it immediately. Run a spatula around edge of cake to loosen it from sides of pan and invert cake onto a clean towel on cake rack. Immediately turn it over again, using another cake rack covered with a clean towel. If left on the rounded side, the cake may crack.

9. Frost cake as soon as it is completely cool. Brush off crumbs gently with hand. Place first layer rounded side down on cake plate. Frost top with icing or filling. Place top layer flat side down on filling so that the two flat sides of cake are together. Frost sides, then top.

TWO-LAYER WHITE CAKE

½ cup butter or shortening
1½ cups sugar
2½ cups sifted cake flour
3 teaspoons double-acting
  baking powder

½ teaspoon salt
1 cup milk
1 teaspoon vanilla
4 (½ cup) egg whites

Cream shortening and sugar.

Stir in combined dry ingredients alternately with milk and vanilla.

Beat egg whites until stiff enough to hold a peak and gently fold them into batter.

Pour batter into prepared pans (two 8-inch layers 1½ inches deep).

Bake at 350° F. for 30 to 35 minutes.

THREE-LAYER WHITE PARTY CAKE

1 cup butter or shortening	½ teaspoon salt
2 cups sugar	1 cup milk
3 cups sifted cake flour	1 teaspoon vanilla
4 teaspoons double-acting baking powder	6 (¾ cup) egg whites

Cream shortening and sugar.

Stir in combined dry ingredients alternately with milk and vanilla.

Beat egg whites until stiff enough to hold a peak and gently fold them into batter.

Pour batter into prepared pans (three 8-inch or two 9-inch layers 1½ inches deep).

Bake at 350° F. 30 to 35 minutes for 8-inch layers; 35 to 40 minutes for 9-inch layers.

DARK CHOCOLATE CAKE

1 cup butter or shortening	¼ teaspoon salt
2 cups sugar	3 teaspoons soda
4 eggs	¾ cup cocoa
1 cup sour milk	⅔ cup boiling water
2½ cups sifted cake flour	1 teaspoon vanilla

Blend shortening, sugar, and eggs very thoroughly.

Add sour milk alternately with the combined flour, salt, and soda.

Stir cocoa into boiling water and stir until dissolved.

Add to batter and mix well.

Stir in vanilla.

Pour into prepared pan or pans (9- or 10-inch tube or three 8-inch layers 1½ inches deep).

Bake at 350° F. about 1 hour and 10 minutes in the tube pan or 35 to 40 minutes in layer pans.

CHOCOLATE BUTTERMILK CAKE

½ cup butter or shortening
1¼ cups sugar
½ teaspoon salt
1 teaspoon vanilla
2 eggs

2 squares unsweetened
   chocolate, melted
1¾ cups sifted cake flour
1 teaspoon soda
1 cup buttermilk

Blend shortening, sugar, salt, vanilla, and eggs.
Add melted chocolate and beat for 2 minutes.
Add flour combined with soda alternately with buttermilk.
Pour into prepared pans (two 8-inch layers 1½ inches deep).
Bake at 350° F. for 30 to 35 minutes.

COFFEE CHOCOLATE CAKE

Use ½ cup cocoa dissolved in 1 cup strong coffee in place of buttermilk and omit melted chocolate.

YELLOW CAKE

½ cup butter or shortening
1 cup sugar
2 eggs
2 cups sifted cake flour
2 teaspoons double-acting
   baking powder

¼ teaspoon salt
¾ cup milk
1 teaspoon vanilla

Blend shortening, sugar, and eggs.
Stir in combined dry ingredients alternately with milk and vanilla.
Pour batter into prepared pans (two 8-inch layers 1¼ inches deep, or one 8-inch square) and bake at 350° F.
Bake layers for 25 to 30 minutes; square cake for 35 to 45 minutes.

GOLD CAKE

1 cup butter or shortening
2 cups sugar
4 eggs
2¾ cups sifted cake flour
3 teaspoons double-acting
   baking powder

1 teaspoon salt
1 cup milk
2 teaspoons vanilla

Blend shortening, sugar, and eggs.

Stir in combined dry ingredients alternately with milk and vanilla.

Pour batter into prepared pans (three 8-inch layers or two 9-inch layers 1¼ inches deep or one 8×12-inch oblong) and bake at 350° F.

Bake layers for 30 to 35 minutes; oblong cake for 45 to 50 minutes.

CUPCAKES

If desired, bake GOLD CAKE batter in cupcake pans rubbed with shortening. Recipe for two 8-inch layers makes about 24 medium cupcakes. Recipe for two 9-inch layers makes about 30 cupcakes.

Bake cupcakes at 375° F. for 15 to 20 minutes.

BRIDE'S CAKE

1¾ cups butter
2 cups sugar
8 eggs, separated
1 teaspoon almond flavoring
2 tablespoons heavy cream
2½ cups sifted all-purpose flour
1 cup chopped seeded raisins
1 cup citron, finely shredded
1 cup blanched almonds
1½ teaspoons double-acting baking powder
¼ teaspoon salt

Cream the butter, gradually add the sugar, and cream together until light and fluffy.

Beat the egg yolks until thick and pale in color and stir into the butter-sugar mixture, along with the almond flavoring and the cream.

Beat thoroughly.

Dredge a little flour over the fruit and nuts and sift the rest together with the baking powder and salt three times.

Stir in the flour, add the nuts and fruit, and lastly fold in the egg whites, which have been beaten until stiff.

Grease a 10-inch tube pan.

Line with waxed paper and grease again.

Pour the batter into the prepared pan and bake at 300° F. for about 2 hours.

Cool on wire cake rack and, when cool, frost the top and sides with ALMOND BUTTER FROSTING, reserving enough to squeeze through pastry tube to decorate the cake with fluted edges, flowers, and leaves.

PERFECT POUND CAKE

1½ cups butter (3 sticks)	1 teaspoon vanilla
1 box (1 pound) 10X confectioners' sugar	1 teaspoon almond extract
	3½ cups sifted enriched flour
7 large eggs (1 pound)	Confectioners' sugar
½ teaspoon salt	

Cream butter and sugar together until light and fluffy.

Beat in eggs, one at a time, beating well after each addition.

Stir in salt, vanilla, and almond extract.

Gradually stir in flour.

Spoon batter into a greased and floured 9-inch tube pan and bake in a preheated 350° F. oven for 1 hour and 15 minutes. For a golden-brown crust, turn off oven heat and leave cake in oven for 15 minutes longer.

Turn out of pan and serve warm or cold sprinkled generously with confectioners' sugar.

MAPLE WALNUT POUND CAKE

¾ cup butter or margarine	¼ teaspoon baking soda
1¼ cups light brown sugar	½ teaspoon salt
4 eggs	1 cup broken walnut meats
2 cups sifted all-purpose flour	1 teaspoon maple flavoring
1 teaspoon baking powder	1 cup light raisins, optional

Beat shortening until pale in color and gradually beat in sugar.

Beat in eggs, one at a time, beating well after each addition.

Combine flour, baking powder, soda, and salt and stir into the egg mixture.

Stir in nuts and flavoring.

Put batter into a greased and floured 5-cup ring mold or angel food pan.

Bake in a preheated 350° F. oven for 35 to 40 minutes, or until cake tests done.

One cup light raisins may be added. If so, bake batter in a 6-cup mold.

Cool and serve, unfrosted, with a brisk cup of tea.

QUICK SPICE CAKE

2⅓ cups sifted cake flour
1 cup sugar
¾ cup brown sugar
1 teaspoon salt
1 teaspoon double-acting
    baking powder
¾ teaspoon soda

1 teaspoon ginger
¼ teaspoon cloves
¼ teaspoon cinnamon
½ cup butter or shortening
1 cup buttermilk
3 eggs

In mixing bowl combine cake flour, sugar, brown sugar, salt, baking powder, soda, ginger, cloves, and cinnamon.

Add shortening and ¾ cup of the buttermilk and beat vigorously for 2 minutes by hand or mixer (medium speed).

Add eggs and remaining buttermilk and beat for 2 minutes longer.

Pour batter into prepared pans (two 9-inch layers 1½ inches deep).

Bake at 350° F. for 35 to 40 minutes.

BROWN SUGAR SPICE CAKE

½ cup butter or margarine
1½ cups brown sugar, firmly
    packed
3 eggs
2½ cups sifted flour
1 teaspoon salt
2½ teaspoons baking powder

1½ teaspoons cinnamon
½ teaspoon cloves
½ teaspoon nutmeg
½ cup chopped pecans
1 cup milk
PECAN TOPPING

Cream butter and sugar until smooth.

Beat in eggs, one at a time.

Combine flour, salt, baking powder, spices, and nuts and stir into egg mixture alternately with the milk.

Pour into a 9-inch square cake pan lined with waxed paper and greased.

Bake in a preheated 350° F. oven for 40 minutes, or until cake tests done.

Remove from oven and spread with pecan topping.

Place under broiler heat for 4 minutes, or until topping is bubbly.

PEANUT RING CAKE

½ cup butter or shortening
½ cup molasses
½ cup chopped peanuts
½ cup sugar
1 teaspoon cinnamon
½ teaspoon ginger
¼ teaspoon salt

1 egg
2 cups sifted cake flour
2 teaspoons double-acting
  baking powder
¾ cup buttermilk
½ teaspoon soda

Beat half the shortening and half the molasses until combined.
Spread mixture in prepared 9-inch 2-quart ring mold and sprinkle with peanuts.
Blend remaining shortening and molasses and the sugar and stir in cinnamon, ginger, and salt.
Add egg and beat well.
Stir in flour mixed with baking powder alternately with milk mixed with soda.
Turn into ring mold.
Bake at 350° F. for 45 minutes.
Cool for 1 minute only. Then turn out on cake rack to cool.

CRUMB AND NUT CAKE

1 cup butter or shortening
1 cup sugar
4 eggs
2 teaspoons vanilla
3 cups fine graham cracker
  crumbs

1 cup finely chopped nuts
3 teaspoons double-acting
  baking powder
1 cup milk

Blend shortening, sugar, eggs, and vanilla.
Combine crumbs, nuts, and baking powder and add to shortening mixture alternately with milk.
Pour into prepared pans (three 8-inch layers 1¼ inches deep).
Bake at 350° F. for 30 to 35 minutes.
Turn out on rack to cool and put layers together with favorite filling.

DATE, NUT, AND GINGER CAKE

1 cup boiling water	1 cup brown sugar
1½ cups cut-up dates	1 egg
½ cup chopped preserved ginger	2 cups sifted cake flour
	½ teaspoon salt
1 cup broken walnuts	1 teaspoon soda
½ cup shortening	2 tablespoons cold water

Pour boiling water over fruit and nuts and let stand.

Cream shortening and sugar thoroughly.

Add egg and beat well.

Combine flour and salt.

Stir soda into dates and nuts.

Add flour and fruit mixture to the egg mixture alternately, stirring after each addition until well blended.

Stir in cold water.

Turn mixture into a greased 5-cup ring mold and bake in a 350° F. oven for 45 minutes.

ALMOND TEACAKE

¾ cup butter or margarine	1 teaspoon nutmeg
1¼ cups light brown sugar	¼ teaspoon salt
4 eggs	½ cup light raisins
2 cups sifted all-purpose flour	½ cup currants
1 teaspoon double-acting baking powder	1 cup seedless raisins
	½ cup chopped mixed fruit peel
¼ teaspoon baking soda	
1 teaspoon cinnamon	1 cup blanched, split almonds

Cream butter or margarine and brown sugar until smooth.

Beat in eggs, one at a time, beating well after each addition.

Combine flour, baking powder, soda, spices, and salt and stir into the egg mixture.

Stir in fruit, peel, and half the almonds.

Put batter into a greased cake pan 8 inches in diameter and 2 inches deep. If your pan is not deep enough, collar it with a strip of greased brown paper cut 2 inches wide.

Smooth top with spatula.

Bake in a preheated 350° F. oven for about 1 hour, or until cake tests done, but after baking for 30 minutes sprinkle top with the remaining almonds.

LEMON STRAWBERRY CAKE

½ cup butter
1 cup fine granulated sugar
2 eggs
Grated rind of 1 lemon
1⅓ cups sifted cake flour
1½ teaspoons double-acting
    baking powder

¼ teaspoon salt
½ cup milk
1 teaspoon lemon extract
Confectioners' sugar
Sliced and sweetened straw-
    berries, fresh or frozen

Cream butter and sugar together until smooth.

Beat in eggs and lemon rind.

Combine dry ingredients and stir them into the butter-sugar mixture alternately with milk and lemon extract.

Pour batter into a buttered and floured 6-cup ring mold or small tube pan and bake in a preheated 350° F. oven for 40 to 45 minutes, or until cake tests done.

Unmold on cake rack to cool.

To serve, place cake on plate and sprinkle generously with confectioners' sugar. Fill center with sliced and sweetened strawberries. *Serves 6.*

JIFFY SPONGECAKE

4 eggs, separated
1⅔ cups sifted cake flour
¼ teaspoon salt
¼ teaspoon double-acting
    baking powder

1½ cups sugar
2 teaspoons cold water
½ cup hot water
1 teaspoon vanilla
MOUNTAIN CREAM FROSTING

Use an electric beater if you have one. Beat egg whites and set aside.

Beat egg yolks at top speed while you sift together the flour, salt, and baking powder.

Add sugar gradually to egg yolks while still beating at top speed.

Reduce speed to medium and add the cold water, hot water, and vanilla.

Remove bowl from beater, fold in dry ingredients, and lastly the stiffly beaten egg whites.

Pour into ungreased tube pan and bake for 40 minutes in a 325° F. oven.

Invert pan over cake rack until cool.

This is nice frosted with a large quantity of mountain cream frosting to which has been added a jar of strawberry jam and a drop of red coloring.

NOTE: To use this cake as a base for desserts or for small iced teacakes, pour it into a large shallow pan or into two round 9-inch pans to a thickness of about 1 inch and bake for 20 minutes.

VELVET SPONGECAKE

4 large eggs, separated
1½ cups fine granulated sugar
½ cup hot water
1 teaspoon vanilla
1½ cups sifted cake flour
¼ teaspoon salt
¼ teaspoon double-acting baking powder

Beat egg yolks and sugar until thick and pale in color.
Beat in hot water and vanilla.
Stir in cake flour mixed with salt and baking powder.
Beat egg whites until stiff but not dry and fold into yolk mixture.
Spoon batter into a 9-inch angel food pan and bake in a preheated 325° F. oven for 55 minutes.
Invert pan and let cake cool for 1 hour before removing from pan.
Serve plain or frosted.

RUM CAKE

3 eggs
1 cup sugar
3 tablespoons cold water
2 teaspoons vanilla
1 cup sifted all-purpose flour
2 teaspoons double-acting baking powder
RUM CREAM TOPPING
Chopped nuts
Candied cherries

Beat eggs until light.
Gradually beat in the sugar and continue beating until the mixture is thick and pale in color. Use electric beater for this, if you have one.
Stir in the water and vanilla.

Fold in the flour, which has been sifted three times with the baking powder.

Pour into a greased 9-inch spring form pan and bake for 30 minutes, (350° F.) or until a cake tester inserted in the middle comes out clean.

Keep the cake in the pan and, when cool, pour over it rum cream topping.

Place in the refrigerator to set, and serve decorated with chopped nuts and candied cherries.

RUSSIAN TEACAKE

6 *egg whites*	½ *teaspoon cream of tartar*
3 *egg yolks*	½ *teaspoon salt*
¾ *cup sugar*	RUSSIAN TEACAKE ICING
⅔ *cup sifted cake flour*	

Beat egg whites until stiff but not dry.

Beat egg yolks with sugar until thick and pale in color and fold into egg whites.

Sift dry ingredients together five times and fold into egg mixture.

Bake in an 8-inch tube pan for 1 hour in a 350° F. oven.

Ice top and sides with Russian teacake icing.

This is really a soufflé that is allowed to fall, then is rolled. It contains no flour.

CHOCOLATE ROLL · *Roulade au Chocolat*

5 *large eggs, separated*	3 *tablespoons strong coffee*
⅔ *cup sugar*	*Cocoa*
6 *squares (ounces) semi-*	1¼ *cups heavy cream,*
sweet chocolate	*whipped*

Butter a large baking sheet (18×12 inches), line it with waxed paper, and butter again.

Beat egg yolks and sugar with a rotary beater until thick and pale in color.

Stir in chocolate, melted with the coffee and slightly cooled, and then fold in egg whites, beaten until stiff.

Spread mixture evenly on prepared sheet and bake in a moderate oven (350° F.) for 15 minutes, or until a knife inserted in the middle comes out clean. Do not overbake.

Remove from oven and cover with a damp cloth for half an hour, or until cool. Loosen cake from baking sheet and dust generously with cocoa.

Turn out on waxed paper, cocoa side down, and carefully remove paper from bottom of cake.

Spread with whipped cream, sweetened and flavored to taste, and roll up like a jelly roll, rolling it sidewise rather than lengthwise to make a thin, long roll that resembles a log. To facilitate the rolling, firmly grasp each corner of the waxed paper on which you turned out the cake and flip over about 2 inches of the edge on top of the cake. Continue to roll by further lifting of the waxed paper. The last roll should deposit the log on a long board or platter. Dust top with a little more cocoa. *Serves 8.*

DARK FRUITCAKE

1 *pound candied cherries*	½ *cup molasses*
2 *pounds sultana raisins*	2 *teaspoons cinnamon*
5 *pounds seedless raisins*	1 *teaspoon allspice*
2 *pounds currants*	1 *teaspoon ground cloves*
½ *pound citron, sliced*	1 *teaspoon ground nutmeg*
½ *pound candied orange and*	1 *teaspoon soda*
lemon, mixed and sliced	2 *teaspoons double-acting*
1 *pound blanched almonds*	*baking powder*
10 *cups sifted all-purpose*	½ *cup sherry*
flour	¼ *cup vanilla*
2 *pounds butter*	½ *cup orange juice*
4 *cups brown sugar*	ALMOND PASTE
12 *eggs*	CONFECTIONERS' SUGAR ICING

Prepare fruit and nuts. If citron, peel, or raisins are hard, soften them by washing them and steaming for 30 minutes.

Mix all together with 2 cups of the flour.

Cream butter and brown sugar well.

Beat in eggs, two at a time, and beat until smooth after each addition.

Stir in molasses.

Add sifted dry ingredients alternately with the liquid.

Finally fold in the floured fruit and nuts.

Bake in 2-pound loaf pans, 8×4×3 inches, which have been lined with heavy brown paper and then greased. Fill pans almost full. Bake at 250° F. for 2 hours. Smaller cakes will require less baking time. Top with a 1-inch-thick layer of almond paste and ice with confectioners' sugar icing.

This recipe will make 8 loaves. Recipe may be halved.

NOTE: To keep fruitcakes for a long time, store them unfrosted in a tightly covered tin box. Every month pour over ½ cup brandy.

LIGHT FRUITCAKE

1 pound sultana raisins
½ pound citron, finely sliced
½ pound candied cherries
½ pound candied pineapple, finely sliced
½ pound candied orange peel, finely sliced
½ pound candied lemon peel, finely sliced

1 pound blanched almonds
4 cups sifted all-purpose flour
1 cup butter
2 cups sugar
2 teaspoons double-acting baking powder
½ teaspoon salt
1 cup white wine
8 egg whites, stiffly beaten

Prepare the fruit and nuts.

If citron, peel, or raisins are hard, soften them by washing and steaming for 30 minutes.

Mix all together with 1 cup of the flour.

Cream butter and sugar together until light and fluffy.

Sift dry ingredients together and add alternately with the wine.

Stir in fruit and nuts and then fold in egg whites.

Bake in loaf pans, 8×4×3 inches, lined with heavy brown paper and then greased.

Bake at 250° F. for 2 hours. *Makes 3 loaves.*

SWEDISH FRUITCAKE

1 cup currants or seedless raisins
1½ cups mixed candied fruits
1¾ cups sifted all-purpose flour
½ teaspoon baking powder

1 cup butter
1 cup sugar
3 eggs, separated
¼ teaspoon cream of tartar
Bread crumbs

Preheat oven to 300° F.

Rinse currants in cold water. Place in a saucepan, cover with water, and bring to a boil. Drain currants and dry thoroughly in a towel.

Chop candied fruits or slice thinly, except cherries, which should be left whole.

Mix fruits thoroughly with one cup of the flour until coated.

Sift remaining flour with baking powder.

Cream butter; gradually add sugar, and cream until white and fluffy. Add one egg yolk at a time, beating well after each addition.

Stir in floured fruit mixture and sifted ingredients. Mix thoroughly.

Beat egg whites a few minutes. Add cream of tartar and continue to beat until they form moist peaks.

Fold in egg whites carefully.

Butter a 9×3½-inch tube pan and sprinkle with fine, dry bread crumbs until evenly coated, shaking off any excess.

Pour batter into pan and bake 1½ to 2 hours, or until done.

Cool cake a few minutes before removing from pan. Keep at least two days before cutting.

NOTE: This cake will keep moist for many months if it is wrapped in aluminum foil and stored in the refrigerator.

DUNDEE CAKE

1 cup butter	1 cup seedless raisins
⅔ cup sugar	1 cup currants
4 eggs	2 tablespoons orange juice
½ cup blanched chopped almonds	⅓ cup candied orange peel, finely cut
2½ cups sifted all-purpose flour	⅓ cup candied lemon peel, finely cut
1 teaspoon double-acting baking powder	½ cup whole blanched almonds
½ teaspoon salt	½ cup candied cherries

Cream butter, add sugar gradually, and blend well.

Add eggs, one at a time, beating well after each addition.

Stir in chopped almonds.

Sift together flour, baking powder, and salt and mix with raisins and currants.

Combine orange juice with orange and lemon peel and add this mixture alternately with the sifted dry ingredients, raisins, and currants.

Grease two small bread pans, line with heavy paper, and grease again.

Divide batter between the two pans and cover tops with the whole almonds and candied cherries.

Bake at 250° F. for 1½ hours, covering tops with greased paper as soon as cakes start to brown.

When baked, remove cakes from the pans and cool on cake rack.

BISCHOFSBROT

5 eggs, separated
¼ teaspoon salt
1¼ cups sugar
¾ cup sliced almonds
½ cup seeded raisins
¼ cup sliced citron

2 squares (ounces) unsweetened chocolate cut into small dice
1¾ cups sifted all-purpose flour

Beat egg yolks until light and foamy, add salt, and add sugar, gradually continuing to beat until mixture is thick and pale in color.

Add almonds, raisins, citron, and chocolate and then fold in the stiffly beaten egg whites.

Sift flour over batter and fold in lightly.

Bake in a long, narrow buttered bread mold at 350° F. for 50 minutes.

Remove cake from tin and allow it to cool on a rack before slicing.

BEST CHEESECAKE

2 graham crackers, crumbed
¼ cup melted butter
1 tablespoon sugar
½ teaspoon cinnamon
1½ pounds cream cheese
3 eggs, lightly beaten

¾ cup sugar
1 tablespoon vanilla
3 cups sour cream
⅓ to 1 cup buttermilk
¼ cup melted butter

Combine graham cracker crumbs, melted butter, the 1 tablespoon sugar, and cinnamon. Line a buttered 8-cup spring form pan.

Soften cream cheese and gradually work in eggs, sugar, and vanilla.

Gradually stir in sour cream and enough buttermilk to make a batter the consistency of pancake batter.

Fold in melted butter.

Bake in a preheated 325° F. oven for 45 minutes.

Cool and chill thoroughly before serving.

Serves 10 to 12.

COTTAGE CHEESE CAKE

1 cup zwieback crumbs
¼ cup sugar
¼ cup melted butter
½ teaspoon cinnamon
1 pound creamed cottage
  cheese
¼ cup sifted cake flour
4 eggs, separated

1 cup sugar
2 tablespoons lemon juice
1½ teaspoons grated lemon
  rind
½ teaspoon vanilla
¼ teaspoon salt
1 cup heavy cream, whipped

Combine zwieback crumbs, the ¼ cup sugar, melted butter, and cinnamon.

Pat three-fourths of this mixture on the bottom of a buttered 8-inch spring form pan.

Force cottage cheese through a coarse strainer twice with the back of a spoon, mix it with the flour, and beat thoroughly until light and fluffy.

Beat egg yolks, add ½ cup of the sugar, and beat until thick and pale in color.

Add lemon juice, lemon rind, vanilla, and salt and fold in the cheese mixture.

Fold in whipped cream; then fold in egg whites beaten until stiff with the remaining sugar.

Blend mixture gently but well and turn into prepared pan.

Sprinkle remaining crumbs on top.

Bake at 325° F. for 1 hour.

Turn off oven, open the door, and without moving cake, leave in oven 1 hour.

Then cool thoroughly, remove spring form, and serve.

CREAM CHEESE CAKE

¾ box zwieback
¼ cup melted butter
7 tablespoons sugar
1 pound cream cheese
1 teaspoon vanilla
4 tablespoons sifted all-
purpose flour

Pinch salt
4 eggs, separated
1 tablespoon lemon juice
1 cup heavy cream

Roll zwieback into fine crumbs or crumb in electric blender and mix with melted butter and 1 tablespoon of the sugar.

Press crumbs firmly onto bottom and sides of a well-buttered 9-inch spring form pan.

Cream the cheese with the vanilla.

Stir in 2 tablespoons of the sugar, the flour, and salt, and cream all together until mixture is fluffy.

Beat egg yolks, add them, and beat thoroughly.

Then stir in lemon juice and cream.

Beat egg whites until almost stiff.

Gradually add the remaining sugar and continue to beat until the meringue is stiff and glossy.

Fold into cheese mixture lightly but thoroughly, and pour into prepared pan.

Bake cake at 325° F. for 1½ hours, or until set in center.

Chill cake before removing the spring form.

GENOISE

Génoise is a very fine-textured, delicate cake used as the basis of some of the finest *gâteaux* and *petits fours*, and for de luxe desserts such as Baked Alaska. Eggs must be beaten with the sugar to the "ribbon stage." That means the mixture must be so thick that it will pull out like a ribbon when the beater is withdrawn and will take some time to level off again. From then on, the batter must be handled gently so that the copious amount of air whipped into the eggs and sugar will not be lost. The batter may be flavored with vanilla or almond extract, or with a little grated orange or lemon rind; and often ½ cup of finely ground grilled hazelnuts or walnuts are folded in with the flour.

Usually a *génoise* is baked in a round or square pan with sides about 1½ inches high, known as a *moule à manqué*. But it may also be baked in layer cake pans, loaf pans, timbale molds, or ring molds. When baked in the ring mold, the cake may be saturated with a rum-flavored syrup and served filled with fresh or canned fruits and whipped cream. Half the batter, in a loaf pan, may be sprinkled with ½ cup chopped preserved fruits or orange peel soaked in rum or curaçao and the fruit covered with the remaining batter.

Once baked, it may be split into two or three layers and reshaped with a filling of marmalade, butter cream, or *crème pâtissière* between the layers. Usually the top and sides of the cake are masked with a thin coating of apricot glaze and iced with fondant, flavored with vanilla, rum, kirsch, or any other appropriate spirit or liqueur. Sometimes only the top is spread with fondant and the sides are thickly covered with finely chopped pistachios or toasted almonds.

Occasionally a slice is cut from the top of a *génoise* and the center is hollowed out. The hollow is then filled with *crème pâtissière* or *crème bourdaloue*, or with whipped cream or ice cream, or with fruits sweetened and flavored with maraschino or kirsch. The top is replaced and the cake is smoothly iced with fondant, simply spread with whipped cream, or lavishly garnished with butter cream.

Just as it is the clothes that make the woman, it is the *décor* that makes the *génoise*. The smooth topping of *glace royale* or of fondant, gaily and colorfully garnished with nuts, candied fruits, and tiny diamonds of preserved peel—or rosettes and scrolls of butter cream pressed through a pastry bag or cone fitted with a decorator's tube —contribute greatly to the popularity of the *génoise*.

The hostess who wishes to establish her culinary reputation will be quick to add the *génoise* cakes to her repertoire.

GENOISE

1 cup sugar	1 cup sifted cake flour
6 eggs	½ cup butter, melted and
1 teaspoon vanilla	cooled

In top of a double boiler combine sugar and eggs and beat with a wire whip over hot water for about 15 minutes, or until the mixture is warmed through and is light and creamy.

Remove pan from heat and beat mixture with a rotary beater until very thick, pale in color, and takes some time to level out when beater is withdrawn.

Stir in vanilla and add the flour gradually by sifting it, a little at a time, over the batter and folding it in gently with a wooden spoon or a rubber scraper.

Gradually and carefully fold in butter. The butter must not be more than lukewarm, and any residue that has fallen to the bottom of the saucepan in which it was melted must not be added to the batter.

Pour batter 1 inch thick into a buttered and floured 9-inch round cake pan and bake in a moderate oven (350° F.) for about 40 minutes, or until cake leaves sides of pan and a cake tester inserted in center comes out clean.

Remove cake immediately from pan to a rack to cool.

FILLED GENOISE NORMANDIE

Split a GENOISE in half and sprinkle the halves with Calvados. Spread the bottom slice with applesauce or apple marmalade and cover this with a thick couch of PASTRY CREAM flavored to taste with Calvados. Place the top slice over the cream and brush cake with APRICOT GLAZE. Warm 2 cups FONDANT over boiling water, flavor with Calvados, and thin with hot water to a spreading consistency. Pour the warm fondant over cake and spread around sides very quickly with a spatula. (GLACE ROYALE may be used instead of fondant.) Decorate top and sides with apple slices cooked in syrup, with blanched almonds, and with diamonds of angelica or citron.

SURPRISE CHEESECAKE • *Fromage de Brie en Surprise*

Bake GENOISE batter in a buttered flan ring placed on a buttered and floured baking sheet. When cool, cut into 2 thin layers and put layers together with a ½-inch-thick layer of BUTTER CREAM flavored with kirsch.

Sprinkle top copiously with granulated sugar tinted pale green by adding a speck of green food paste and rubbing sugar and coloring between palms of the hands. Sprinkle confectioners' sugar heavily over the green sugar. The cake will resemble a Brie cheese.

CHESTNUT CREAM CAKE · *Gâteau Régent aux Marrons*

Bake GENOISE batter in three buttered flan rings. When layers are cool, put them together with thick layers of CHESTNUT BUTTER CREAM between. Spread top and sides of cake with APRICOT GLAZE. In center of the cake put a thin slice of green candied cherry, and surround with blanched almond halves to imitate the petals of a daisy.

Warm 2 cups RUM FONDANT over boiling water and thin it with hot water to a very thin consistency. Pour the warm rum fondant over the cake, spreading it around the sides very quickly with a spatula, covering cake and decoration with a thin veil of icing. The surplus that runs off the cake may be retrieved and used another time.

GATEAU SANS GENE

Bake GENOISE batter in a buttered and floured cake pan 9 inches in diameter and 1½ inches deep. When cool, split and put layers together with PRALINE BUTTER CREAM or CHOCOLATE BUTTER CREAM. Frost top and sides smoothly with more of the same cream, and press finely chopped toasted almonds around the side.

On top, radiate from the center 6 CORNETS filled with cream. Make a large rosette of cream in the center and insert the pointed end of another cornet in the rosette.

WALNUT CREAM CAKE · *Le Lutétia*

Bake GENOISE batter in a buttered and floured cake pan 9 inches in diameter and 2 inches deep. When cool, split into 3 layers and put the layers together with WALNUT BUTTER CREAM. Spread top and sides with a thin coating of APRICOT GLAZE and ice the cake with CHOCOLATE FONDANT.

Fill a pastry cone fitted with a small round tube with CHESTNUT PUREE and press out the purée, letting it fall at random in the center of the cake to form a nestlike effect. Decorate around the mound of purée and around the side of the cake with some perfect walnut halves.

MACARONI CAKE • *Le Baquet de Macaroni au Gratin*

Bake GENOISE batter in a buttered flan ring placed on a buttered and floured baking sheet. When cool spread top and sides with a layer of BUTTER CREAM.

Cut 15 CAT TONGUES in half crosswise, and place them close together all around the side of the cake, cut side down, to imitate the staves of a basket. Fill "basket" with butter cream, letting cream fall at random from a pastry cone fitted with a small round tube, to simulate macaroni. Sprinkle with finely chopped toasted almonds to represent bread crumbs.

PEACH PYRAMID

Bake GENOISE batter in a 9-inch cake pan about 2 inches deep and, when cool, pour over it ¼ cup sherry or Madeira. Rub some apricot jam through a sieve and coat sides and top of cake with it. Sprinkle cake thickly with chopped pistachio nuts and place on a serving dish. Whip 1 cup heavy cream, reserve a little for decoration, and pile the rest in the center of the cake in pyramid form. Drain some preserved peaches and mount them in rows all over the cream. Put reserved cream into a pastry bag fitted with an open-star tube and pipe a small rosette of cream between the peach halves.

ORANGE ICE BOMBE

Bake GENOISE batter in two melon molds and, when cool, scoop out center from each cake, leaving a thick shell. When ready to serve, fill cakes with ORANGE ICE and put the two halves together to form a whole melon. Frost with orange ice.

STRAWBERRY CREAM CAKE

Bake GENOISE batter in a timbale mold and, when cool, scoop out inside, leaving sides and bottom ½ inch thick. Rub a little apricot jam through a sieve and spread it over outside of the cake. Cover thickly with chopped nuts and place on serving dish. Fill inside with alternate layers of VANILLA BAVARIAN CREAM and STRAWBERRY BAVARIAN CREAM, allowing each layer to set before putting in the next. When ready to serve, whip 1 cup cream, flavor and sweeten to taste, and pile on top of cake in the shape of a pyramid. Cover pyramid with halved strawberries.

KIRSCH CAKE • *Citeau au Kirsch*

Sprinkle a GENOISE about 9 inches in diameter and ¾ inch thick with ¼ cup kirsch.

Make VANILLA BAVARIAN CREAM and turn it into an 8-inch round mold about 1 inch high. Chill the cream in the refrigerator and, when set, unmold onto cake.

Put a slice of pineapple in the center of the cream and half a candied cherry in the center of the pineapple slice. Around the cream, on the cake, arrange quarters of pineapple slices and candied cherries. *Serves 6.*

GATEAU ALEXANDRA

3 egg yolks	¼ cup sifted flour
1 egg	¾ cup sifted cornstarch
⅝ cup sugar	3 egg whites, stiffly beaten
⅓ cup grated blanched almonds	⅓ cup butter, melted and cooled
4 ounces dark sweet chocolate	Apricot marmalade
3 tablespoons coffee	CHOCOLATE FONDANT

Beat egg yolks and egg until light and fluffy.

Add sugar and continue to beat until mixture is thick and pale in color.

Stir in almonds, and chocolate melted over a low flame with the coffee and cooled.

Fold in flour, sifted with cornstarch, then the stiffly beaten egg whites.

Finally fold in melted butter.

Turn batter into a buttered and floured square cake pan with sides about 1½ inches deep and bake in a slow oven (325° F.) for about 50 minutes, or until a cake tester comes out clean.

Remove cake from pan to a rack to cool, and when cold mask top and sides with apricot marmalade, and ice with chocolate fondant.

PINEAPPLE BOURDALOUE

Bake a GENOISE in a buttered and floured 8-inch ring or savarin mold. Unmold on a round platter and arrange on top thin slices of fresh pineapple, poached for 10 minutes in VANILLA SYRUP. The slices should overlap and take the shape of the *génoise*.

Fill center with BOURDALOUE CREAM or FRANGIPANE CREAM piled into a dome. Sprinkle with macaroon crumbs or chopped almonds, sprinkle with butter, and brown in a hot oven. Brush pineapple with apricot syrup flavored with kirsch and decorate with preserved cherries and angelica.

TORTES

Tortes, like the *génoise*, contain no other leavening but the air beaten into the eggs.

DOBOS TORTE

7 *eggs, separated*	CHOCOLATE CREAM FOR DOBOS
¾ *cup sugar*	TORTE
1 *cup sifted cake flour*	CARAMELIZED SUGAR
¼ *teaspoon salt*	

Beat egg yolks until fluffy, add sugar gradually, and continue to beat until mixture is thick and pale in color.

Fold in flour and then fold in egg whites, beaten with salt until stiff but not dry.

Butter seven shallow 8-inch layer cake pans, line bottoms with waxed paper, and butter again. The bottom tins of spring molds may be used. If you have only two or three pans, these may be prepared, the layers baked, and the operation repeated.

Spread layers evenly with 4 or 5 tablespoons of batter and bake in a moderate oven (350° F.) for 8 minutes, or until the thin sheets of cake are lightly browned.

Remove pans from oven and turn out layers onto cake racks to cool.

Remove waxed paper immediately.

When all the layers have been baked and cooled, spread chocolate cream for Dobos torte between the layers and over top and sides of cake.

Chill thoroughly, then cover top with caramelized sugar (¾ cup sugar melted in a small pan; 1 tablespoon butter added and stirred until mixture is golden brown). Use a spatula and spread the caramel over the top of the cake. *This must be done quickly, or the sugar will harden.* When sugar has hardened, heat a knife and make wedge-shaped incisions through the sugar coating.

This torte will taste better the day after it is made. Keep it in the refrigerator, where it will stay fresh for a week.

CHOCOLATE CREAM FOR DOBOS TORTE

5 ounces unsweetened chocolate	Pinch salt
3 tablespoons coffee	½ cup sugar
4 egg yolks	1 cup sweet butter, creamed

Melt chocolate with coffee over boiling water, stirring until the mixture is smooth. Beat egg yolks with salt until light, add sugar gradually, beating until the mixture is thick and pale in color.

Stir in melted chocolate and cook over hot water for 5 to 6 minutes, stirring constantly until cream is thick and smooth.

Remove cream from the fire and add butter bit by bit, beating briskly after each addition.

Chill until cream reaches a spreading consistency, stirring occasionally.

MOCHA TORTE

12 ounces semi-sweet chocolate	4 tablespoons strong coffee
4 large or 5 medium-sized eggs	½ cup unsifted all-purpose flour
½ cup sugar plus 1 tablespoon	MOCHA BUTTER CREAM

Melt 8 ounces of the chocolate over boiling water.

Cut circles 2½ inches in diameter from waxed paper and spread these rounds with a thin coating of the melted chocolate.

Place rounds on a cooky sheet and chill.

Butter a round cake pan 9 inches in diameter and 2 inches deep. Line bottom with waxed paper and butter again.

Beat eggs and sugar until light and pale in color—ribbon stage, 5 minutes. (Use an electric beater for this, if possible. If you do not have an electric beater, place the bowl containing the sugar and eggs over hot water and beat vigorously with a rotary beater.)

Melt remaining 4 ounces of chocolate with coffee and stir into the batter.

Sift flour twice and fold into the batter.

Pour batter into prepared pan and bake in a moderate oven (350° F.) for 35 minutes, or until a cake tester comes out clean.

Turn out immediately on a wire cake rack to cool. Frost generously with half of the mocha butter cream and make a circle of large rosettes on top with the remaining cream pressed from a pastry bag fitted with an open-star tube.

Peel waxed paper from back of the chocolate rounds and place the rounds, slightly overlapping, all around the sides of the cake.

HAZELNUT TORTE

1 heaping cup shelled hazelnuts	3 teaspoons vanilla
	1 teaspoon lemon juice
4 egg whites	1 cup heavy cream
1⅓ cups fine granulated sugar	2 tablespoons sugar
	Confectioners' sugar

Roast hazelnuts in a very hot oven (450° to 500° F.) for about 10 minutes, or until skins crack open and nuts are toasted. Shake pan occasionally so they will brown evenly. Empty out onto a clean towel and rub briskly together to remove the skin.

Pick out nuts, discarding skins, and put them through a nut grater or grind in an electric blender.

Sift grated nuts through a sieve to eliminate any large pieces of nuts. You should have about 1½ cups of finely powdered toasted nuts.

Beat egg whites until stiff, then beat in gradually the fine granulated sugar. Continue to beat for several minutes.

Add 2 teaspoons of the vanilla and the lemon juice, and beat for 2 or 3 minutes longer to make sure all the sugar has been thoroughly dissolved in the egg whites.

Fold in carefully 1¼ cups of the nuts and spread mixture evenly in two 9-inch paper-lined layer cake tins.

Bake in a slow oven (300° F.) for about 30 minutes.

Remove paper immediately and cool.

When ready to serve, whip cream until just stiff, add the 2 tablespoons of sugar and remaining vanilla, fold in the rest of the powdered nuts, and spread between the layers. Sprinkle top with confectioners' sugar and serve.

FILBERT TORTE

10 eggs, separated, at room
  temperature
1½ cups sugar
3 tablespoons cake flour
2 cups finely ground, skinned
  filberts

1 twelve-ounce jar of apricot
  preserves
Juice of one lemon
1 pint heavy cream
½ cup dark brown sugar
Shaved filberts for garnish

Line the bottoms of three 9-inch layer pans (preferably with removable bottoms) with parchment paper or greased and lightly floured waxed paper.

Beat egg yolks until thick.

Gradually add sugar, beating until mixture is light and fluffy.

Fold in flour and nuts.

Beat egg whites until stiff but not dry. Mix one-third of the egg whites into nut mixture. Fold in remainder gently.

Pour into prepared pans and bake in a preheated 350° F. oven for 30 to 35 minutes, until browned and set.

Remove from oven and cool slightly. The layers will shrink. Set layers, still on paper, on racks to cool.

Mix preserves with lemon juice.

Beat cream with the brown sugar until it reaches spreading consistency.

Carefully remove paper from one layer and place layer on a cake plate. Spread with apricot mixture and then two tablespoons of the whipped cream.

Remove paper from a second layer and place on top. Repeat the spreading process and top with the third layer.

Frost the torte all over with remaining cream. Garnish with shaved filberts and refrigerate.

Spread the nuts in a shallow pan and bake in a 350° oven for 15 to 20 minutes.

Remove the filberts and cover them with boiling water.

Drain immediately and rub the nuts back and forth between two towels, loosening the skin. Any skin remaining after this process will not be detrimental to the dishes prepared.

VIRGINIA TORTE

⅔ cup blanched almonds
½ cup sugar
½ cup butter
3 teaspoons all-purpose flour
2 tablespoons light cream

CUSTARD CREAM FILLING
1 cup heavy cream, whipped, sweetened to taste
Candied violets or chocolate bits, optional

Grind or chop almonds or grate in an electric blender.

Combine almonds with the sugar, butter, flour, and cream and cook over low heat until butter melts. Then stir vigorously until mixture pulls away from sides of saucepan.

Butter three cooky sheets generously and dust with flour.

Spoon one-third of the almond mixture into the center of each cooky sheet.

Bake in a preheated 375° F. oven for 4 minutes or until cooky mixture has spread out.

Remove from oven and shape into 9-inch rounds.

Return to oven and bake 3 to 4 minutes longer, or until golden brown.

Cool 1 minute and remove rounds with a sharp knife.

Transfer to a double piece of waxed paper.

Place one cooky on a dessert dish and top with a layer of custard cream filling.

Add another almond layer, another round of custard, and a final almond layer.

Garnish with whipped cream and, if desired, candied violets or chocolate bits.

WALNUT TORTE

2½ cups ground walnuts
¾ cup sugar
7 egg whites

WALNUT FILLING
Confectioners' sugar

Combine walnuts and sugar.

Beat egg whites until stiff and fold in the walnut-sugar mixture.

Divide batter evenly between three buttered and floured 9-inch cake pans and bake in a hot oven (400° F.) for 15 to 20 minutes, or until delicately browned.

Let layers cool in pans before removing them.

Spread walnut filling between layers. Sprinkle top with confectioners' sugar.

COFFEE PRALINE TORTE

6 eggs, separated
¼ cup strong coffee
1 cup sugar
¾ cup walnut meats
⅓ cup all-purpose flour

⅛ teaspoon salt
PRALINE BUTTER CREAM
CHOCOLATE WATER ICING
PRALINE POWDER

Into container of the electric blender put egg yolks, coffee, sugar, walnuts, flour, and salt.

Cover and blend on high speed for 15 seconds, stopping to stir down if necessary.

Beat egg whites until stiff but not dry and fold into egg yolk mixture.

Spread batter in 3 greased and waxed paper-lined 8-inch layer cake pans.

Bake in a preheated 375° F. oven for 30 minutes.

Immediately run spatula around each cake to loosen from edge of pan. Cake will sink slightly but evenly.

Cool.

Then turn out and carefully remove paper.

Spread praline butter cream between cake layers and top with chocolate water icing.

Sprinkle top with additional praline powder.

FOUR-TIERED CAKES

Many people with enough time on their hands and sufficient ambition can make wedding cakes at home; however, everybody can make small tiered cakes, simply but attractively decorated, for birthdays and other special occasions. The set of pans is available at most five-and-dime stores and at housewares sections of department stores. The pans measure in diameter: 9, 7¼, 5½ and 3¼ inches in diameter.

Any packaged mix for two 9-inch pans or any homemade cake designed to fit in two 9-inch pans is suitable for the tier pans, the largest and smallest tier pans and the two middle tiers each being equivalent to one 9-inch layer. The following five cakes, however, have been designed and tested to perfectly fit the four tiers.

GOLDEN CLIFF CAKE

1 cup butter or shortening
1½ cups granulated sugar
1 teaspoon vanilla extract
4 eggs, separated
3 cups sifted cake flour

3 teaspoons double-acting
  baking powder
¼ teaspoon salt
1 cup milk

Cream shortening and sugar until light and fluffy.

Beat in vanilla and egg yolks.

Combine cake flour, baking powder, and salt.

Add dry ingredients to egg yolk mixture alternately with the milk, stirring well after each addition until batter is smooth.

Beat egg whites until stiff, but not dry, and fold into batter.

Pour into greased and floured tier cake pans, filling the pans half full, and bake in a preheated 375° F. oven—25 minutes for the two small layers, 30 minutes for the two large layers.

WHITE CLIFF CAKE

Omit egg yolks from above recipe and fold into the batter 6 egg whites, beaten until stiff but not dry.

CHIFFON CAKE

1¾ cups sifted cake flour
1 cup plus 2 tablespoons
    granulated sugar
2¼ teaspoons double-acting
    baking powder
¾ teaspoon salt
6 tablespoons salad oil

4 egg yolks
9 tablespoons cold water
1½ teaspoons vanilla extract
Grated rind of 1 lemon
¾ cup egg whites (5 to 6)
½ teaspoon cream of tartar

Sift flour, sugar, baking powder, and salt into a bowl.

Add oil, egg yolks, water, vanilla, and lemon rind.

Beat until smooth. Use an electric beater if possible.

Beat egg whites and cream of tartar until they form and hold very stiff peaks. Do not underbeat.

Pour egg yolk mixture over beaten egg whites and fold gently with a rubber spatula until blended.

Pour into ungreased tier cake pans, filling the pans two-thirds full.

Bake in a preheated 350° F. oven—30 minutes for the two small layers, 35 minutes for the two large layers.

Remove from oven and let cool for 10 minutes.

Loosen cake from sides of pan with spatula and turn cake out on cake rack to cool.

CREOLE CAKE

1 cup butter or shortening
2½ cups light brown sugar
4 eggs
2 teaspoons vanilla extract
3½ cups sifted cake flour

3½ teaspoons double-acting
    baking powder
½ teaspoon salt
¾ cup strong cold coffee

Cream shortening and sugar thoroughly.

Add eggs, one at a time, beating well after each addition.

Beat in vanilla extract.

Combine flour, baking powder, and salt.

Add dry ingredients to the egg mixture alternately with the cold coffee, stirring well after each addition until batter is smooth.

Pour batter into greased and floured tier cake pans, filling pans half full.

Bake in a preheated 350° F. oven—30 minutes for the two small layers, 35 minutes for the two large layers.

CHOCOLATE CAKE

¾ cup butter or shortening
2 cups granulated sugar
3 eggs
3 cups sifted all-purpose flour
1½ teaspoons baking soda
1 teaspoon salt
1½ cups buttermilk

1 teaspoon vanilla extract
1½ teaspoons lemon juice
3 squares unsweetened chocolate, melted and cooled
½ cup chopped nuts, optional

Cream shortening and sugar thoroughly.

Add eggs, one at a time, beating well after each addition.

Combine flour, baking soda, and salt.

Add dry ingredients to the egg mixture alternately with the buttermilk, stirring well after each addition until batter is smooth.

Stir in vanilla, lemon juice, and chocolate. One-half cup chopped nuts may be added.

Pour batter into greased and floured tier cake pans, filling the pans half full.

Bake in a preheated 350° F. oven—30 minutes for the two small layers, 35 minutes for the next-largest layer, and 40 minutes for the large layer.

EASY DECORATIVE IDEAS FOR SMALL FOUR-TIERED PANS

Many decorative ideas are possible without any extra equipment. But if you wish to decorate them with fluted edgings, rosebuds, and leaves, see section on cake decorating.

TO ASSEMBLE CAKE LAYERS

Place the largest cake tier on a cake plate and spread icing, white or tinted, smoothly over top and sides, using a long steel spatula. Place next-size layer on top and spread smooth with icing. Continue until all layers are frosted. Let icing set for 30 minutes before adding decoration.

BIRTHDAY CAKE

CREAMY FROSTING on top of layers; CHOCOLATE BUTTER CREAM on sides. Decorate with candied cherries and either fresh leaves or slices of green gumdrops.

EASTER BUNNY CAKE

Frost cake with pink or white icing and decorate with jelly beans in coconut nests. A candy Easter bunny on top.

VALENTINE CAKE

Frost cake with white icing. Decorate with red candy hearts. Paper valentine cutout on top.

HALLOWEEN CAKE

Frost cake with ORANGE ICING and drip CHOCOLATE BUTTER CREAM, thinned with a little milk or water, around edges. Decorate with candy pumpkins. Wax-candle cat for top.

BABY SHOWER CAKE

Frost cake with white, pink, or blue icing and decorate with tinted coconut on top and around base of layers. Arrange tiny ribbon bows on edges and top with a paper stork.

MOTHER'S DAY CAKE

CREAMY FROSTING on top of layers; CHOCOLATE BUTTER CREAM on sides. Frost all but the top of top layer. Tie ribbon around sides and bring over top in large bow, then set on cake.

CHRISTMAS CAKE

Frost cake with green icing. Set candles in nests of red-tinted coconut. Candy stick canes on top and holly leaves around base.

CAKE DECORATING

Anyone with patience and the desire can learn to decorate cakes as beautifully as or better than those turned out by professionals. You need a large assortment of pastry tips or tubes, which are available at housewares sections of department stores throughout the country. In addition, you need a supply of grease-proof or plastic pastry bags or a quantity of parchment paper to cut into triangles and roll into cones. These are easily formed and can be discarded after use. If you can't find a source for parchment, you can use any freezer wrapping paper, butcher's paper, or even paper garbage bags. The essential requirement is that it be strong and grease-proof; otherwise the butter or shortening used in the frosting will ooze through and you'll find it dripping down your wrist. This is not as serious as the fact that you will be losing the creamy quality of your frosting, which is important not only in fashioning the flowers but in the final palatability of the finished cake.

For any ambitious or extensive cake decorating you should have a professional cake-decorating turntable, or a Lazy Susan, which you can pick up at secondhand stores or thrift shop outlets.

ICING THE CAKE

The cake you are going to decorate must first be frosted as smoothly as possible with a MERINGUE FROSTING. This may be white or delicately tinted pink, green, blue, or yellow. A two-egg white ITALIAN MERINGUE FROSTING is usually sufficient for any normal two-layer cake. For a larger cake or a four-tiered wedding cake you will need to use a four-egg white meringue.

When cake layers are completely cool, brush off crumbs gently with hand. Cover a serving plate with 4 triangles of waxed paper that can be slipped out after the cake is decorated, leaving your plate clean. The points of the triangles should extend under the cake toward the center of the platter, leaving about 2 inches of the wide angles extending from the outer sides of the cake.

Place the first layer flat side up on the paper and spread the top with a thin layer of the meringue frosting. Place the second layer flat side down so that the two flat sides are together. If the top of the cake is too rounded, level it off by cutting a thin slice away with a serrated knife to give you a flat surface on which to apply the decorations. Frost sides, working quickly. Use a large flexible spatula to cover the sides roughly with frosting. Pile remaining frosting on top and smooth off with spatula, letting any excess run over sides of cake. Finish by holding the spatula, in a vertical position, lightly against side frosting and turn cake plate to smooth and even the frosting around the sides. Let frosted cake stand for at least 30 minutes, until the frosting sets and forms a light surface skin over the cake.

HOW TO ROLL A PAPER CONE

Cut 12-inch squares of parchment or other grease-proof strong paper. Cut the squares in half from corner to corner to make triangles.

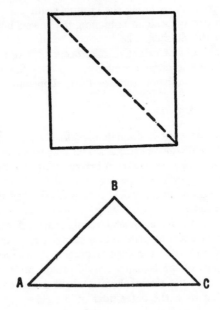

Hold a triangle in the left hand with thumb in center of the wide side of triangle and point of triangle upward. Bring corner A up to corner B and hold points and paper together with right hand.

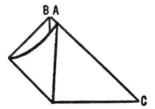

Bring corner C around front of cone to back so that points A, B, and C are together. Hold all points in right hand.

Fold points down into the cone and cut off the bottom tip.

Drop in one of the metal tubes (whichever kind you are working with).

Fill paper cone two-thirds full with butter cream.

Flatten top making corners D and E.

Fold corners D and E down and toward center.

Fold top down and over.

MAKE DECORATOR'S BUTTER CREAM*

TO COLOR THE BUTTER CREAM

Use a separate cup or bowl for each color, reserving a large amount of white for shading. Tint a portion of the white butter cream with a

* See Index.

small quantity of food color and work it in thoroughly. Add more if needed to give you the shade you want, keeping in mind that colors on all cakes should be kept delicate, except for such once-a-year decorations as the red berries on Christmas holly. Even in this case, it is almost impossible to get a dark red from commercial liquid food coloring, so one is better off to make the holly leaves and use cinnamon candies for the berries.

Continue to tint portions of the cream to make as many colors as you are going to use. Should you wish to mix the basic colors, remember:

Blue and yellow make green
Blue and red make lavender or purple
Yellow and red make orange
Yellow, red, and green make brown.

GREEN LEAF BUTTER CREAM

Mix your basic leaf green color. For green leaves surrounding pink flowers, add a small quantity of pink butter cream and mix well. For green leaves add a small quantity of yellow butter. Cream and mix.

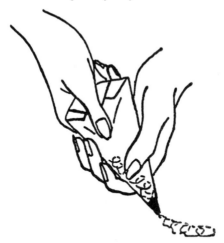

BASIC TECHNIQUE

Always hold the cone firmly at the back. If your hand gets too near the tube, the butter cream will squeeze out the back of the cone instead of through the tip. Keep the cream pushed well down in the cone as you do toothpaste in the tube. Use your hand to squeeze the butter cream through the tip, and keep your wrist pliable so that you will develop a facility to move the cone in any direction and at any angle. You can't decorate with a stiff wrist. *You* move the cone and regulate the pressure, and the amount of pressure on the cone determines the thickness of the lines, dots, leaves, or petals. The tip or tube does the forming of the flute, petals, or leaves.

DECORATING TUBES

All tubes are numbered; the larger the number, the larger the opening.

For beginners, the most important pastry tubes are:

1. *Plain tubes* with round openings, which make straight or curved lines and stems, dots and buds. These are numbered from 1 to 12.

2. *Leaf tubes* with flat notched openings, which form leaves and may be used to make such flowers as poinsettias, whose petals look like leaves. These are numbered from 65 to 70.

3. *Star tubes* with round, saw-toothed openings, which make fluted borders, stars, and "fantasy flowers." These are numbered from 13 to 22.

4. *Rose tubes* with slits, narrower at tip than at the base. These are numbered from 123 to 126.

FLUTED BORDERS · *Tube No. 16*

This is only one of the many tubes that make an attractive border around the edge of cakes. Hold it almost parallel and close to surface. Point cone in the direction the border will run. Press on cone until a flute is made. The harder the pressure, the larger the flute. Move tube ⅛ to ¼ inch away, depending on size of flute, and repeat until border is complete. Or continue pressing on the cone as you slowly pull tube and cone around edge of cake making a continuous border. By means of various movements with your wrist, by a variety of pressures on the cone, a great number of decorative effects may be made.

PLANNING A FLOWERED DESIGN

Flowers grow on stems and the positions of the major stems determine your design. You may wish to roughly sketch the design on paper before duplicating it on your cake. As in designing a flower arrangement, there is usually one major stem line and two shorter stems, one of which is slightly shorter than the others. You may wish to use more than three, but keep the design simple at first and make the stems curved and graceful.

LINES OR STEMS • *Tube No. 2 or 3*

The opening in these tubes is very small. A bit of soft butter, the size of a large pea, blended into ½ cup of the butter cream helps the cream flow more easily through the tiny openings. Hold tube almost parallel and close to surface of the cake. Press out green butter cream and, while pressing, draw tube slowly in direction the line is to flow.

FANTASY FLOWERS • *Tube No. 13, 14, 15, or 16*

Fantasy flowers actually resemble no flower but give the effect of a tiny flower or star. Used in groupings along a stem they look like a sprig of forget-me-nots. Used in clusters they look like lilacs. The tube does the work. Hold the tube upright, directly over the spot where the star is to appear. Press out a bit of the butter cream. The heavier the pressure, the larger the star will be.

DOTS • *Tube No. 2 or 3*

Hold tube upright, directly over and close to the spot where the dot is to appear. Press out the size dot desired.

SMALL LEAVES · *Tube No. 65*

Press out tiny leaves along the stems, making them larger at the base of the stem and gradually decreasing in size to the terminal end. Add leaves sparingly, as more may be added later.

Flat Leaves: Twist tube in cone so that one of the flat surfaces is parallel to surface of cake. Hold tip of tube close to where you wish the leaf to be. Press and, while pressing, draw tube away to make a leaf.

Upright Leaves: These take a little more practice and are more difficult to make than leaves that lie flat on the surface of the cake. Hold tube at a 45 degree angle directly over the spot where leaf is to appear. Press hard and, while pressing, raise the tube quickly. The harder you press, the sturdier the base of the leaf will be and you must have this sturdy base if your leaf is to remain upright.

GREEN BUDS · *Tube No. 3*

Hold tube almost parallel and touching surface. Keep it steady and press out bud of desired size. Without removing tube, continue to press and gently pull tube away making a slender stem which joins onto the major stem of your design.

FORGET-ME-NOTS • *Tube No. 13 or 14*

Press out tiny fantasy stars of pale blue butter cream along slender stems. Finish stem ends with a tiny dot of green butter cream pressed from tube No. 2. A few dots of pale pink butter cream on top of the green dots make a pretty effect.

LILACS • *Tubes No. 14 and 2*

Make a few graceful stems with tube No. 2. Around and over the stems press out clusters of small stars in any shade of lilac you wish. Add stars on top of stars until you build up a cluster and give it shape like a lilac. With tube No. 2 make tiny dots for buds around the cluster.

A FANTASY ROSE · *Tube No. 3*

Hold tube No. 3 almost parallel and touching surface, with tip of cone pointing away from you. Press hard and steadily until a curled petal is formed. Swing point of tube to another angle and press out second petal. Press out 6 or 7 petals, all radiating from center. A dot in the center and 2 upright leaves complete the flower.

DAISIES · *Tube No. 3*

Hold tube almost parallel and touching surface. Press out butter cream and, while pressing, draw tube slowly away from center of flower to make a slender petal. Press out 4, 6, or 12 petals radiating from center. Complete with a center dot, a stem, and 2 flat leaves.

SWEETHEART ROSES • *Two No. 3 tubes*

Hold cone filled with pink or yellow butter cream almost parallel and touching surface. Press out bud. With second cone filled with a slightly lighter or darker pink or yellow butter cream, press out an *S* over the bud. Add a green dot at base of bud with an adjoining slender stem.

LILIES OF THE VALLEY · *Tubes No. 81, 2, and 3*

With tube No. 2 make green stems. Press out white butter cream along the stems through tube No. 81. Hold tube with the hollow side down and press gently away from you as each little flower is made. With tube No. 2 put a small yellow dot in center of each little flower. With tube No. 3 add 2 or 3 white buds at the terminal ends of the stems.

WILD ROSES · *Tubes No. 126, 3, and 2*

A wild rose has five pale pink petals all radiating from a green center. It takes a little practice to make the petals because you must remember to move your wrist in a swinging motion as the tube extrudes each petal. Hold tube No. 126 close to the spot where you want the first petal to be, with narrow tube opening in position to form the outer thin edge of the petal. With a swing of the wrist, press out the first petal. Hold the cone in such a position that the base of the petal lies flat against the cake and the outer edge flares up and out. In the same manner press out a second petal that partly overlaps the first. Remember that the petals all must radiate from the center of the flower. This means turning the cake each time you add a petal, or moving yourself to another position. If you work on a small, narrow table, you can actually move around the cake as you decorate. Continue until you have pressed out the five petals. With tube No. 3 press out a dot of pale green butter cream the size of a pea in the center of the flower and surround this with tiny yellow stamens (see directions).

CLOSED BUDS • *Tube No. 2*

Press out a small dot of green butter cream at the terminal end of a stem. Release the flow of cream but keep tube in place and press out a larger amount of cream while gently drawing tube away to make the pointed tip of the bud.

BREAKING BUDS • *Tube No. 2*

Begin by first making a closed bud as above. Then with pink or yellow butter cream and tube No. 2 insert tip of tube right into the pointed end of the green bud. Press gently until the cream bursts out of the bud to form a rosebud on the verge of breaking into bloom.

STAMENS · *Tube No. 2*

Press out a dot of bright yellow butter cream and, while pressing, pull tube quickly up and away.

THE FULL-BLOWN ROSE · *Tubes No. 126, 124, 3, and 2*

These are made very much like the wild rose. First make a wild rose with tube No. 126. Remember to hold tube opening with the narrow part in position to form the outer edge of the petals and to radiate each petal from an imaginary center. With same tube press out another layer of petals on top of and in between the first circle of petals. Then with tube No. 124 make a third layer of smaller petals. Fill in center with a large dot of soft green butter cream through tube No. 3 and surround the mound with yellow stamens through tube No. 2.

RAMBLER ROSES · *Tube No. 104*

A spray of rambler roses is quite easy to make. Use pink, white, or red butter cream and press out many small petals close together, keeping the flower round and mounded in shape. Surround by small flat green leaves.

NARCISSUS • *Tubes No. 61, 3, and 2*

With tube No. 61, press out 5 or 6 small white petals radiating from a center circle about the size of the head of a pin. Press out a green dot in the center through tube No. 3 and surround the dot with a thin circular line of bright yellow cream pressed through tube No. 2.

VIOLETS • *Tubes No. 61 and 2*

The violet has five petals. With tube No. 61 and blue, pink, or lavender butter cream, press out the two top petals, one slightly over-lapping the other. Then press out the two side petals, which should be made a little longer and more slender than the others. Finally make the slightly larger bottom petal, overlapping the side petals Make a small yellow dot with tube No. 2 in the center of each blossom.

VIOLET LEAVES • *Tube No. 104*

The violet leaves are made with the same tube that makes small rose petals. Press out green butter cream and, while pressing, move wrist until a circle is almost completed.

SWEET PEAS • *Tubes No. 123, 104, and 68*

With pale pink butter cream and tube No. 123 press out a circular petal. Place a second petal inside and over the first one, holding the cone in such a position that the outer edge of the second petal flares up. With tube No. 104 and white butter cream press out 2 tiny white petals on top of second petal. With tube No. 68 press out a green leaf at the bottom of each blossom as follows: Do not pull the tube up, but press down and release the flow of cream quickly so that a cleft is left in the leaf. With tube No. 2 press out soft green butter cream lines in delicate curling tendrils.

THE SMALL ROSE • *Tubes No. 61 and 104*

The rose is the most difficult flower to fashion out of butter cream and should not be attempted until you have developed quite a flair at fashioning all the other flowers in this section. If you begin with it, you are bound to be discouraged and will probably never look another pastry cone in the tube for the rest of your culinary life! However, once you have mastered the wild rose and the full-blown rose, try your hand at these. You may wish to begin working with a cupcake before trying them on a large cake. The center of the rose is made first. Hold tube No. 61 in a vertical position with the wide part of the curved opening touching the cake. Using gentle pressure, guide the flow of butter cream to make a closed or partially closed, partially upright petal. It must stand at such an angle as to allow you to press out other petals both under and over it. Around this center and with the same tube press out several small curved petals. The outer petals are made with tube No. 104. Hold wide part of the tube opening close to the base of the center petals and add as many petals as you wish to make desired effect. Remember to swing your wrist as you work.

LARGE ROSES • *Tubes No. 123 and 126*

These are made in exactly the same way as the smaller roses, using tube No. 123 for the inner bud and No. 126 for the outer petals.

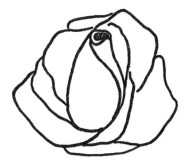

ROSE LEAVES • *Tube No. 68*

These are made in the same way as the smaller upright leaves. Place one flat side of the tube on the cake under a rose petal and squeeze hard on the cone, forming a sturdy base. Still pressing, raise tube quickly upward and release the flow of cream.

CHAPTER 13

Small Cakes and Cookies

D_{AINTY} cakes, dipped in colored fondant and attractively garnished, are France's contribution to the tray of Lilliputian cakes and cookies that graces many a tea table or wedding buffet and, with little more than time and patience, can be skillfully made in the home kitchen.

The second group of petits fours, embracing all the small dry cookies—such as *Palets de Dames, Tuiles, Langues de Chat,* and macaroons—is known as *petits fours secs,* or dry petits fours. (Petits fours are party fare, the "dainties last to make the end most sweet.") Very different are these sweet or buttery dainties from the everyday favorites—the plump gingerbread cooky—that fill the cooky jar on the pantry shelf with more robust nourishment.

SMALL FROSTED CAKES • *Petits Fours Glacés*

Almost any cake batter may be used to make these tiny decorative bits, but the most suitable is a fine-textured butter cake, spongecake, *Génoise,* or angel food.

Put a layer of cake batter about ¾ inch deep in a buttered and floured shallow pan, and bake until a cake tester comes out clean. Cool the sheet of cake on a rack, then cut it into small squares, crescents, diamonds, hearts, rectangles, or circles.

Flavor some FONDANT with vanilla, almond, rum or kirsch, and stir over a very low flame until just warm to the touch. (Take care not to overheat it, or it will be dull when cool instead of glossy.) If the consistency is too thick, stir in a little warm water. It should be thick enough to mask the little cakes, yet soft enough to flow smoothly. Tint the warm fondant mixture with a drop or two of liquid food coloring.

Keep the mixture warm over hot water. Put the cut pieces of cake on a two-tined fork, one at a time, and dip them into it. Put them on waxed paper to dry for an hour, then decorate with candied cherries or pineapple, strips of candied peel, chopped pistachio nuts, blanched almonds, or crystallized violets. Dip the end of the decorations in the fondant to make them stick.

FILLED PETITS FOURS GLACES

Cut a sheet of cake about ¾ inch thick into small squares, diamonds, hearts, or circles. Cut a ¼-inch slice from the top of each cutout and lay it aside. Hollow out the center of each piece of cake, fill it with whipped cream, ALMOND PASTE, PASTRY CREAM, or BUTTER CREAM, and press the cover gently on top. Dip the filled cakes into warm, delicately tinted and flavored FONDANT. Put them on waxed paper to dry and decorate gaily with candied fruit, nuts, or crystallized flowers.

FROSTED PETITS FOURS

Small cake cutouts may be iced smoothly with ROYAL ICING and decorated with colored BUTTER CREAM pressed through a pastry bag fitted with a small open-star tube. Or the entire surface of the little cakes may be covered closely with tiny rosettes of varicolored butter cream.

BRESILIENS

Cut a sheet of cake into small rounds, split each round, and put together again with MOCHA BUTTER CREAM. Dip each cake into white FONDANT flavored with rum, and press grated toasted almonds around the sides.

PETITES CARAQUES

Cut a sheet of cake into rectangles, split each rectangle, and put together again with CHOCOLATE BUTTER CREAM. Frost top and sides with the same cream, garnish the tops heavily with granulated chocolate, and sprinkle with confectioners' sugar.

CENDRILLONS

Cut a sheet of cake into little squares, split the squares, and put them together again with COFFEE or CHOCOLATE BUTTER CREAM between. Dip the filled squares into FONDANT colored and flavored with coffee or chocolate to match the flavor used in the filling. Put on waxed paper to dry and top each little cake with half a toasted almond.

MARTINIQUES

Cut a sheet of cake into squares, split each square, and put together again with COFFEE BUTTER CREAM mixed with grated blanched almonds and flavored with rum. Dip each little cake into COFFEE FONDANT flavored with rum.

CHOCOLATINES

Cut a sheet of cake into little squares. Split the squares and put together again with CHOCOLATE BUTTER CREAM between. Frost each little cake with chocolate butter cream and dip the sides in grated toasted almonds. Press rosettes of butter cream through a pastry bag fitted with a fluted tube on top of each *chocolatine*.

MOKATINES

Mokatines are made in the same way as CHOCOLATINES, except the cake is cut into tiny rounds instead of squares. Fill and frost them with MOCHA BUTTER CREAM, roll the sides in crystallized sugar or in grated toasted nuts, and put rosettes of mocha butter cream on top.

COOKIES

PETITS FOURS SECS

Any sweet, dainty cooky may be correctly labeled a *petit four sec*, and most cookbooks contain an adequate number of cooky recipes to satisfy the average needs. The following dainties are typically French and are not found in many American books.

CIGARETTES · *Gaufrettes*

2 egg whites	½ teaspoon vanilla
½ cup sugar	Confectioners' sugar, PASTRY
⅓ cup flour	CREAM, or whipped cream,
3 tablespoons butter, melted and cooled	optional

Beat egg whites until stiff.

Gradually fold in sugar, a little at a time.

Sift flour over the meringue a little at a time and fold in.

Fold in butter and vanilla.

Butter and flour a baking sheet and heat in a very hot oven (450° F.).

Drop batter by the tablespoonful onto the hot pan, and spread it as thinly as possible with a spatula.

Bake in a very hot oven (450° F.) for about 3 minutes, or until cookies are golden brown.

While still hot, roll cookies quickly around a pencil; and when the *gaufrettes* thus formed are cool, serve them plain, sprinkled with confectioners' sugar, or filled with PASTRY CREAM or whipped cream.

Before baking all the batter, bake a trial cooky. If the finished *gaufrette* is so fragile that it breaks when it is handled, the batter needs a little more flour.

If, on the contrary, the *gaufrette* is thick and difficult to roll, add a little more melted butter. *Makes 2 dozen.*

VANILLA WAFERS · *Petits Gâteaux Tailles*

1 cup soft butter	Pinch salt
1 cup fine granulated sugar	1 teaspoon vanilla
2½ cups sifted all-purpose flour	

Cream butter and sugar together until light and fluffy.

Stir in flour, salt, and vanilla and mix into a firm dough.

Shape dough into a roll 2 inches in diameter, wrap it in waxed paper, and chill for 2 hours.

Slice the roll of dough 1/16 inch thick with a sharp knife, place the slices on a buttered baking sheet, and bake in a hot oven (400° F.) for 8 minutes. *Makes 4 dozen.*

Petits gâteaux tailles may be delicately colored with a few drops of food coloring and the flavor changed accordingly.

Red Food Coloring: Flavor with rose water.

Green Food Coloring: Flavor with peppermint or wintergreen.

Yellow Food Coloring: Flavor with almond.

LADIES' TONGUES • *Palets de Dames*

4 tablespoons currants	½ cup sugar
2 tablespoons rum	3 eggs
½ cup butter	⅞ cup sifted all-purpose flour

Soak currants in rum for 1 hour.

Cream butter until light, add sugar, and cream together until fluffy.

Add eggs, one at a time, beating well after each addition.

Then stir in flour and, when well combined, stir in currants and rum in which they were soaked.

Put mixture in a pastry bag fitted with a large plain tube, and pipe mounds about the size of macaroons on a buttered and floured baking sheet.

Bake in a very hot oven (450° F.) for 5 minutes.

Remove from the sheet to a cake rack to cool. *Makes 2 dozen.*

LADYFINGERS • *Biscuits à la Cuiller*

3 eggs, separated	1 tablespoon hot water
⅓ cup fine granulated sugar	½ cup sifted cake flour
1 teaspoon vanilla or lemon juice	Egg white, CONFECTIONERS' SUGAR ICING, jam, or jelly
Pinch salt	

Beat egg whites until stiff enough to hold their shape but still moist, then beat in sugar a little at a time.

Beat egg yolks until thick and pale in color, and fold into egg whites with vanilla or lemon juice, salt, and hot water.

Then fold in flour, sifted twice.

Put batter in a pastry tube fitted with a plain tube.

Press out 2½-inch strips, not too close together, onto cooky sheets covered with heavy paper.

Sprinkle with fine granulated sugar and bake in a moderate oven (350° F.) for 12 minutes, or until a very delicate brown.

The fingers should still feel soft to the touch when removed from the oven.

Cool slightly and remove from the paper, wetting the back of the paper if necessary.

Brush the flat side of half the fingers with egg white and press the underside of a second cake on each. Or they may be sandwiched together with confectioners' sugar icing or with jam or jelly. *Makes 2 dozen.*

MADELEINES

1 *lump sugar*	3 *eggs*
1 *orange or lemon*	2 *egg yolks*
¾ *cup sugar*	1 *tablespoon brandy*
1¼ *cups sifted cake flour*	*Pinch salt*
10 *tablespoons* (1¼ *sticks*)	
sweet butter	

Rub the lump of sugar on the skin of an orange or lemon until it is saturated with fruit oil, or zest.

Then crush or grate the sugar.

Sift together the ¾ cup sugar and flour and stir in the crushed sugar.

Melt butter, skim off the white foam that forms on top, and cool to lukewarm.

Put a few drops of this clarified butter into eighteen small, shell-shaped tins.

Tip *madeleine* shells so they are coated with butter.

Drain excess butter back into rest of butter, then repeat the operation so that each mold gets two coats of butter.

Beat together eggs and yolks.

With a wooden spoon stir in gradually the sugar-flour mixture.

Add brandy and salt and continue to stir until batter is smooth and free from lumps.

Let it rest for 2 or 3 minutes, then beat vigorously for 1 minute.

Stir in the warm butter, being careful not to include any sediment that has settled to the bottom of the saucepan in which the butter was heated.

Place batter in an enamel pan on a very low flame and stir vigorously for 1 to 2 minutes, or until mixture is heated through.

Pour immediately into buttered shells, filling them not quite full, and bake in a moderate oven (350° F.) for 15 minutes, or until a delicate brown.

Turn immediately onto a cake rack, shell side up, to cool. *Makes 2 dozen.*

CAT TONGUES • *Langues de Chat*

¼ cup butter	2 egg whites
¼ cup sugar	½ cup flour
½ teaspoon vanilla	

Cream butter, add sugar and vanilla, and cream together until light and fluffy.

Add egg whites, one at a time, mixing well after each addition.

Sift flour, a little at a time, over surface of the mixture and carefully fold it in.

Press batter through a pastry bag fitted with a small plain tube onto a buttered and floured baking sheet, making thin strips about 2 inches long and as big around as a pencil.

Bake in a very hot oven (450° F.) for about 4 minutes, or until the edges of the *langues de chat* are lightly browned.

Remove from baking sheet to cool on cake rack. *Makes 30.*

LITTLE FRUITED CAKES • *Petits Gâteaux aux Fruits*

¼ cup citron, shredded	1 cup butter
¼ cup candied cherries, cut into small pieces	1 cup sugar
½ cup chopped raisins	5 eggs, separated
¼ cup shredded blanched almonds	2½ cups sifted all-purpose flour
2 tablespoons rum	¼ teaspoon salt

Combine fruit and nuts and moisten with rum.

Cream butter until light and gradually add sugar, creaming together until fluffy.

Add egg yolks, one at a time, stirring well after each addition, and then gradually stir in sifted flour.

When all the flour has been incorporated, add fruits and nuts and lastly fold in the egg whites, beaten with salt until stiff.

Fill tiny fluted baking cups ¾ full with the mixture and bake in a moderate oven (325° F.) for 25 to 30 minutes, or until the cakes are delicately browned. *Makes 4 dozen.*

FORTUNES • *Fortunés*

½ cup grated blanched
  almonds
½ cup fine granulated sugar
1 egg
1 cup flour, sifted

1 tablespoon heavy cream
1 tablespoon melted butter
1 tablespoon kirsch
Candied cherries

Combine almonds and sugar.

Add egg and mix thoroughly.

Stir in flour alternately with the cream, butter, and kirsch and mix into a very soft batter.

Spoon batter into tiny paper cups and top each with half a candied cherry.

Bake in a moderate oven (350° F.) for 6 to 8 minutes.

Cool and serve the fortunes in the cups. *Makes 16.*

SHINGLES • *Tuiles*

2 egg whites
½ cup sugar
½ cup flour, sifted
¼ cup grated blanched
  almonds

¼ cup butter, melted and
  cooled

Beat egg whites until frothy.

Add sugar gradually and continue to beat until the meringue is light and fluffy.

Fold in flour, almonds, and butter.

Drop batter onto a buttered baking sheet by the teaspoonful 2 inches apart.

Flatten each mound a little with a fork and sprinkle with sugar.

Bake in a hot oven (400° F.) for 4 or 5 minutes, or until delicately browned.

Take the cookies from the oven and while still warm press them over a thin rolling pin or broom handle into a curve. *Makes 2 dozen.*

ALMOND COOKIES • *Milanais*

1 cup sifted all-purpose flour	Grated rind of 1 lemon
⅓ cup sugar	1 egg
½ cup grated blanched almonds	Pinch salt
	1 beaten egg
⅓ cup soft butter	Candied fruit or nuts

Sift flour into a bowl and make a well in the center.

Into the well put sugar, almonds, butter, lemon rind, egg, and salt, and mix these ingredients together thoroughly with a wooden spoon or with the hand.

Gradually work in flour.

Form dough into a ball, wrap in waxed paper, and chill for 2 hours.

Roll out dough ¼ inch thick on a lightly floured board and cut into small cookies with fancy cooky cutters.

Put cookies on a buttered baking sheet, brush with beaten egg, and decorate with candied fruit or nuts.

Bake in a moderate oven (350° F.) for about 15 minutes, or until brown. *Makes 2 dozen.*

ALMOND SQUARES • *Amandines*

⅔ cup butter	1 teaspoon vanilla
½ cup sugar	1 beaten egg
2 cups sifted all-purpose flour	½ cup blanched almonds, finely chopped
½ teaspoon baking powder	
2 eggs, lightly beaten	¼ cup sugar

Cream butter and the ½ cup sugar until light and fluffy.

Stir in flour sifted with baking powder, then eggs and vanilla, and mix well.

Form dough into a ball, wrap in waxed paper, and chill for 1 hour.

Roll out dough ¼ inch thick on a lightly floured board and cut into long strips 1 inch wide.

Put strips on a buttered baking sheet and brush with a little beaten egg.

Combine almonds and the ¼ cup sugar and sprinkle the mixture over the strips, score strips every inch, and bake in a moderate oven (375° F.) for about 15 minutes, or until delicately browned.

When cold, cut strips apart where they were scored, to make tiny square cookies. *Makes 4 dozen.*

MACAROONS • *Massepain*

1 cup ALMOND PASTE	3 to 4 egg whites
1 cup confectioners' sugar	½ cup fine granulated sugar

Work the almond paste and sugar together until well mixed.

Add egg whites, one at a time, mixing thoroughly after each addition.

It may not be necessary to add any or all of the last egg white.

The consistency of the dough should be soft enough to be easily pressed through a pastry bag fitted with a plain round tube, and yet hold its shape on the baking sheet.

Line baking sheet with waxed paper and press out rounds of the dough the size of a twenty-five-cent piece.

Sprinkle rounds with fine granulated sugar and bake in a slow oven (300° F.) for 12 to 15 minutes.

Remove the macaroons from the paper to a cake rack to cool. *Makes 2 dozen.*

CORNETS • *Petits Cornets*

2 egg whites	Whipped cream, PASTRY
½ cup sugar	CREAM, or CHESTNUT CREAM
⅓ cup flour	
3 tablespoons butter, melted and cooled	

Beat egg whites until stiff, sprinkle sugar over them, and fold it in gently.

Fold in flour and butter in the same way.

Butter and flour a baking sheet and heat it in a hot oven (400° F.).

Drop batter onto the hot sheet by tablespoons and spread it thinly.

Bake for about 3 minutes, or until the wafers are golden brown.

Remove wafers quickly from the sheet with a spatula and roll them while still warm into cones.

When cool, fill with whipped cream, pastry cream, or chestnut cream. *Makes 2 dozen.*

FRENCH LACE COOKIES

1 cup sifted enriched flour
1 cup finely chopped nuts
½ cup corn syrup

½ cup butter
⅔ cup brown sugar, firmly packed

Combine flour and nuts.

Put corn syrup, butter, and brown sugar in top of double boiler and bring to a boil over direct heat.

Remove from the heat and gradually stir in flour and nuts.

Drop batter 3 inches apart from teaspoon onto baking sheet covered with aluminum foil.

Bake at 325° F. for 8 to 10 minutes.

Let cool for 1 minute and remove from foil by gently pulling foil away from cookies.

Keep batter over boiling water to keep it warm between batches. *Makes 3 dozen 3¾-inch cookies.*

FRENCH CURL COOKIES

½ cup butter
1⅔ cups sugar
5 to 6 egg whites (¾ cup)

¼ teaspoon salt
1 cup sifted enriched flour

Blend butter and sugar and beat in unbeaten egg whites and salt. Beat until mixture is thick.

Stir in flour.

Drop batter 3 inches apart from tablespoon onto baking sheet rubbed with shortening and sprinkled with flour.

Spread out batter with back of spoon into large rounds and bake at 350° F. for 8 to 10 minutes.

Cool for 1 minute.

Remove cookies from sheet with spatula and quickly roll them around rolling pin or wooden spoon handle.

Hold firm until set. *Makes 5 dozen 3½-inch cookies.*

FLORENTINES

½ cup cream
3 tablespoons butter
½ cup sugar
1¼ cups finely chopped
  almonds

⅓ cup sifted enriched flour
¾ cup finely chopped
  candied orange peel
Melted chocolate, optional

In a saucepan combine cream, butter, and sugar and bring to a boil.

Remove from heat and stir in remaining ingredients.

Drop batter from tablespoon onto baking sheet rubbed with shortening, keeping drops 3 inches apart.

Bake at 350° F. for 10 minutes.

Cool for 5 minutes and remove immediately with spatula to cake rack.

If desired spread tops with melted chocolate. *Makes 2 dozen 3-inch cookies.*

SOME OLD COOKY JAR FAVORITES

BASIC DROP COOKIES

1 cup butter
1½ cups sugar
2 eggs
4 cups sifted enriched flour
¼ teaspoon salt
1 teaspoon cream of tartar
1 teaspoon soda
1 cup milk
2 teaspoons vanilla
1 teaspoon cinnamon, ½
  teaspoon nutmeg, and ½
  teaspoon ginger, optional

1 cup chopped nuts, chopped
  dates, or seedless raisins
1 package (6 ounces) semi-
  sweet chocolate
½ teaspoon cinnamon
1 square unsweetened chocolate, melted

Blend butter, sugar, and eggs. Stir in combined dry ingredients alternately with milk and vanilla.

Divide dough into four equal parts.

Leave one part plain or stir in 1 teaspoon cinnamon, ½ teaspoon nutmeg, and ½ teaspoon ginger to make spice drops.

To the second part: Add 1 cup chopped nuts, chopped dates, or seedless raisins.

To the third part: Add 1 package (6 ounces) semi-sweet chocolate pieces.

To the fourth part: Add ½ teaspoon cinnamon and 1 square unsweetened chocolate, melted.

Drop batter from teaspoon onto baking sheet rubbed with shortening and bake at 375° F. for 10 to 12 minutes. *Makes 8 to 8½ dozen 2-inch drops.*

TO MAKE A DOUGH THAT CAN BE HAND-FORMED INTO BALLS OR STICKS:

Increase the amount of flour in recipe for BASIC DROP COOKIES to 4½ to 5 cups.

TO MAKE A DOUGH THAT CAN BE ROLLED OUT ON A LIGHTLY FLOURED BOARD:

Increase the amount of flour in recipe for BASIC DROP COOKIES to 5 to 5½ cups.

CHOCOLATE DROPS

1 package (6 ounces) semi-sweet chocolate pieces	1 cup sifted enriched flour
½ cup butter	½ teaspoon soda
½ cup sugar	½ teaspoon salt
1 egg	¼ cup water
	1 cup chopped nuts

Melt half the chocolate pieces.

Blend butter, sugar, egg, and melted chocolate.

Stir in combined dry ingredients alternately with the water.

Stir in nuts and remaining chocolate pieces.

Drop batter from a teaspoon onto baking sheet and bake at 350° F. for 12 to 15 minutes. *Makes 3 dozen 2-inch drops.*

MOLASSES DROPS

½ cup butter
⅓ cup sugar
1 egg
½ cup molasses
2 cups sifted enriched flour
1 teaspoon soda

½ teaspoon salt
½ teaspoon nutmeg
1 teaspoon cinnamon
½ teaspoon ginger
¾ cup sour milk

Blend butter, sugar, egg, and molasses.

Combine flour, soda, salt, and spices and add alternately with the sour milk.

Drop batter from tablespoon onto baking sheet rubbed with shortening and bake at 375° F. for 10 minutes. *Makes 2 dozen 3½-inch cookies.*

OATMEAL DROP COOKIES

1 cup butter
1½ cups brown sugar
¼ cup sour milk
2 eggs
1 teaspoon salt
1 teaspoon cinnamon

½ teaspoon cloves
1¾ cups sifted enriched flour
¾ teaspoon soda
1½ cups rolled oats
1 cup chopped nuts
1 cup seedless raisins

Blend butter and sugar.

Beat in milk and eggs.

Stir in salt, spices, flour, soda, oats, nuts, and raisins.

Drop batter by tablespoon onto baking sheet rubbed with shortening and bake at 375° F. for 15 minutes. *Makes 5 dozen 3-inch cookies.*

DATE DROP COOKIES

½ cup butter
¾ cup brown sugar
1 egg
1 teaspoon vanilla
2 cups sifted enriched flour

2 teaspoons double-acting
    baking powder
½ teaspoon salt
1 cup sliced dates
¼ cup milk

Blend butter, sugar, egg, and vanilla.

Combine flour, baking powder, and salt and stir in sliced dates.

Add flour-date mixture alternately with milk to butter mixture.

Drop batter from teaspoon onto baking sheet rubbed with shortening and bake at 350° F. for 12 to 15 minutes. *Makes 2 dozen 2-inch cookies.*

SPRITZKUCHEN

½ cup butter	2 cups sifted enriched flour
1 cup sugar	¼ teaspoon salt
1 egg	1 teaspoon vanilla
2 tablespoons milk	

Blend butter and sugar, beat in egg, and stir in milk alternately with flour.

Stir in salt and vanilla.

Fill a cooky press half full and press out cookies on ungreased baking sheet.

Bake at 375° F. for 8 to 10 minutes. *Makes 5 dozen 2-inch cookies.*

CHOCOLATE SPRITZKUCHEN

Follow recipe above but add 2 squares unsweetened chocolate, melted.

PEANUT BUTTER COOKIES

½ cup butter	1 tablespoon hot water
½ cup sugar	½ cup peanut butter
½ cup brown sugar	1¼ cups sifted enriched flour
1 egg	½ teaspoon soda

Blend butter and sugars.

Beat in egg, water, and peanut butter.

Combine dry ingredients and stir them into butter-sugar mixture.

Fill a cooky press half full and press out cookies on ungreased baking sheet.

Bake at 375° F. for 10 to 12 minutes. *Makes 4 dozen 1½-inch cookies.*

MOLASSES SPICE COOKIES

½ cup butter
½ cup sugar
1 egg
¼ cup molasses
¼ teaspoon soda
2 cups sifted enriched flour

¼ teaspoon salt
½ teaspoon ginger
1 teaspoon cinnamon
½ teaspoon allspice
½ teaspoon cloves
½ teaspoon mace

Blend butter and sugar. Beat in egg and the molasses mixed with soda.

Gradually stir in flour mixed with salt and spices.

Fill a cooky press half full and press out cookies on ungreased baking sheet.

Bake at 375° F. for 10 to 12 minutes. *Makes 5 dozen 1½-inch cookies.*

MOLASSES LOGS

2½ cups sifted enriched flour
½ cup confectioners' sugar
¼ teaspoon salt
¾ cup butter

½ cup molasses
2 teaspoons vanilla
1 cup chopped nuts

Blend flour, sugar, and salt.

Cut in butter.

Stir in molasses and vanilla until dough is smooth.

Chill dough for at least 1 hour.

Break off small lumps of dough and shape into "logs" about 3 inches long.

Roll in chopped nuts and arrange on ungreased cooky sheet.

Bake at 325° F. for 15 minutes. *Makes 3 dozen 3½-inch logs.*

ALMOND BALLS

1 cup butter
1½ cups sifted confectioners' sugar
1 egg
1 teaspoon vanilla
1 teaspoon almond extract

2½ cups sifted enriched flour
1 teaspoon salt
1 teaspoon soda
1 teaspoon cream of tartar
5 dozen blanched almonds

Blend butter and sugar.

Beat in egg, vanilla, and almond extract.

Stir in combined dry ingredients and chill for at least 1 hour.

Form small balls with floured fingers, place on baking sheet rubbed with shortening, and press a blanched almond into center of each.

Bake at 375° F. for 12 to 15 minutes. *Makes 5 dozen 2-inch cookies.*

CHERRY BALLS

1 cup butter	1¾ cups sifted cake flour
¾ cup sugar	1 teaspoon salt
2 eggs, separated	1 tablespoon sugar
1 cup finely chopped walnuts	Cherries, candied

Blend butter and ¾ cup sugar.

Beat in egg yolks.

Stir in nuts, flour (do not substitute enriched flour), and salt and chill for 1 hour.

Form dough into small balls and place on baking sheet rubbed with shortening.

Beat egg whites with 1 tablespoon sugar until they hold a soft peak.

Brush each ball with egg white and top with a cherry.

Bake in a 400° F. oven for 12 to 15 minutes. *Makes 4 dozen 2-inch cookies.*

SUGAR COOKIES

½ cup butter	2½ cups sifted enriched flour
1 cup sugar	½ teaspoon cream of tartar
1 egg	½ teaspoon soda
⅓ cup milk	¼ teaspoon salt
2 teaspoons vanilla	

Blend butter, sugar, egg, milk, and vanilla.

Gradually stir in the combined dry ingredients.

Roll out ⅛ inch thick on floured board and cut into desired shapes.

Place on ungreased baking sheet and bake at 400° F. for 5 to 7 minutes. *Makes 5 dozen 2-inch cookies.*

SUGAR SPICE COOKIES

Omit vanilla and add ½ teaspoon nutmeg and ¼ teaspoon cinnamon to dry ingredients.

BUTTERSCOTCH PECAN COOKIES

Use 1½ cups brown sugar in place of granulated sugar. Add 1 cup finely chopped nuts with the dry ingredients.

COCONUT COOKIES

Add 1 cup chopped shredded moist coconut with the flour.

ORANGE COOKIES

Add 2 tablespoons grated orange rind and use orange juice in place of milk.

BROWN SUGAR FANS

1½ *cups dark brown sugar*	1 *teaspoon vanilla*
½ *cup (1 stick) butter*	2 *cups sifted all-purpose flour*
1 *egg*	3 *dozen pecans*

Cream sugar and butter.
Beat in egg and vanilla.
Gradually stir in flour.
Roll out dough thinly on floured board and cut into 5-inch circles.
Cut circles into quarters with floured knife and place quarters 1 inch apart on greased baking sheet.
Press with floured tines of fork to make fans and press a pecan at base of each fan.
Bake in a preheated 375° F. oven for 12 minutes. *Makes 3 dozen.*

COFFEE WALNUT CAKES

½ *cup sifted all-purpose flour*	¼ *cup butter*
½ *cup ground walnuts*	COFFEE BUTTER CREAM
¼ *cup granulated sugar*	1 *dozen walnut halves*

In mixing bowl combine flour, walnuts, and sugar.

Cut in butter.

Work together until mixture forms a ball.

Roll out on floured surface ¼ inch thick.

Cut into circles with floured 1½-inch cooky cutter.

Place circles on greased cookie sheet.

Bake in a preheated 375° F. oven for 12 to 15 minutes, or until golden.

Cool on wire tray. (Makes 2 dozen circles.)

Sandwich together 2 cookies with coffee butter cream between.

Pipe one large rosette of butter cream in the center of each cake.

Top each with a walnut half. *Makes 1 dozen.*

SHORTBREAD FANS

1 cup sifted all-purpose flour	½ cup butter
⅓ cup granulated sugar	Fine sugar
Dash salt	

In mixing bowl sift together flour, granulated sugar, and salt.

Rub in butter with the tips of fingers, until mixture resembles fine bread crumbs.

Work together until it forms a ball.

Roll out ¼ inch thick on floured surface.

Cut out 4 circles using a 4½-inch cutter.

Mark each circle across diagonally with back of knife 8 times.

Mark center of each circle with a 2-inch cooky cutter.

Cut into quarters, using 2 of the marked lines.

Place on a greased cooky sheet.

Bake in a preheated 350° F. oven for 12 to 15 minutes, or until pale golden.

Sprinkle at once with fine sugar.

Place on wire tray to cool. *Makes 16.*

CHOCOLATE AND VANILLA PINWHEELS

½ cup butter	3 tablespoons milk
½ cup sugar	2 teaspoons vanilla
1 egg yolk	1 square unsweetened chocolate, melted
1¾ cups sifted enriched flour	
¼ teaspoon salt	

Blend butter and sugar and beat in egg yolk.

Combine dry ingredients and stir them into butter mixture alternately with the milk and vanilla.

Divide dough in half and into one half work in melted chocolate.

Roll out chocolate dough thinly on lightly floured board into a rectangle.

Roll out vanilla dough to same size and thickness and place on top of the chocolate dough.

Trim edges and roll lengthwise like a jelly roll.

Wrap in waxed paper and chill for several hours.

Then slice crosswise ¼ inch thick.

Place cut side down on baking sheet rubbed with shortening and bake at 350° F. for 8 to 10 minutes. *Makes 3 dozen 2-inch pinwheels.*

COCOA AND VANILLA COOKIES

1 *cup butter*	½ *teaspoon salt*
¼ *cup sugar*	2 *teaspoons vanilla*
2½ *cups enriched flour*	2 *tablespoons cocoa*

Blend butter and sugar thoroughly.

Stir in flour, salt, and vanilla and divide dough in half.

To one half work in the cocoa.

Shape dough into two rolls about 1 inch in diameter and cut each roll in half crosswise.

Place one chocolate and one vanilla roll close together on waxed paper.

Place second vanilla roll on top of chocolate, and second chocolate roll on top of vanilla roll.

Press firmly together, wrap in waxed paper, and chill for several hours.

Slice crosswise about ¼ inch thick, place slices cut side down on baking sheet rubbed with shortening, and bake at 350° F. for 8 to 10 minutes. *Makes 4 dozen 2-inch cookies.*

BORDERED COOKIES

To make these, two cutters of the same shape, one slightly smaller than the other, are necessary. With larger cutter cut a cooky from each shade of dough. With smaller cutter, cut center from each cooky.

Transfer the center of the light dough to the center of the dark dough and transfer the center of the dark dough to the center of the light dough, thus making two bordered cookies. Chill before baking.

STRIPED AND CHECKERBOARD COOKIES

To make checkerboard cookies, you first must make striped cookies. Roll out light dough and dark dough about ¼ inch thick. Cut 4 oblongs of identical size from each dough. Stack oblongs one atop the other, alternating colors. Press stack together firmly. Wrap the stack in waxed paper and chill.

For checkerboards: Before chilling striped dough, slice the dough crosswise ¼ inch thick. Stack 8 slices, one atop the other, turning every other slice so that a dark stripe rests on a light stripe. Press firmly together, wrap tightly in waxed paper, and chill. When ready to bake, cut striped or checkered dough across stripes or checks into ¼-inch slices. Lift slices carefully with spatula to a baking sheet rubbed with shortening and bake at 350° F. for 8 to 10 minutes.

ALMOND GINGER COOKIES

1 cup butter	1 teaspoon soda
1 cup sugar	1 teaspoon salt
½ cup molasses	1 cup blanched almonds,
1 tablespoon ginger	chopped
2 teaspoons cinnamon	3½ cups sifted enriched flour
2 teaspoons cloves	

Blend butter and sugar.

Stir in molasses, spices, soda, salt, almonds, and flour.

Turn onto floured board and knead until dough is smooth.

Shape into thick rolls or oblongs, wrap in waxed paper, and chill.

Cut crosswise into ¼-inch-thick slices, place on baking sheet rubbed with shortening, and bake at 350° F. for 8 to 10 minutes. *Makes 8 dozen 2-inch cookies.*

DATE AND NUT SQUARES

½ cup butter
1 cup sugar
2 eggs
2 cups chopped pitted dates
1 cup chopped pecan meats
½ cup cut candied cherries

1 teaspoon vanilla
⅔ cup sifted enriched flour
1 teaspoon double-acting baking powder
Confectioners' sugar

Blend butter and sugar and beat in eggs.

Stir in remaining ingredients except confectioners' sugar and spread batter in a 9-inch square pan rubbed with shortening.

Bake at 350° F. for 40 to 45 minutes.

Cut into squares while warm and roll in confectioners' sugar. *Makes 3 dozen 1½-inch squares.*

CHAPTER 14

Yeast Cakes, Large and Small

Eggs and butter added to sweet yeast dough are responsible for the rich flavor, the golden color, and the delicate structure of a group of dessert cakes that has been modified and adapted into the cuisine of almost every nation. From the light-textured simplicity of the sugar-powdered Austrian *Kougelhof* through the rum-bathed Polonese *baba* and the French *savarin* to the high-bonneted, fruit-filled *kulitch* of Russia, sweet leavened cakes have contributed to the popular entremets of the world.

The *Kougelhof* is the most ancient of these honorable cakes. It is recorded as having been made in 1609 at Lemberg, Poland, more than two hundred years before it made its debut in Paris. It was King Stanislas, the gourmand Polish monarch, who conceived the notion of soaking the *Kougelhof* in rum syrup and blazing it in the same manner as one flames a plum pudding. The nectared *Kougelhof* became the vogue at the court of Lorraine, where it was served with a sweet sauce flavored with spices and Malaga wine. King Stanislas named his creation after the hero of his favorite tale, *Ali Baba*.

It was not until the beginning of the eighteenth century that the *Ali Baba* was introduced into Paris by *pâtissier* Sthorer, who made it the *spécialité de la maison* on the Rue Montorgueil where he was pastry chef. Before long it was in high favor throughout all of France and the Continent, and its name became simply *baba*.

In 1840 another French pastry chef, Julien, used the same yeast dough that make the *Kougelhof* and the *baba*, but changed its shape and name. He eliminated the raisins and currants, baked the dough in a ring mold, modified the syrup in which it was soaked, and named it for the philosopher, Brillat-Savarin. As with the *Ali Baba*, the name of this cake was shortened to *savarin*.

At the same time, the *Kougelhof* itself, progenitor of this entire group of yeast desserts, was made by *pâtissier* Georges in his pastry shop on the Rue de Coq. Certain historians prefer the theory that it was Carême who recreated the *Kougelhof* in France from a recipe he obtained from the *chef des cuisines* of the Austrian ambassador, but it is very possible that it was Marie Antoinette, the luxury-loving, pampered darling of the French courts, who popularized it in Paris.

KOUGELHOF

1 cake or envelope yeast	½ teaspoon salt
¼ cup lukewarm water	1½ tablespoons fine gran-
2½ cups all-purpose flour	ulated sugar
2 eggs	½ cup sultana raisins
1 cup lukewarm milk	Blanched halved almonds
½ cup butter	Confectioners' sugar

In a warm bowl soften yeast in the ¼ cup lukewarm water.

Stir in about ½ cup of the flour to make a soft dough and sift remaining flour over dough.

Do not mix, but put bowl in a warm place until the soft yeast dough rises up through the dry flour.

Then mix dry flour and dough lightly and, with the hand, beat in eggs, one at a time, and the 1 cup lukewarm milk.

Continue to beat batter vigorously for 5 or 6 minutes until it is very elastic, adding a little more flour if needed.

Cream butter, salt, and sugar until mixture is soft and fluffy.

Distribute it over batter and beat thoroughly.

Add raisins and beat again to distribute the raisins throughout.

Butter generously a *Kougelhof* pan or a tube pan, 8 or 9 inches in diameter, and decorate the bottom with blanched halved almonds.

Fill pan half full of batter and put the pan, covered, in a warm place until batter doubles in bulk and pan is full.

Bake in a hot oven (400° F.) for 40 to 45 minutes. Remove the *Kougelhof* from the pan while still hot, and cool on a cake rack.

Serve sprinkled generously with confectioners' sugar.

FILLED KOUGELHOF

KOUGELHOF *batter*	6 *tablespoons chopped raisins*
6 *tablespoons ground*	1 *teaspoon cinnamon*
almonds	*Grated rind 1 lemon*
2 *tablespoons sugar*	*Confectioners' sugar*

Make a *Kougelhof* batter omitting the raisins.

Butter generously a *Kougelhof* pan or a tube pan and fill it ¼ full with the batter.

Sprinkle over the batter the almonds, sugar, raisins, cinnamon, and grated lemon rind.

Pour batter over the filling until pan is half full, let rise in a warm spot, and bake in a hot oven (400° F.) for 40 to 45 minutes.

Remove cake from pan while still hot and cool on a cake rack.

Serve dusted with confectioners' sugar.

KOUGELHOF WITH CHOCOLATE

KOUGELHOF *batter with no*	3 *tablespoons milk*
raisins and with additional	1 *teaspoon vanilla*
flour	2 *tablespoons sugar*
2 *ounces sweet chocolate*	

Make a *Kougelhof* batter, omitting the raisins and adding enough additional flour to make a dough that is soft but not sticky.

Divide dough into two parts.

Melt chocolate in the milk.

Add vanilla and sugar.

Mix this into one part of the dough.

Roll out each part on a lightly floured sheet and place the chocolate dough over the white dough.

Roll up like a jelly roll and put in a well-buttered *Kougelhof* pan or a tube pan.

Let rise until double in bulk and bake in a hot oven (400° F.) for 10 minutes.

Lower heat to 350° F. and bake for 45 minutes longer.

RUM CAKE • *Baba au Rhum*

1 cake or envelope yeast
½ cup lukewarm milk
2 cups all-purpose flour
4 eggs, lightly beaten
½ teaspoon salt
1 tablespoon currants
1½ tablespoons sultana
  raisins

1 tablespoon fine granulated
  sugar
⅔ cup soft butter
RUM SYRUP
Ice cream and fruit, optional
Blanched almonds and
  candied cherries, optional

Soften yeast in the lukewarm milk.

Sift flour into a mixing bowl and make a well in the center.

Into the well pour the softened yeast and milk and the eggs.

Mix flour into the liquid ingredients to make a soft sticky dough.

Add a little more milk if necessary, for the amount of liquid depends greatly on the size of the eggs used.

Beat dough with the hand for 2 minutes, raising it up with the fingers and letting it fall back again into the bowl.

Cover bowl lightly with a towel and put in a warm place for about ¾ hour, or until double in bulk.

Stir dough down and sprinkle over it the salt, currants, raisins, sugar, and the butter, divided into small bits.

Beat again with the hand for 3 to 4 minutes.

Turn dough into a well-buttered, high-sided decorative mold.

Put in a warm place until dough rises to top of mold.

Bake in a very hot oven (450° F.) for 10 minutes to destroy the action of the yeast, reduce oven temperature to 350° F., and continue to bake for 35 to 40 minutes until cake is lightly brown and a cake tester comes out clean.

Unmold the baba onto a serving plate and, while still warm, pour rum syrup over.

Just before serving, pour a little more rum over the baba.

The center of the mold may be filled with ice cream and fruit, such as apricot halves or pitted black cherries, piled high on top, or it may be simply and attractively garnished with blanched almonds and candied cherries.

FLAMING BABA • *Baba Flambé*

Keep the soaked baba (see preceding recipe) in a warm place and, just before serving, sprinkle top generously with confectioners' sugar. Pour over ¼ cup warm rum. Light the rum and serve ablaze.

SMALL RUM BABAS • *Petits Babas au Rhum*

Bake baba dough for about 20 minutes in small individual molds. Unmold and drop into a saucepan of hot RUM SYRUP. Marinate in the syrup for several hours. When ready to serve, put the babas into the blazer of a chafing dish with any syrup left in the saucepan that they did not absorb. When hot, sprinkle with confectioners' sugar, pour ¼ cup warm rum over them, and blaze.

BABA SAVOUREUX

Fill a well-buttered fluted brioche mold half full with baba dough, put it in a warm place, covered, until double in bulk, and bake in a very hot oven (450° F.) for 10 minutes. Reduce temperature to 350° F. and continue to bake for about 30 minutes, or until a cake tester comes out clean. Unmold, cut a slice off the top, and hollow out the middle of the cake slightly. Soak the baba and the top in ALMOND MILK. Garnish center with whipped cream, sweetened and flavored with vanilla. Replace top and spread top and sides with CONFECTIONERS' SUGAR ICING. Sprinkle with toasted slivered almonds.

The savarin is made in exactly the same way as the *baba au rhum* and with the same yeast dough, but the raisins and currants are omitted.

SAVARIN

Follow the recipe for RUM CAKE, omitting the raisins and currants. Turn dough into a well-buttered ring mold, filling it two-thirds full. Put in a warm place until dough rises to top of mold. Bake in a hot oven (400° F.) for 30 to 35 minutes, or until a cake tester comes out clean, watching carefully that it does not overbrown.

Unmold the savarin onto a serving plate and, while still warm, drench it with a RUM- or KIRSCH-FLAVORED SYRUP. The center may be filled with a macédoine of fruits marinated in kirsch, rum, or brandy, or it may be filled with brandy- or rum-flavored whipped cream and served with APRICOT SAUCE.

SAVARIN AU RHUM FLAMBE

Unmold a SAVARIN carefully while it is still warm and spoon over it a hot RUM SYRUP until cake is saturated. Keep the soaked cake in a warm spot and, just before serving, pour ¼ cup warm rum over it. Touch a match to the savarin and serve blazing.

PETITS SAVARINS

Bake SAVARIN dough in small individual ring molds and, while the *petits savarins* are still hot from the oven, drop into a RUM or KIRSCH SYRUP. They may be flambéed in the same manner as small rum babas. The centers may be garnished with whipped cream, PASTRY CREAM, marmalade, or fresh or poached fruit.

SAVARIN CHANTILLY

Soak a SAVARIN or small individual savarins in KIRSCH SYRUP. Coat with APRICOT GLAZE and fill centers with whipped cream, piling it high in the center. Garnish the border of the cakes with whipped cream pressed through an open-star pastry tube.

SAVARIN A LA CREME

Soak a SAVARIN or small individual savarins in syrup flavored with rum or a liqueur and garnish the centers with a PASTRY CREAM.

SAVARIN AUX FRAISES

Soak a SAVARIN or small individual savarins in a syrup flavored with Madeira and a dash of Cointreau instead or rum. Fill the centers with whole or sliced strawberries, fresh or frozen, sugared to taste and flavored with vanilla.

SAVARIN AUX FRUITS

Soak a SAVARIN or small individual savarins in KIRSCH SYRUP and spread with APRICOT GLAZE. Garnish centers with a compote of fruits or with marmalade.

CHERRY CAKE · *Gâteau aux Cerises*

2 *pounds sour cherries*	SAVARIN
1½ *cups sugar*	1 *cup heavy cream, whipped,*
½ *cup kirsch*	*flavored with kirsch*

Pit cherries and put them in a bowl with 1 dozen of the pits, crushed and tied in cheesecloth.

Sprinkle sugar over the fruit and pits and let stand overnight, or until enough juice has been drawn from the cherries to almost cover them.

Cook cherries slowly for 5 minutes in their own juice without adding any other liquid.

Discard pits, add the kirsch, and spoon the cherry syrup over a savarin until it is saturated.

Let cherries cool and, when ready to serve, turn them into the center of the cake, reserving a few for decoration.

Cover cherries with the whipped cream flavored with kirsch, piling it high in the middle, and decorate with the reserved cherries.

BASKET CAKE · *Gâteau Marignan*

Bake SAVARIN dough in a large oval buttered mold. Unmold the cake and, while it is still warm, drench it with a KIRSCH SYRUP. Split cake from both sides, almost but not quite in half, leaving 2 inches uncut in the center, so that the sides may be lifted to give the appearance of a basket. Coat top and sides with APRICOT GLAZE. Fill the basket with ITALIAN MERINGUE flavored with kirsch. Soften a long strip of angelica in warm water, bend it into the shape of a basket handle, and insert the ends in either side of the *marignan*.

The basket may also be filled with SAINT-HONORE CREAM or with a mixture of fresh berries and whipped cream.

MARIGNANS

Fill small buttered boat-shaped molds half full with SAVARIN dough. Put them in a warm place to rise until the dough reaches tops of molds and bake in a hot oven (400° F.) for 15 to 20 minutes.

Remove from molds and saturate with a syrup flavored with rum or kirsch or any liqueur.

When ready to serve, split the *marignans* sidewise, without cutting them all the way through, much as you would split a frankturter roll, and insert in the pocket of each a small baked, fluted MERINGUE or a spoonful of whipped cream. Glaze the top of the *marignans* with APRICOT SAUCE.

GATEAU MANON

Fill a well-buttered *brioche mousseline* mold or a timbale mold half full with SAVARIN dough made as for the savarin recipe. Let dough rise until it reaches top of the mold. Tie a band of buttered paper around the top of mold, letting it extend 2 inches above mold. Bake in a hot oven (400° F.) for 30 to 35 minutes.

When the savarin is cool, unmold and cut crosswise into 5 slices. Soak slices lightly in a KIRSCH SYRUP and reconstruct the cake, putting a layer of PASTRY CREAM between each slice. Spread top and sides with apricot marmalade and cover the marmalade with blanched slivered almonds, browned in butter. Sprinkle with confectioners' sugar.

APPLE RING · *Bórdure de Pommes Brillat-Savarin*

Fill the center of a baked SAVARIN with PASTRY CREAM mixed with an equal amount of applesauce and flavored with rum to taste. Cover the cake with a ring of apple halves, poached until tender in a light syrup flavored with vanilla and the juice of ½ lemon. Glaze the apples with APRICOT GLAZE and decorate with candied cherries and toasted almonds.

Many of the sweet yeast breads and traditional Christmas breads of other lands deserve to be included in a book on desserts, for all of them make delicious desserts. They may be served with fruit, fresh or poached, or simply by themselves with a steaming cup of coffee.

NORWEGIAN JULE KAGE

2 cakes or packages yeast	½ cup chopped candied
½ cup lukewarm water	cherries
2 cups milk	½ cup chopped blanched
1 cup sugar	almonds
2 teaspoons salt	1 tablespoon ground
1 cup shortening	cardamom
8 cups all-purpose flour	CONFECTIONERS' SUGAR ICING
1 cup chopped raisins	Bits of fruit and nuts
½ cup shredded citron	

Dissolve yeast in the lukewarm water.

Scald the milk, add sugar, salt, and shortening, and cool to luke-warm.

Add yeast and beat in 4 cups of the flour.

Place in a warm spot to rise until it doubles in bulk.

Punch down and add the fruit and nuts and the rest of the flour.

Turn out on a lightly floured board and knead until smooth and satiny, adding more flour, if necessary, to make a medium-firm dough.

Round up the dough, place in a greased bowl, grease the surface of the dough, cover, and place in a warm spot to double again in bulk.

Punch down, knead again, form into loaves, and place in greased loaf pans.

Allow to rise until double in bulk and bake at 400° F. for 10 minutes.

Reduce oven temperature to 350° F. and bake for 50 minutes longer.

When cool, frost with confectioners' sugar icing and decorate with bits of fruit and nuts. *Makes 3 loaves.*

CHRISTMAS FRUIT BREAD

½ cup shredded citron
½ cup chopped raisins
½ cup chopped candied
    cherries
1 tablespoon grated lemon
    rind
½ cup chopped blanched
    almonds
1 teaspoon cinnamon
½ teaspoon ground cloves
½ teaspoon nutmeg

¼ cup brandy
1 cake or package yeast
2 tablespoons lukewarm water
1 cup milk
⅓ cup shortening
¼ cup sugar
1 teaspoon salt
1 egg, beaten
4 cups all-purpose flour
Melted butter
CONFECTIONERS' SUGAR ICING

Soak fruit, nuts, and spices in the brandy overnight.

Soften yeast in the lukewarm water.

Scald milk, add to it the shortening, sugar, and salt, and cool to lukewarm.

Add softened yeast, egg, and 2 cups of the flour.

Beat thoroughly, then add the rest of the flour.

Allow to rise in a warm place until double in bulk, turn out on a floured board, and knead, adding more flour if necessary, to make a medium-firm dough.

Allow to rise again until double in bulk.

Punch down, knead the fruit mixture into the dough, and form into loaves.

Place loaves in greased loaf pans and allow to rise again until double in bulk.

Brush tops of the loaves with melted butter.

Bake at 400° F. for 10 minutes, reduce oven temperature to 350° F., and bake for another 50 minutes.

Cool and frost with a thin confectioners' sugar icing flavored with almond extract. *Makes 1 large or 2 small loaves.*

YUGOSLAVIAN SWEET YEAST BREAD · *Putica*

4 cups all-purpose flour
1½ cups sugar
¼ teaspoon salt
4 tablespoons soft butter
1 cake or package yeast
½ cup lukewarm milk

2 eggs, lightly beaten
½ pound chopped walnuts
¼ pound chopped raisins
¼ pound bitter chocolate,
    shaved
½ cup honey

In a mixing bowl combine flour, sugar, and salt, and rub into it the soft butter.

Soften yeast in the milk and add it along with the eggs.

Mix well and let rise until double in bulk.

Roll out the dough ½ inch thick and spread with the walnuts, raisins, chocolate, and honey, all mixed together.

Roll as a jelly roll, place on a greased baking sheet, and bake at 350° F. for 25 minutes. *Makes 1 large roll.*

SPAETZEL

1 cake or package yeast	5 egg yolks, beaten
2 tablespoons lukewarm water	1 cup ground unblanched almonds
1 cup milk	½ cup melted butter
2 tablespoons butter	½ cup raisins
1 tablespoon sugar	2 teaspoons cinnamon
½ teaspoon salt	½ cup sugar
5 cups all-purpose flour	

Soften yeast in the lukewarm water.

Scald milk and add to it the butter, sugar, and salt.

Cool to lukewarm and then add softened yeast and 2 cups of the flour.

Beat well and allow to rise in a warm place until light and foamy.

Stir in egg yolks and the rest of the flour and knead well on a floured board.

Allow to rise until double in bulk.

Punch down and roll dough into a thin sheet.

Cut dough into cooky-shaped rounds.

Sprinkle a greased loaf pan lightly with some of the almonds.

Dip the rounds of dough in melted butter and place them in layers in the prepared pan until pan is half full.

Sprinkle each layer with ground almonds, raisins, cinnamon, and sugar and sprinkle the top with melted butter.

Allow to rise until double in bulk and bake at 350° F. for 45 minutes. *Makes 2 loaves.*

ITALIAN CHRISTMAS BREAD · *Panettone de Natale*

1 cake or package yeast
¼ cup milk, scalded and
   cooled to lukewarm
4 cups all-purpose flour
¾ cup shortening
½ cup sugar
2 egg yolks, beaten
3 whole eggs, beaten
1 teaspoon vanilla

½ teaspoon salt
½ cup raisins
¼ cup shredded candied peel
¼ cup shredded citron
¼ cup chopped blanched
   almonds
Whole almonds and sugar,
   optional

Dissolve yeast in the milk, add ½ cup of the flour, and allow to stand in a warm place until bubbly.

Cream together the shortening and sugar.

Add beaten eggs and then the yeast-milk mixture.

Add vanilla, salt, and enough flour to make a dough that is soft but not sticky.

Turn out on floured board and knead in fruit and nuts.

Place in a warm spot to rise until double in bulk.

Punch down and knead again for 3 minutes.

Shape into a round loaf, place in a greased baking pan, and allow to rise again until double in bulk. This will take longer than usual because of the fruit.

Bake at 400° F. for 10 minutes.

Reduce oven temperature to 350° F. and bake for 50 minutes longer.

This may be baked in a *Kougelhof* pan, the bottom of which is covered with whole almonds and sprinkled with sugar. *Makes 1 large loaf.*

MEXICAN EGG BREAD · *Pan de Huevos*

2 cakes or packages yeast
2 tablespoons lukewarm
   water
12 egg yolks
½ cup sugar

2 tablespoons melted shortening
3 tablespoons anise seed
12 egg whites, stiffly beaten
3½ cups all-purpose flour

Soften yeast in the water and allow to stand for 10 minutes.

Beat egg yolks until thick and pale in color.

Add sugar gradually, continuing to beat.

Then stir in shortening and the softened yeast.

Stir in anise seed and egg whites and blend thoroughly and then add enough flour to make a dough that is light but not sticky.

Allow to rise in a warm place until double in bulk, punch down, and knead for 3 minutes.

Roll out ½ inch thick and cut into large squares.

Places the squares on greased baking pans and allow to rise again until double in bulk.

Bake at 350° F. for 45 minutes.

SWEDISH SWEET BREAD • *Christollen*

2 cakes or packages active yeast	3 tablespoons lemon juice
¼ cup lukewarm water	1½ cups seedless raisins
1 cup milk	½ cup shredded citron
1 cup sugar	½ cup chopped candied cherries
1 teaspoon salt	1½ cups chopped nuts
½ cup soft butter	2 tablespoons soft butter
5 cups enriched flour	Confectioners' sugar or
2 eggs, beaten	CONFECTIONERS' SUGAR ICING
1 teaspoon mace	
1 tablespoon grated lemon peel	

Soften yeast in the lukewarm water for 5 minutes, then stir until blended.

Scald milk, add sugar, salt, and butter, and cool to lukewarm.

Add 2 cups of the flour to make a thick batter and beat well.

Add yeast, eggs, mace, lemon peel, and lemon juice and beat until the batter is elastic.

Stir in 2 more cups flour, then with floured fingers work in enough additional flour to make a soft dough that does not stick to the hands.

Turn out dough on a lightly floured board and knead until smooth, about 100 kneading strokes.

Place dough in a greased bowl, cover, and let rise until double in bulk, about 1½ hours.

Punch dough down, turn out on a lightly floured board, and knead in the raisins, citron, candied cherries, and nuts.

Shape the dough into 2 balls.

Flatten each ball into an oval about ¾ inch thick and spread lightly with 2 tablespoons soft butter, using about 1 tablespoon for each oval.

Fold over like large Parker House rolls.

Pinch the ends firmly together and place the *stollen* on greased baking sheets.

Cover and let rise until almost double in bulk, about 1 hour.

Bake at 350° F. for 35 minutes.

While still warm dust heavily with confectioners' sugar or spread with confectioners' sugar icing.

Another group of sweet tea or dessert breads is made from a basic sweet yeast dough. Make the full quantity of dough in the recipe below, use half for sweet buns or rolls, and make the rest into a delicious dessert.

BASIC SWEET DOUGH

2 *cakes or packages yeast*	½ *cup shortening (part*
¼ *cup lukewarm water*	*butter)*
1 *cup milk*	5 *cups all-purpose flour*
½ *cup sugar*	2 *eggs, beaten*
1 *teaspoon salt*	

Soften yeast in the lukewarm water.

Scald milk, add sugar, salt, and shortening, and cool to lukewarm (80°–85° F.).

Add part of the flour to make a thick batter and mix well.

Add softened yeast and eggs and beat thoroughly.

Add enough additional flour to make a dough that is soft but does not stick to the hands.

Turn out on a lightly floured board and knead until smooth and satiny.

Place in a greased bowl, cover, and allow to rise in a warm place until double in bulk (about 1½ hours).

Punch down and allow to rest for 10 minutes.

Then shape into rolls, tea rings, or coffeecakes.

Allow to rise until double (about 1 hour).

Bake at 350° F. for 30 minutes for coffeecakes, 20 to 25 minutes for rolls. *Makes 3 dozen rolls, 3 coffeecakes, or 3 medium-sized loaves.*

SWEDISH TEA RINGS

½ recipe BASIC SWEET DOUGH	Melted butter
3 tablespoons melted butter	1 cup confectioners' sugar
½ cup brown sugar	3 tablespoons light cream
2 teaspoons cinnamon	¼ cup chopped nuts
½ cup raisins, if desired	Candied fruit

When basic sweet dough is light, punch down and allow it to rest for 10 minutes.

Roll into a rectangle about ½ inch thick and 8 inches wide.

Brush with melted butter, sprinkle with brown sugar and cinnamon and raisins, if used, and roll up like a jelly roll, sealing the edge.

Place on a greased baking sheet with sealed edge down, moisten ends slightly, and join securely to form a ring.

With kitchen scissors make deep slantwise cuts in the ring about two-thirds through and at intervals of 1 inch.

Turn each slice partly on its side to give a petallike appearance.

If you wish to make a double ring, lift every other cut slice to the center of the ring.

Brush lightly with melted butter, cover with a towel, and allow to rise in a warm place until double in bulk (about 45 minutes).

Bake at 350° F. for 30 minutes.

Remove from the oven and while still slightly warm frost with 1 cup confectioners' sugar which has been mixed to a paste of spreading consistency with 3 tablespoons light cream.

Sprinkle with chopped nuts and decorate with bits of candied fruit.

BUBBLE LOAF

½ recipe for BASIC SWEET
DOUGH
CARAMEL GLAZE

When basic sweet dough is light and doubled in bulk, punch down and allow it to rest for 10 minutes.

Break off pieces of dough about the size of walnuts and shape into balls.

Place a layer of balls on the bottom of a greased loaf pan, slightly apart.

Arrange a second layer on top of the first, placing the balls between the spaces in the first layer.

Arrange a third layer in the same manner.

Pour caramel glaze over all and allow to rise in a warm place until doubled in bulk (about 1 hour).

Bake at 350° F. for 35 minutes and allow to cool in the pan for 5 minutes before turning out.

JAM SWIRL CAKE

½ recipe BASIC SWEET DOUGH	¼ cup sugar
½ cup jam or marmalade	¼ teaspoon cinnamon

When the basic sweet dough batter is light and doubled in bulk, stir down.

Spread batter evenly in a greased, deep layer cake pan 9 inches in diameter.

With a floured spoon make 5 grooves in a swirl design from the edge to the center.

Fill grooves with jam.

Mix together sugar and cinnamon and sprinkle over top.

Allow to rise in a warm place until double in bulk (about 45 minutes) and bake at 375° F. for 30 minutes.

DUTCH APPLECAKE

½ recipe for BASIC SWEET DOUGH	2 tablespoons sugar
1 tablespoon melted butter	½ teaspoon nutmeg
2 tart apples	Butter

When basic sweet dough is light, punch down and allow it to rest for 10 minutes.

Pat it out to fit a greased, 8-inch square cake pan.

Brush top with melted butter.

Cover with a clean towel and allow to rise until double in bulk.

Pare and core apples, cut into sections ⅓ inch thick, and arrange in even rows on top of the dough, pressing edges slightly into the dough.

Sprinkle with sugar and nutmeg mixed.

Dot with butter and allow to rise another 15 minutes.

Bake at 375° F. for 40 minutes.

Cover top at first with buttered paper to aid in cooking the apples.

Remove paper the last 10 minutes to allow cake to brown.

HONEY TWIST

> *⅓ recipe for* BASIC SWEET
>   DOUGH
> HONEY TOPPING

When the basic sweet dough is light, punch down and allow it to rest for 10 minutes.

Shape into a long roll about 1 inch in diameter.

Coil the roll loosely into a greased, 9-inch layer pan or an 8-inch square pan, beginning at the center and working out.

Brush with honey topping and allow to rise until doubled in bulk (about 1 hour).

Bake at 350° F. for 30 minutes.

HONEY TOPPING

Combine and mix until smooth ¼ cup butter, ⅔ cup confectioners' sugar, 1 egg white, and 2 tablespoons honey.

HUNGARIAN COFFEECAKE

Make ½ the recipe for BASIC SWEET DOUGH. When dough is light, punch down and allow it to rest for 10 minutes. Break dough into pieces the size of walnuts and form into balls. Dip balls in ½ cup melted butter and then roll in a mixture of ¾ cup brown sugar, 1 teaspoon cinnamon, and ½ cup finely chopped nuts. Place a layer of the balls very lightly in a greased 9-inch tube pan and sprinkle raisins and more nuts in the crevices. Continue in this manner until all the balls are in the pan. Cover with a towel and allow to rise for about 1 hour, or until double in bulk. Bake at 375° F. for 35 minutes.

BUTTERSCOTCH PECAN ROLL

Make ½ recipe BASIC SWEET DOUGH. When light, punch down and allow it to rest for 10 minutes. Roll out into a rectangle about ⅓ inch thick, spread surface liberally with softened butter, and sprinkle with ½ cup brown sugar mixed with 2 teaspoons cinnamon. Roll up lengthwise like a jelly roll and place seam side down in a greased loaf pan 10×5×3½ inches. Cover with a clean towel, place in a warm spot, and allow to rise until double in bulk. Bake at 350° F. for 30 minutes. Remove from oven and coat surface of loaf with a mixture of ½ cup brown sugar and ½ cup melted butter and sprinkle over 1 cup chopped pecans. Return to oven and bake 15 minutes longer.

APRICOT PRUNE CAKE

Make ½ recipe BASIC SWEET DOUGH and, when light, punch down and allow it to stand for 10 minutes. Pat out dough to fit a 9-inch square greased cake pan. Place dough in pan and arrange on top in even rows alternate halves of stewed prunes and apricots. Mix together ¼ cup brown sugar, 2 tablespoons melted butter, and 1 teaspoon cinnamon and sprinkle over the fruit. Place in a warm spot to double in bulk and bake at 350° F. for 45 minutes.

CHAPTER 15

Pies and Tarts

Oᴜʀ forefathers ate double-crust apple and mince pie, deep-dish cherry and berry pies, and one-crust pumpkin pies—pies that can be considered truly American desserts. While these are undoubtedly good, no one should limit his repertoire of pies to these few. There are more ethereal creations and ones that perhaps cater to more delicate appetites: the smooth light custard pies with berry toppings, the creamy chocolate and butterscotch cream pies in which cornstarch is the distinctive ingredient to give it its smooth texture. Then we come to the frothy chiffon and meringue-topped pies of which lemon chiffon or lemon meringue heads the list of notable pie desserts. They are all here in logical progression but, again, because of space limitations only the best have been included.

We begin with how to make pastry—a basic creative cooking art so simple that it is hard to believe that many feel it is beyond their culinary talents. A really fine flaky crust can be made from flour, shortening, salt, and water in less that 5 minutes and made equally well each time. The most important part of good pastry making is equipment. And I recommend that if you go to your local department store and invest in a pastry cloth and a stocking to fit your rolling pin you will find it is one of the best investments you have ever made for your kitchen and your family table. Incidentally, there is no reason why anyone needs to sift flour to make a pie dough.

GOOD PLAIN PASTRY FOR A TWO-CRUST PIE

2 cups all-purpose flour   ¾ cup shortening
1 teaspoon salt   6 tablespoons water

In a mixing bowl combine flour and salt.

With a pastry blender or two knives cut in shortening until mixture looks like coarse corn meal.

Sprinkle water over mixture, one tablespoon at a time, and mix lightly with a fork until all flour is moistened.

With hands gather dough into a ball and divide in half.

On a lightly floured board or pastry cloth roll out half the pastry ⅛ inch thick and about 1½ inches larger than pie plate.

Gently fit circle into plate and trim off overhanging edge.

Add filling according to recipe.

Roll out other half of pastry ⅛ inch thick and fold in half.

Cut several slits for steam to escape.

Unfold and place on filled pie.

Trim off extra edge leaving ½ inch overhanging.

Fold edge of top pastry under edge of lower pastry and press firmly together.

To flute edge: Take rim of pastry between thumb and forefinger of both hands held ½ inch apart. Pull rim held in right hand down and toward you, holding rim in place with other hand. Move hands, placing thumb and finger of left hand in ripple made by right hand; repeat all around edge.

For a shiny top: Brush top lightly with milk just before baking.

For a glazed crust: Brush top with 1 egg yolk lightly beaten with 1 teaspoon cold water.

Bake according to directions for each recipe.

LATTICE-TOP PIES

Allow bottom pastry to hang ½ inch over the edge of pan. Roll pastry for the top the exact size of the pan and cut into strips ½ inch wide. Lay half the strips about 1 inch apart one way across the filling. Then place the other half of the strips diagonally across to make diamond-shaped openings. Seal ends of strips to pastry on edge of the pan. Moisten overhanging edge with a little cold water, turn it over the ends of the strips, and flute in the regular way. The edge may be crimped with the tines of a fork if you wish.

To interweave the strips, place half the strips one way on waxed paper. Weave the other strips in and out across the other way, beginning with the center strip and working out to the sides. Chill thoroughly, transfer to the top of the filling, seal, and flute.

PASTRY FOR A SIX-INCH PIE OR ONE CRUST

Use 1½ cups flour, ½ teaspoon salt, ½ cup shortening, and 3 tablespoons water and follow directions for GOOD PLAIN PASTRY.

FOR A ONE-CRUST PIE

Fit pastry loosely into pie plate and trim off edge, leaving ½ inch overhanging. Fold overhanging edge back and under. Build up a fluted edge: Place left forefinger against inside of pastry rim and pinch outside with right thumb and forefinger. Repeat all around rim. Fill and bake according to directions for each recipe.

SERVINGS:

A 9-inch pie serves 8.
An 8-inch pie serves 6.
A 6-inch pie serves 4.

ORANGE PASTRY

Add grated rind of 1 orange to flour-shortening mixture. Use orange juice in place of water.

NUT PASTRY

Add ½ cup ground walnuts or pecans to flour-shortening mixture before adding water.

CHEESE PASTRY

Roll each half of pastry in a circle ⅛ inch thick and about 1½ inches larger in diameter than pie plate. Sprinkle each half with 2 tablespoons grated American cheese. Cover with a piece of waxed paper and gently roll cheese into pastry. Remove waxed paper and use pastry for double-crust pies.

SWEET PASTRY

Add ¼ cup sugar to flour and salt in mixing bowl.

CHOCOLATE PASTRY

Roll each half of pastry in a circle ⅛ inch thick and about 1½ inches larger in diameter than pie plate. Sprinkle each half with 4 tablespoons finely chopped semi-sweet chocolate. Cover with a piece of waxed paper and gently roll chocolate into dough. Remove waxed paper and use pastry for two single-crust pies or baked pie shells.

FLAKY PASTRY

Make GOOD PLAIN PASTRY and chill as usual. Roll it out lengthwise ⅓ inch thick and spread the surface with thin shavings of hard butter. Fold into thirds, lapping one part over the other, then roll out thin and fold again. Chill in the refrigerator for several hours or overnight before rolling out and lining pie plate.

RICH FLAKY PASTRY

Make FLAKY PASTRY as above and roll dough out lengthwise ⅓ inch thick. Spread the surface again with thin shavings of hard butter. Fold into thirds, lapping one part over the other, then roll out thin and fold again. Chill in the refrigerator for several hours or overnight before rolling out and lining pie plate and using for various other pastry desserts.

NOTE: Adding the flakes of butter once will make a pastry rich and flaky enough for ordinary use.

SOUR CREAM PASTRY

2 cups sifted all-purpose flour	1 cup butter
Pinch salt	1 egg yolk
1 tablespoon sugar	1 cup sour cream

Sift flour, salt, and sugar into mixing bowl.

Cut in the butter and add the egg yolk and enough of the sour cream to make a smooth dough.

Roll out thin and fold like a napkin. Wrap in waxed paper and chill in the refrigerator overnight.

When ready to make the pie, roll out two crusts (9-inch pie) according to general directions in GOOD PLAIN PASTRY recipe.

CREAM CHEESE PASTRY

1 cup butter	Pinch salt
8 ounces cream cheese	2½ cups sifted all-purpose
½ cup cream	flour

Cream together the butter and cheese until light and fluffy.

Stir in the cream and salt and mix until all the ingredients are well combined.

Stir in the flour and mix into a smooth dough.

Chill in refrigerator before rolling out to line pie plate (9-inch) or tart pans or for various other pastries.

This pastry will keep for several days in the refrigerator.

TWO-CRUST PIES

APPLE PIE

6 cups sliced apples	1 tablespoon flour
¾ to 1 cup sugar	Pastry for a two-crust pie
1 teaspoon cinnamon or nutmeg	2 tablespoons butter

Mix sliced apples with sugar, spice, and flour.

Fill pastry-lined pan.

Dot with butter.

Cover with top pastry and bake in a 450° F. oven for 10 minutes.

Reduce heat to 350° F. and continue to bake for 30 to 40 minutes, or until crust is nicely browned and apples are soft.

HONEY APPLE PIE

Pastry for a two-crust pie	*1 teaspoon cinnamon*
Sliced apples	*1 teaspoon vanilla*
¾ cup honey	*2 tablespoons butter*

Fill pastry-lined pie plate with apples and pour honey over them.
Sprinkle with cinnamon and vanilla.
Dot with butter.
Cover with slashed top crust and bake at 400° F. for 30 to 40 minutes or until apples are tender.

COLONIAL APPLE PIE

Sprinkle over apples ½ cup each chopped pecans and seedless raisins.

CRUMB-TOPPED APPLE PIE

Pastry-lined pie plate	*1 cup flour*
Sliced apples	*½ cup brown sugar*
½ cup sugar	*¼ cup butter*
1 teaspoon nutmeg	*Cream*

Fill pastry-lined pie plate with apples mixed with sugar and nutmeg.
Combine flour and brown sugar and cut in butter to make crumbs.
Sprinkle the crumbs over the apple filling and bake at 400° F. for 30 to 40 minutes or until apples are tender.
Serve warm with cream.

CHERRY APPLE PIE

4 cups sliced pared apples	*1 tablespoon orange juice*
1 tablespoon flour	*Pastry for a two-crust pie*
¼ teaspoon salt	*2-4 tablespoons cherry pre-*
½ cup sugar	*serves*

Combine apples, flour, salt, sugar, and orange juice.
Turn mixture into pastry-lined pie plate.
Drop preserves by tablespoon over filling.

Cover with slashed top crust.

Bake at 400° F. for 30 to 40 minutes, or until apples are tender.

CHERRY PIE

1 cup cherry juice	2½ cups canned red sour
2 tablespoons tapioca or	cherries, drained
cornstarch	Pastry for a 9-inch two-crust
1 cup sugar	pie
⅛ teaspoon salt	1 tablespoon butter

Combine juice, tapioca, sugar, and salt and pour over cherries in pastry-lined plate.

Dot with butter.

Cover with slashed top crust; flute edges.

Bake at 400° F. for 30 to 40 minutes, or until browned.

FRESH CHERRY PIE

1 quart sour cherries, pitted	2 tablespoons cornstarch
1 cup sugar	Pastry for two-crust pie
⅛ teaspoon salt	1 tablespoon butter

Place cherries and their juice in a saucepan.

Add sugar and salt mixed with cornstarch.

Bring to a boil and cook, stirring, until slightly thickened.

Line a 9-inch pie plate with pastry, fill with the fruit, dot with butter, and cover with a lattice topping.

Bake at 400° F. for 45 minutes, or until the pie is delicately browned.

FRESH PEACH PIE

3 cups sliced peeled peaches	⅛ teaspoon ginger
¼ cup flour	Pastry for a two-crust pie
½ cup brown sugar	1 tablespoon butter

Combine peaches, flour, brown sugar, and ginger. (If frozen peaches are used, no sugar is needed.)

Turn mixture into pastry-lined pie plate and dot with butter.

Cover with slashed top crust and flute edges.

Bake at 400° F. for 30 to 40 minutes, or until browned.
For a fuller pie, increase peaches to 4 cups.

FRESH RHUBARB PIE

Select early tender strawberry rhubarb. Remove the leaves, wash
the stalks, and cut into 1-inch pieces. The amount of sugar will have
to be adjusted to the tartness of the rhubarb and to the individual
taste.

Pastry for two-crust pie	*2 pounds (4 cups) cut-up*
3 tablespoons flour	*rhubarb*
1½–2 cups sugar	*2 tablespoons butter*
	Sugar

Line a 9-inch pie plate with pastry and chill.

Combine flour and sugar and sprinkle one fourth of it over bottom
of pastry.

Fill with rhubarb, piling it up in the center, and sprinkle with remaining sugar and flour mixture.

Dot with butter and cover with pastry.

Sprinkle top crust with sugar and bake at 450° F. for 10 minutes.

Reduce heat to 350° F. and bake for about 45 minutes longer, or
until the crust is nicely browned and the rhubarb is soft.

BLUEBERRY PIE

3 cups berries	*2 tablespoons cornstarch*
Pastry for two-crust pie	*⅛ teaspoon salt*
½–¾ cup sugar	

Wash and sort berries.

Line a 9-inch pie plate with pastry and fill with berries.

Combine sugar, cornstarch, and salt and sprinkle over berries.

Cover with pastry and bake at 450° F. for 10 minutes.

Reduce temperature to 350° F. and bake for another 35 to 40
minutes, or until the crust is nicely browned and the berries are
tender.

CRANBERRY PIE

2 cups cranberries	Pinch salt
Pastry for two-crust pie	Butter
2 cups sugar	½ cup seeded raisins,
2 tablespoons flour	optional

Wash cranberries and cut in half.

Line a 9-inch pie plate with pastry and fill with the cranberries.
Combine sugar, flour, and salt and sprinkle over the top of berries.
Dot with butter and cover with pastry.

Bake at 450° F. for 15 minutes.

Reduce the temperature to 350° F. and bake for another 35 minutes.

Serve hot or warm.

One-half cup seeded raisins makes a nice addition to this pie.

STRAWBERRY OR RASPBERRY PIE

3 cups berries	2 tablespoons cornstarch
Pastry for two-crust pie	Pinch salt
1 cup sugar	Butter

Wash berries, sort, and hull.

Line a 9-inch pie plate with pastry and fill with berries.

Mix together sugar, cornstarch, and salt and sprinkle over top of berries.

Dot with butter.

Cover with pastry or with a lattice topping and bake at 450° F. for 10 minutes.

Reduce temperature to 350° F. and bake for another 30 minutes, or until the crust is nicely browned.

Serve slightly warm.

DEEP-DISH BERRY PIE

4 cups fresh blueberries, blackberries, raspberries, or boysenberries	⅛ teaspoon salt
	Grated rind of ½ lemon
	1 tablespoon lemon juice
¾ cup sugar	1 tablespoon butter
1½ teaspoons tapioca or flour	Pastry for one-crust pie

Combine fruit, sugar, tapioca or flour, salt, rind, and juice and turn mixture into an oblong baking dish (8×6×2 inches).

Dot with butter.

Roll pastry into a rectangle ⅛ inch thick and about 1½ inches larger than dish.

Arrange pastry lightly over berries and trim edges, leaving ½ inch overhanging.

Moisten rim of dish, turn overhanging edge of pastry under, and press it onto rim.

Flute or crimp edge with tines of a fork.

Cut slits in pastry for steam to escape and bake at 400° F. for 30 to 45 minutes, or until browned.

DEEP-DISH STRAWBERRY RHUBARB

2 cups fresh or frozen strawberries
2 cups cut-up fresh rhubarb
1 cup sugar
2 tablespoons tapioca or flour
⅛ teaspoon salt
1 tablespoon grated orange rind
1 tablespoon orange juice
1 tablespoon butter
Pastry for one-crust pie

Combine fruit, sugar, tapioca or flour, salt, rind, and juice and turn mixture into an oblong baking dish (8×6×2 inches).

Dot with butter.

Roll pastry into a rectangle ⅛ inch thick and about 1½ inches larger than dish.

Arrange pastry lightly over berries and trim edges, leaving ½ inch overhanging.

Moisten rim of dish, turn overhanging edge of pastry under, and press it onto rim.

Flute or crimp edge with tines of a fork.

Cut slits in pastry for steam to escape and bake at 400° F. for 30 to 45 minutes, or until browned.

MINCEMEAT PIE

There are many good prepared mincemeats in stores today, but for those who wish to make their own, here is a delicious one.

½ pound lean boiled beef, chopped	3 ounces each candied orange rind, lemon rind, and citron, chopped
½ pound beef kidney suet, chopped	
3¾ pounds raw apples, peeled and chopped	Grated rind of 2 lemons
	5 cups brown sugar
½ pound currants	3 tablespoons cinnamon
1 pound seeded raisins, chopped	2 teaspoons nutmeg
	1 teaspoon ginger
1 tablespoon salt	½ teaspoon ground cloves
	5 cups cider

Combine all ingredients in a large kettle and simmer gently for 2 hours, stirring occasionally. Cool and place in clean quart jars, seal tightly, and store in a cool place. It will keep for 6 months.

TO MAKE PIE:

Line a 9-inch pie plate with pastry, fill with mincemeat, and cover the top with pastry according to standard directions in GOOD PLAIN PASTRY recipe.

Bake at 450° F. for 10 minutes, reduce temperature to 350° F., and continue baking for about 30 minutes longer.

While the pie is still hot insert a small funnel into one of the slits in the crust and pour in ¼ cup brandy.

Serve warm.

While the number of two-crust fruit pies is limited to the numbers of combinations of fruit and berries in season, canned, or frozen, the majority of pie "recipes" are for those baked in a single crust or for creamy and chiffon fillings poured into a baked crust.

This type of pie is technically known as a tart or, when made in diminutive sizes, tartlets. The word "tart" is derived from the French word *tartine*, meaning a slice of bread. For a long period in France, when china was a scarce commodity, the undercrust of a loaf of bread served as a plate, and host or guest could, if he wished, eat his dinner plate after consuming his dinner. In time, these plates of bread crust were made finer, richer, more cakelike. They were filled

with sweet or savory foods and were called tarts or tartlets according
to their size.

There are many kinds of pastry used for tarts. In Germany the
favorite tart paste is called *mürber teig,* and France has a variety of
names for the same rich, flaky undercrust—*pâte brisée, pâte à foncé,
pâte sucrée,* or *pâte sèche.* America has devised other types of crusts
suitable for framing a tart filling—those of crumbs and of nuts, or
the ethereal base made of meringue. Or you can use the recipe for
GOOD PLAIN PASTRY at the beginning of this Chapter.

Here is the recipe for *mürber teig* or *pâte à foncé.* Work it gently
and chill it for at least an hour or overnight in the refrigerator before
rolling out.

TART PASTE

1 *cup flour*	½ *cup soft butter*
1 *egg yolk*	*Grated rind of 1 lemon*
1 *tablespoon sugar*	*Pinch salt*

Sift flour onto a pastry board or into a bowl.

Make a well in the center and put into the well the egg yolk,
sugar, butter, lemon rind, and salt.

Mix these center ingredients with one hand into a smooth paste.

Then quickly work in the flour, adding a very little ice water if
needed to moisten the dough so that it can be gathered together and
will clean the board or bowl.

Wrap dough in waxed paper and chill for at least 1 hour. *Makes
one 9-inch shell.*

Tarts may be made in standard pie tins or in flan rings. A flan
ring is simply a ring of metal about 1 inch high.

TO LINE A FLAN RING

Roll out chilled TART PASTE into a circle ⅛ inch thick. Lift
dough carefully and place it over a buttered flan ring. Press dough
into the ring and round the sides with the thumb so that it sticks
to the sides. Make a small tuck of the dough all around the inner top
edge of the ring and cut away the paste that rises above the ring.
Use a floured knife, or simply press the rolling pin over the edge and

the excess dough will fall cleanly away. Then raise the little tuck to make a border and flute the border with thumb and index finger, or pinch it all around with a pastry pincher. Put the lined flan ring on a buttered baking sheet and prick bottom with the tines of a fork. Chill for 30 minutes before covering the dough with fruit, sugar, and spices.

TO BAKE A TART SHELL

Cover TART PASTE in a flan ring with waxed paper and cover paper with dry rice or beans to keep the dough in shape while it is baking. Bake in a hot oven (400° F.) for 10 minutes, reduce the oven temperature to moderate (350° F.), and bake for another 15 minutes, or until the crust is golden brown. Remove the paper, discard the rice or beans, and cool.

BRAZIL NUT PASTRY SHELL

Mix 2 cups ground brazil nuts with 4 tablespoons sugar and press firmly onto bottom and sides of a 9-inch pie plate.

MERINGUE PASTRY SHELL

3 egg whites
Pinch salt
¼ teaspoon cream of tartar

¾ cup fine granulated sugar
1 teaspoon vanilla

Beat egg whites and salt until foamy.

Add cream of tartar and continue to beat until egg whites will stand in a soft peak when beater is withdrawn.

Gradually beat in sugar, about 1 tablespoon at a time, and continue to beat until sugar is completely blended and mixture is very stiff and glossy.

Beat in vanilla.

Spread meringue thickly over bottom and sides, building it up a good ½ inch above edge of plate to form a nestlike shell.

Bake shell at 300° F. for 50 minutes, or until meringue is dry and delicately colored.

Loosen from the pan while still warm and allow to cool before adding filling.

ZWIEBACK PASTRY SHELL

Crumb a few zwieback at a time in an electric blender or crush 1 box zwieback with a rolling pin and put through a sieve. Crush again any large pieces that remain in the sieve. Combine 1½ cups crumbs with 3 tablespoons sugar and ¼ cup melted butter. Butter a pie plate generously and press mixture on sides and bottom. Chill for a short time. Zwieback pastry shells may be flavored with a little grated lemon rind and a little cinnamon, if desired.

GRAHAM CRACKER PASTRY SHELL

Make the same as for ZWIEBACK PASTRY SHELL.

WAFER SHELL

Crush 1 box vanilla, chocolate, or ginger wafers and put through a sieve. Crush again any large pieces that remain in the sieve. Mix the crumbs with ¼ cup each sugar and melted butter. Butter a pie plate generously and pat the cooky crumbs thickly over the bottom and sides. Chill in the refrigerator for a short time.

CORNFLAKE SHELL

Combine 2 cups crushed cornflakes with ½ cup melted butter, 4 tablespoons sugar, and 1 teaspoon cinnamon. Press on bottom and sides of a buttered pie plate.

TARTLETS

The following recipes may be made into individual tarts, or tartlets, instead of one large tart. One tart equals six 3-inch tartlets. Let your personal preference be your guide.

FRUIT TARTS

Fruit tarts are made in several ways, but the name of the tart need not dictate the actual fruit used. Peaches or large plums may be substituted for fresh apricots; small plums may be used in place of cherries, and so on. Juicy fruits such as plums and cherries may need a few stale cake crumbs sprinkled on the dough to absorb some of the juice. Tarts are glazed with either apricot jam or red currant jelly thinned to sauce consistency with warm water. The yellow apricot glaze is usually used for peaches, apricots, and apples. Use the red currant glaze with cherries or red- or blueberries.

APPLE TART

Line a pie tin or flan ring with TART PASTE. Fill lined plate three-fourths full of applesauce, sweetened to taste, and arrange thin apple slices on top, overlapping them in orderly fashion. Sprinkle apple slices with sugar and bake in a moderate oven (350° F.) for 35 minutes, or until crust is brown and apples tender. When cool, glaze top with apricot jam or marmalade diluted with water to make a thin sauce.

APRICOT TART

Line a flan ring or pie plate with TART PASTE and sprinkle the paste with ½ cup sugar. Cover sugar with fresh apricots, peeled, pitted, and halved. Place the fruit cut side down in a spiral from the center, each half slightly overlapping the previous one. Bake in a moderate oven (350° to 375° F.) for 30 to 40 minutes, or until the crust is golden brown. When cool, spread the fruit with APRICOT GLAZE.

PEACH TART

Line a flan ring or pie plate with TART PASTE. Cover dough with peach wedges in an attractive pattern, each section slightly overlapping the previous one. Sprinkle fruit with ½ cup sugar and ½ teaspoon nutmeg or 1 teaspoon cinnamon. Dot generously with butter and bake in a moderate oven (350° F.) for 15 minutes. Beat egg yolk with 3 tablespoons heavy cream and drip over the fruit. Continue to bake for another 15 minutes, or until the dough is lightly browned and the fruit is tender.

UNCOOKED PEACH TART

Fill a baked TART SHELL level with whipped cream sweetened and flavored to taste. Put slices of fresh peaches over the cream and brush surface of the slices with a little apricot or peach jam heated with an equal amount of water. Sprinkle over all some blanched almonds, shredded and toasted in the oven to a golden brown.

UPSIDE-DOWN FRUIT TART

Spread a pie plate thickly with butter and sprinkle butter with ½ cup sugar. Cover sugar with apple quarters or peach or apricot halves. Sprinkle with a little more sugar, dot with butter, and cover fruit with a circle of TART PASTE. The edge may be fluted, but do not press it against the rim of the plate. Bake the tart in a hot oven (400° F.) for about 25 minutes, or until the crust is brown, the fruit is tender, and the sugar has started to caramelize. Test fruit by slipping the point of a knife under the crust.

Cover tart with the plate on which it is to be served, upside down. Quickly reverse plate and tart. The crust will be on the bottom and the fruit, glazed with syrup, will be on top. Serve warm with a big dollop of lightly whipped cream on each serving.

CHERRY TART

Line a flan ring with TART PASTE. Pit 1 pound dark sweet cherries and place them in the lined ring close together and in neat array. Sprinkle with ½ cup sugar and bake in a moderate oven (350° F.) for 25 to 30 minutes. When cool, glaze the cherries with diluted red currant jelly.

CHERRY TART COUNTRY-STYLE

TART PASTE
2 cups pitted sweet cherries
1 egg, beaten
3 tablespoons flour

½ cup heavy cream
1 tablespoon sugar
Pinch salt

Line a flan ring or pie plate with tart paste.
Cover dough with 2 cups cherries.

Combine remaining ingredients and pour over cherries.

Bake in a moderate oven (375° F.) for 30 to 35 minutes, or until the top is delicately browned.

BLACK CHERRY TART

3 tablespoons cornstarch	1 teaspoon vanilla
1¼ cups sugar	½ cup heavy cream, whipped
Pinch salt	½ cup water
½ cup cold milk	1 teaspoon lemon juice
1½ cups hot milk	2 cups pitted black cherries
3 egg yolks, beaten	Baked TART SHELL

In top of a double boiler beat cornstarch, ¼ cup of the sugar, the salt, and the cold milk, until smooth.

Gradually stir in hot milk and cook over a low flame, stirring constantly, until sauce is thickened. Then cook over boiling water for 10 minutes.

Stir a little of the hot sauce into the egg yolks, and gradually stir yolks into the rest of the sauce.

Cook over the boiling water for another 2 minutes, stirring constantly.

Remove cream from the fire, stir in vanilla, and let cool.

When cream is cool, fold in whipped cream.

Meanwhile, dissolve remaining sugar in the water and lemon juice, bring to a boil, and simmer for 5 minutes.

Add cherries, cover, and simmer gently for 15 minutes.

Remove cherries from syrup with a slit spoon and spread them on a platter to cool. Continue to cook syrup until it is thick.

Spread cream in the bottom of a baked tart shell.

Cover cream with cherries and pour the thickened syrup over them.

PRUNE PLUM TART

Wash 1 quart fresh prune plums, make four incisions lengthwise to within ½ inch of one end, and remove pits. Place plums, cut side up, in an attractive pattern in a flan ring or pie plate lined with TART PASTE. Sprinkle with ¾ cup sugar, 1 tablespoon lemon juice, and 1 teaspoon cinnamon. Dot with butter and bake in a moderate oven (350° F.) for 30 to 40 minutes, or until the crust is lightly browned and the fruit is tender.

BLUEBERRY TART

Line a flan ring or pie plate with TART PASTE. Wash and pick over 1 quart blueberries and put them in the lined pan. Sprinkle with ½ cup sugar, 2 tablespoons lemon juice, and 1 teaspoon cinnamon. Bake in a moderate oven (350° F.) for 15 minutes. Beat yolk of an egg with 3 tablespoons heavy cream and drip over the berries. Continue to bake for another 20 minutes, or until the crust is lightly browned.

GOOSEBERRY TART

Line a pie plate or flan ring with TART PASTE. Wash and pick over 1 quart ripe gooseberries and put them in the lined pan. Sprinkle with 1 cup sugar and bake in a moderate oven (350° F.) for 20 minutes. Beat the yolk of an egg with 3 tablespoons heavy cream and drip over the berries. Continue to bake for another 15 minutes, or until the dough is lightly browned and the fruit is tender.

STRAWBERRY TART

3 tablespoons flour
3 tablespoons sugar
1 egg
1 egg yolk
2 teaspoons gelatin (1 envelope)
¾ cup hot milk

2 egg whites, stiffly beaten
¾ cup heavy cream
2 tablespoons Jamaica rum
Baked TART SHELL
Strawberries
Red currant jelly

In a saucepan combine flour, sugar, egg, and egg yolk and beat until smooth.

Stir in gelatin and gradually add hot milk. Stir mixture over a low flame until it almost, but not quite, reaches the boiling point.

Then stir custard over a bowl of cracked ice until it is cool and begins to set.

Fold in egg whites, ½ cup of the cream, whipped, and the rum. Turn the cream into a baked tart shell.

Cover top closely with whole strawberries and glaze berries by brushing them with 2 tablespoons red currant jelly diluted with 1 tablespoon water to make a sauce.

Whip remaining cream and pipe a fluted border of cream around the edge of the tart.

PEACH TART A LA NAPOLITAINE

Spread a 1-inch-thick layer of PASTRY CREAM in a baked TART SHELL. Cover cream with fresh peach halves, poached until tender in syrup, or canned peach halves, cut side down. Spread the fruit with APRICOT GLAZE and sprinkle with shredded, blanched, toasted almonds.

PEAR TART A LA BOURDALOUE

Spread a 1-inch layer of BOURDALOUE CREAM in a baked TART SHELL. Over the cream arrange pear quarters, cooked in syrup, in a circle around the tart, overlapping the sections and leaving a small circle in the center of the tart uncovered. Brush fruit with red currant jelly diluted with a little warm water and sprinkle with crushed macaroon crumbs.

FRUIT CREAM TARTS

Other creams, such as FRANGIPANE CREAM, may be used to fill a TART SHELL. The cream may be covered with fresh or cooked berries, or with sliced fruit, fresh or canned.

CUSTARD PIE

4 eggs	2⅔ cups milk
⅔ cup sugar	1 teaspoon vanilla
½ teaspoon salt	Pastry for one-crust pie
½ teaspoon nutmeg	

Beat eggs with rotary beater until thoroughly blended.
Add sugar, salt, nutmeg, milk, and vanilla and stir until smooth.
Pour into pastry-lined pie plate (9-inch).
Bake at 425° F. for 15 minutes, reduce temperature to 350° F., and bake for 30 minutes longer, or until blade of a silver knife inserted in filling about 1 inch from pastry edge comes out clean.

COCONUT CUSTARD

Stir in 1 cup chopped shredded coconut before pouring filling into pie plate.

RASPBERRY CUSTARD

Mash 1 cup fresh or frozen raspberries and stir in 1 to 2 tablespoons sugar. When custard is cool, spread the raspberry mixture over surface of custard and serve with whipped cream.

CHOCOLATE FROSTED CUSTARD

Melt 1 square unsweetened chocolate and 2 tablespoons butter. Stir in ½ cup confectioners' sugar and 2 tablespoons cream. Spread the frosting over custard pie just before serving.

RICH CUSTARD PIE • *Crème de la Crème*

3 cups heavy cream	FLAKY PASTRY for one-crust
⅓ cup sugar	pie
6 egg yolks	½ cup brown sugar
Vanilla	Fruit sauce or SABAYON SAUCE

Heat cream over boiling water until it is hot but not scalding.
Stir in sugar until thoroughly dissolved.
Beat egg yolks lightly and pour over them the hot cream, stirring constantly.
Flavor with vanilla.
Line a 9-inch pie plate with flaky pastry and sprinkle the brown sugar over the bottom. Pour in custard.
Bake at 350° F. for 35 minutes, or until almost set in the center.
Serve with a fruit sauce or sabayon sauce.

RASPBERRY CUSTARD PIE

2 cups hot milk	1 box raspberries
4 tablespoons sugar	3 tablespoons sherry
6 egg yolks, beaten	Whipped cream
Pastry for one-crust pie	

Combine milk and sugar and pour gradually over the beaten egg yolks, stirring rapidly.

Line a 9-inch pie plate with pastry and strain into it the custard mixture.

Bake at 350° F. for 35 minutes, or until almost set in the middle. Cool.

Wash and pick over the raspberries and pass them through a fine sieve.

Sweeten the resulting purée with sugar to taste.

Pour the sherry over the surface of the custard, spread a layer of the raspberry purée on top, and serve with whipped cream.

PUMPKIN PIE

1½ cups canned pumpkin
¾ cup sugar
½ teaspoon salt
½ teaspoon ginger
¼ teaspoon nutmeg

3 eggs
1¼ cups milk
¾ cup cream
Pastry for one-crust pie
Whipped cream

Mix pumpkin, sugar, salt, and spices.

Add eggs, milk, and cream and blend well.

Pour into 9-inch pastry-lined pie plate and bake at 425° F. for 15 minutes.

Reduce temperature to 350° F. and bake 30 to 40 minutes longer, or until set.

Serve with whipped cream sweetened to taste and spiced with a little ginger.

RUM PECAN PUMPKIN PIE

Make filling as above but use ¼ cup dark rum in place of ¼ cup of the milk. Before pouring filling into pastry-lined pie plate, sprinkle pastry with ½ cup chopped pecans or walnuts.

CREAM OF PUMPKIN PIE

2 cups strained cooked
pumpkin, fresh, frozen, or
canned
2 teaspoons cinnamon
⅔ cup brown sugar

½ teaspoon ginger
½ teaspoon salt
2 cups heavy cream
2 eggs
Pastry for a one-crust pie

Combine pumpkin, cinnamon, sugar, ginger, and salt. Gradually beat in 1 cup of the cream (or blend all these in an electric blender).

Beat eggs with remaining cream and stir into pumpkin mixture. Mix thoroughly.

Pour into a 9-inch pie plate lined with pastry. Sprinkle top with additional cinnamon.

Bake in a preheated 325° F. oven for about 50 minutes, or until cream is set in center.

PECAN PIE

3 eggs	1 teaspoon vanilla
1 tablespoon sugar	¼ teaspoon salt
2 tablespoons flour	1 cup pecan halves
2 cups dark corn syrup	Pastry for one-crust pie

Beat eggs until light.

Mix sugar and flour, add it to the eggs, and beat well.

Stir in corn syrup, vanilla, salt, and pecans.

Pour mixture into a 9-inch pastry-lined pie plate and bake at 350° F. for 45 to 50 minutes, or until filling is set.

MOLASSES PECAN PIE

Make filling as above but use 1 cup sugar and 1 cup light or dark molasses in place of the 2 cups corn syrup. Pour filling into pastry-lined pie plate and dot with 1 tablespoon butter.

SHOOFLY PIE

1½ cups enriched flour	½ teaspoon soda
1 cup brown sugar	⅔ cup hot water
½ cup butter	⅔ cup molasses
¼ teaspoon salt	Pastry for one-crust pie

Make crumbs by combining flour, sugar, butter, and salt and rubbing mixture between hands.

Dissolve soda in hot water and combine with molasses.

Pour into a 9-inch pastry-lined pie plate. Top with crumbs.

Bake at 350° F. for 35 to 40 minutes, or until filling is set.

CHOCOLATE CAKE PIE

Pastry for one-crust pie
1 cup sugar
2 tablespoons all-purpose
flour
Pinch salt

3 eggs, separated
2 squares (ounces) unsweet-
ened chocolate, melted
1 cup rich milk

Make pastry, line a 9-inch pie plate, and chill.

Sift together sugar, flour, and salt.

Beat egg yolks until light and fluffy and stir in sifted dry ingredients.

Stir in melted chocolate and milk.

Beat egg whites until stiff and fold in the chocolate-egg yolk mixture.

Pour into prepared pan and bake at 450° F. for 15 minutes.

Reduce the temperature to 350° F. and bake for another 30 minutes.

LEMON CAKE PIE

½ cup butter
1 cup sugar plus 2 table-
spoons
4 eggs, separated
2 tablespoons all-purpose
flour

Grated rind of 1 lemon
Juice of 2 lemons
1 cup rich milk
Pastry for one-crust pie

Cream butter and sugar.

Beat egg yolks until light and stir into the butter-sugar mixture along with the flour and the grated lemon rind.

Add lemon juice and milk and mix thoroughly.

Beat egg whites until stiff and fold into the lemon custard.

Turn into a 9-inch pie plate, lined with pastry, and bake at 450° F. for 15 minutes.

Reduce oven temperature to 350° F. and bake for another 30 minutes.

VANILLA CREAM PIE

2 tablespoons flour	3 egg yolks
2 tablespoons cornstarch	1 teaspoon vanilla
½ teaspoon salt	1 tablespoon butter
⅔ cup sugar	Baked 9-inch TART SHELL
2 cups milk	

Blend flour, cornstarch, salt, and sugar in a saucepan.
Stir in milk and bring to a boil over low heat.
Cook until thickened, stirring constantly.
Stir in egg yolks lightly beaten with a little of the hot sauce.
Cook, stirring, over low heat for 2 minutes.
Stir in vanilla and butter. Cool slightly.
Pour into baked tart shell.
Serve cold.

CHOCOLATE CREAM PIE

Use VANILLA CREAM PIE recipe above but increase sugar to ¾ cup and add 2 squares unsweetened chocolate along with the milk.

ALMOND CREAM PIE

Use VANILLA CREAM PIE recipe above but use almond extract instead of vanilla and stir ½ cup toasted blanched slivered almonds into the cooked filling. Cool pie and top with whipped cream, sweetened to taste. Stud the cream with blanched toasted almonds.

BUTTERSCOTCH PIE

Use VANILLA CREAM PIE recipe above but use ¾ cup brown sugar in place of the ⅔ cup sugar. If desired, when pie is cool top with whipped cream, sweetened to taste, or with a 3-egg-white MERINGUE.

RUM CREAM FRUIT TART

Use VANILLA CREAM PIE recipe above but omit vanilla. Stir 2 tablespoons dark rum into the cooked filling. Cool pie and arrange halved peaches or apricots or whole berries on top of filling. Brush fruit with 4 tablespoons apricot jelly mixed with 1 tablespoon boiling water.

BANANA CREAM PIE

Line baked pastry shell with sliced bananas and pour VANILLA CREAM PIE filling over the slices. Cool pie, top with a 3-egg-white MERINGUE, and brown in oven. Just before serving press sliced bananas between meringue and pastry edge.

NESSELRODE PIE

Use VANILLA CREAM PIE recipe above. Stir in 2 tablespoons dark rum or 1 teaspoon rum flavoring and ½ cup cut-up maraschino cherries. Fold in ½ cup heavy cream, whipped. Garnish with additional whipped cream and sprinkle with grated unsweetened chocolate.

Meringue, whether a thin layer swirled prettily on top of creamy fillings or a veritable mountain, always adds a festive touch to pies.

For Extravagant Toppings: Use 4 egg whites
For Ordinary Toppings: Use 2 or 3 egg whites
For a Garnish: Use 1 egg white

MERINGUE

Beat egg whites until frothy. Add ¼ teaspoon cream of tartar and continue to beat until egg whites are stiff enough to hold a peak. Gradually beat in sugar, using 2 tablespoons sugar for each egg white, and beat until meringue is stiff and glossy.

Putting Meringue on Pies or Tarts: Pile meringue lightly on cooled pie, making sure it touches edges of pastry to prevent it from shrinking. With tablespoon or spatula swirl large graceful curls and bake at 425° F. until delicately browned, about 5 to 6 minutes.

LEMON MERINGUE PIE

1 *cup sugar*	1 *tablespoon butter*
Pinch salt	¼ *cup lemon juice*
¼ *cup enriched flour*	*Grated rind of 1 lemon*
3 *tablespoons cornstarch*	*Baked 9-inch* TART SHELL
2 *cups water*	MERINGUE
3 *eggs, separated*	

Combine sugar, salt, flour, and cornstarch and gradually stir in water.

Cook, stirring constantly, until thickened.

Gradually stir hot mixture into beaten egg yolks, return to low heat, and cook, stirring, for 2 minutes.

Stir in butter, lemon juice, and rind and cool slightly.

Pour into baked tart shell and cool.

Top with 3-egg-white meringue and brown in oven.

LIME MERINGUE PIE

Use lime in place of lemon in recipe above. Cautiously add a few drops of green food coloring to brighten color.

ORANGE MERINGUE PIE

Use orange juice in place of water in recipe for LEMON MERINGUE PIE. Add only 1 tablespoon lemon juice and use grated orange rind in place of lemon rind.

LEMON, LIME, OR ORANGE FLUFF PIE

Follow directions for LEMON, LIME or ORANGE MERINGUE PIE but do not top with meringue. Instead, cool filling slightly. Beat 3 egg whites until stiff but not dry and fold them into filling. Pour into baked pastry shell and chill.

RUM CREAM PIE

6 egg yolks	1 pint heavy cream, whipped
⅞ cup sugar	½ cup Jamaica rum
1 tablespoon (envelope)	Baked 9-inch PASTRY SHELL
gelatin	Shaved bittersweet chocolate
½ cup cold water	

Beat egg yolks until light, add sugar gradually, and continue to beat until mixture is thick and pale.

Soak gelatin in the cold water for 5 minutes, then place it over boiling water until it becomes very hot.

Strain gelatin into egg-sugar mixture and stir briskly to thoroughly combine.

Fold in whipped cream, stir in rum, and pour mixture into the baked pastry shell.

Chill until set, then cover top generously with shaved curls of chocolate.

CHOCOLATE ANGEL PIE

Make a MERINGUE PASTRY SHELL, folding into the meringue ¾ cup finely chopped walnuts or pecans and 1 teaspoon vanilla. Make a nestlike shell, building up the sides of the shell a good ½ inch above the edge of the plate. Bake at 300° F. for 50 to 55 minutes and allow it to cool.

4 ounces sweet chocolate	1 teaspoon vanilla
3 tablespoons strong black coffee	1 cup heavy cream, whipped

Melt chocolate with coffee over low heat, stirring until mixture is smooth.

Cool and stir in vanilla.

Fold this chocolate mixture into the whipped cream and turn into the meringue pastry shell.

Chill for 2 hours before serving.

BANANA CREAM

3 tablespoons cornstarch	3 egg yolks, well beaten
4 tablespoons sugar	1 banana
¼ cup cold milk	1 teaspoon vanilla
1½ cups hot milk	½ cup heavy cream, whipped
½ cup warm heavy cream	Baked 9-inch TART SHELL

In top of double boiler combine cornstarch and sugar.

Stir in cold milk and, gradually, the hot milk.

Stir mixture constantly over boiling water for about 10 minutes, or until thickened.

Stir in the warm cream and the beaten egg yolks and continue to cook, stirring, for another 5 minutes.

Remove cream from heat and stir in the banana, riced or mashed, and cool.

When cool, stir in vanilla and whipped cream.
Turn into tart shell.

BUTTERSCOTCH CREAM

1½ cups firmly packed brown
  sugar
9 tablespoons flour
Pinch salt
3 cups hot milk

3 egg yolks, beaten
3 tablespoons butter
2 teaspoons vanilla
Baked 9-inch TART SHELL
Whipped cream

In top of a double boiler combine sugar, flour, and salt.

Gradually stir in the hot milk and the beaten egg yolks and cook over boiling water, stirring constantly, until cream is smooth and thickened.

Cover pan, lower heat so water beneath does not boil, and cook the cream for 10 minutes longer.

Remove from heat and stir in butter and vanilla.

Turn into a 9-inch baked pie shell or into baked tart shells, cool, and top with whipped cream.

EGGNOG CREAM

3 large or 4 medium eggs,
  separated
⅓ cup sugar
1 tablespoon gelatin
1 cup hot milk

1 cup heavy cream
2 tablespoons dark rum
Baked 9-inch TART SHELL
Nutmeg

In top of double boiler beat egg yolks and sugar until thick and pale in color.

Stir in gelatin and, gradually, the hot milk.

Cook over boiling water, stirring, until cream is very hot, smooth, and thickened.

Stir over cracked ice until cream cools and begins to set.

Whip egg whites until stiff and whip cream until light and fluffy.

Fold beaten whites and half the whipped cream into the egg cream, stir in rum, and turn into the baked tart shell.

Decorate with the remaining whipped cream, dust with nutmeg, and chill in the refrigerator until ready to serve.

LEMON OR LIME CREAM

2 cups sugar
9 tablespoons flour
Pinch salt
2½ cups hot water
6 egg yolks, beaten
4 tablespoons butter

½ cup lemon or lime juice
1 teaspoon grated lemon or
   lime rind
Baked 9-inch TART SHELL
MERINGUE, optional

In top of double boiler combine sugar, flour, and salt.

Gradually stir in water and then the beaten egg yolks.

Cool mixture over boiling water, stirring constantly, until thickened and smooth.

Cover pan, reduce heat so water does not boil, and cook for 10 minutes.

Stir in butter, juice, and rind; cool.

Pour into a baked tart shell or individual tart shells, top with meringue if desired, and brown meringue in a hot oven (425° F.).

RICH CHOCOLATE PASTRY CREAM

2 eggs
2 egg yolks
6 tablespoons sugar
6 tablespoons flour
2 tablespoons gelatin
12 ounces (squares) semi-
   sweet chocolate

10 tablespoons strong coffee
1½ cups hot milk
4 egg whites, stiffly beaten
1 cup heavy cream, whipped
2 tablespoons Jamaica rum
Baked 9-inch TART SHELL

In saucepan beat eggs, egg yolks, sugar, and flour until light and fluffy.

Stir in gelatin.

Cut chocolate into small pieces, add coffee, and stir over a low flame until chocolate is melted and mixture is smooth.

Stir hot milk gradually into the chocolate and then stir this chocolate milk into the egg mixture.

Cook over low heat until cream is hot and thickened.

Stir over a bowl of cracked ice until cool.

Fold in egg whites, cream, and rum.

Turn into baked shell and serve.

RUM PASTRY CREAM

3 tablespoons flour	½ cup heavy cream, whipped
3 tablespoons sugar	Rum
1 egg	Baked 9-inch TART SHELL
1 egg yolk	Sliced fresh fruit or berries
2 teaspoons gelatin	Jelly glaze
¾ cup hot milk	Whipped cream
2 egg whites, stiffly beaten	

In a saucepan combine flour, sugar, egg, and yolk and beat until the mixture is smooth.

Stir in gelatin and gradually pour in the hot milk, stirring rapidly.

Stir cream over low heat until it almost reaches the boiling point, but do not let it boil.

Put saucepan over a bowl of cracked ice and stir until cream is cool and thick.

Fold in egg whites, the whipped cream, and a generous stream of dark rum.

Line tart shell or individual tartlet shells with the rum cream.

Cover with sliced fresh fruit or berries and coat fruit with a jelly glaze.

Pipe a fluted ring of whipped cream around edge.

FLAN MERINGUE

Fill a baked pastry shell with VANILLA, CHOCOLATE, or RUM PASTRY CREAM and chill. Put the pie on a heavy wooden board and spread top and sides with a thick, even layer of ORDINARY MERINGUE. Decorate top with circles and scrolls of meringue pressed through a small open-star tube, and sprinkle with fine granulated sugar. Bake in a very hot oven (450° F.) for about 5 minutes, or until the meringue is lightly browned. Fill center of the circles on the top *décor* with currant jelly or apricot marmalade.

CHIFFON PIES

APRICOT CHIFFON PIE

1 tablespoon gelatin
2 tablespoons cold water
3 eggs, separated
¾ cup sugar
½ cup canned apricot nectar
⅛ teaspoon salt

1 tablespoon lemon juice
1 cup cooked, dried apricots,
  puréed*
½ cup heavy cream, whipped
Baked 9-inch TART SHELL

Soak gelatin in cold water.

Combine egg yolks, ½ cup of the sugar, apricot nectar, and salt and cook over low heat until thickened, stirring constantly.

Remove from heat, add softened gelatin, and stir until dissolved.

Stir in lemon juice and apricot purée and cool until mixture begins to set.

Fold in whipped cream.

Beat egg whites until stiff and gradually beat in remaining sugar.

Fold gelatin mixture into egg whites, pile lightly into baked tart shell, and chill until firm.

CHERRY CHIFFON PIE

2 teaspoons gelatin
2 tablespoons cold water
4 eggs, separated
½ cup cherry juice
¼ teaspoon salt
¾ cup sugar
1½ teaspoons grated lemon
  rind

1½ cups red sour cherries,
  drained and chopped
Baked 8-inch TART SHELL
Whipped cream
Cherries

Soften gelatin in cold water.

Beat egg yolks and add cherry juice, salt, and ½ cup of the sugar. Cook over low heat until thickened, stirring constantly.

Remove from heat, add softened gelatin, and stir until dissolved. Cool slightly and stir in lemon rind and cherries.

* *Fruit Purée:* Press cooked fruit or berries or soft fresh or frozen fruits and berries through a fine sieve. Blend the resulting juice and pulp to make a purée.

Beat egg whites until stiff but not dry, gradually beat in the remaining sugar, and fold egg whites into gelatin mixture.

Pile lightly into baked tart shell and chill until firm.

Top with whipped cream and decorate with cherries.

CRANBERRY CHIFFON PIE

1 tablespoon gelatin	3 egg whites
¼ cup cold water	6 tablespoons sugar
1 cup jellied cranberry sauce	Baked 8-inch TART SHELL
⅛ teaspoon salt	Whipped cream
1 teaspoon grated lemon rind	Cranberry jelly, optional
2 teaspoons lemon juice	

Soak gelatin in water.

Heat cranberry sauce until steaming, add softened gelatin, and stir until thoroughly dissolved.

Stir in salt, lemon rind, and juice and cool until mixture begins to set.

Beat egg whites until stiff and gradually beat in sugar.

Fold in cranberry mixture and pour into pastry shell.

Chill until firm and top with whipped cream.

If desired decorate with mounds of whipped cream. Make a little hollow on top of each mound of cream and fill with a spoonful of cranberry jelly.

BLACK BOTTOM PIE

1 tablespoon gelatin	1 teaspoon vanilla
¼ cup cold water	Baked 9-inch TART SHELL
1 cup sugar	1 teaspoon rum flavoring
½ teaspoon salt	¼ teaspoon cream of tartar
4 tablespoons cornstarch	Whipped cream
2 cups milk	Shaved chocolate
4 eggs, separated	
6 ounces semi-sweet chocolate pieces	

Soften gelatin in water.

In a saucepan combine ½ cup of the sugar, salt, and cornstarch and gradually stir in milk.

Cook over low heat, stirring constantly, until thickened.

Stir the hot mixture slowly into beaten egg yolks, return to heat, and cook, stirring, for 2 minutes.

Remove from heat and blend 1½ cups of the mixture with the chocolate pieces.

Add vanilla and pour into baked pie shell. Chill.

Add gelatin to remaining custard mixture and cool to lukewarm. Add rum flavoring.

Beat egg whites and cream of tartar until stiff and gradually beat in remaining sugar.

Fold egg whites into the rum-flavored custard, pour over chocolate custard in baked pie shell, and chill.

Serve topped with whipped cream and garnished with shaved chocolate.

LEMON CHIFFON PIE

1 tablespoon (envelope) gelatin	Pinch salt
¼ cup cold water	4 eggs, separated
1 cup sugar	1 teaspoon grated lemon rind
½ cup lemon juice	Baked 9-inch TART SHELL
	Whipped cream, if desired

Soak gelatin in the cold water for 5 minutes.

In top of a double boiler combine ½ cup of the sugar, lemon juice, salt, and the slightly beaten yolks of eggs.

Cook over boiling water, stirring, until mixture coats the spoon.

Stir in softened gelatin and lemon rind and cool.

Beat egg whites until stiff.

Gradually beat in remaining sugar and continue beating until meringue is stiff and glossy.

Fold into the cooled custard, turn into baked shell, and chill.

Whipped cream may be spread on top at serving time, if desired.

ORANGE CHIFFON PIE

Make according to the directions for LEMON CHIFFON PIE. Substitute 1 teaspoon lemon juice, 1 tablespoon grated orange rind, and ½ cup orange juice for the lemon juice and rind.

LIME CHIFFON PIE

4 eggs, separated
1 cup sugar
½ cup lime juice
1 tablespoon (envelope) gelatin

½ cup cold water
Grated rind of 1 lime
Pinch salt
Baked 9-inch TART SHELL
Whipped cream

Beat egg yolks lightly and stir in ½ cup of the sugar and the lime juice.

Cook mixture over boiling water until it coats the spoon.

Soak gelatin in cold water for 5 minutes and stir into the hot custard.

Add rind and stir over cracked ice until mixture begins to thicken.

Beat egg whites with the salt until stiff and then gradually beat in remaining sugar and continue beating until meringue is thick and glossy.

Fold into the lime custard and pour into baked tart shell.

Just before serving, spread the surface with whipped cream.

BUTTERSCOTCH CHIFFON PIE

1 tablespoon (envelope) gelatin
¼ cup cold water
3 eggs, separated
1 cup hot milk

½ cup brown sugar
¼ teaspoon salt
1 teaspoon vanilla
1 cup heavy cream, whipped
Baked 9-inch TART SHELL

Soak gelatin in cold water for 5 minutes.

In top of double boiler combine egg yolks, hot milk, sugar, and salt and cook over boiling water until mixture coats the spoon, stirring constantly.

Add gelatin and stir until thoroughly dissolved. Cool.

Stir in vanilla and fold in stiffly beaten egg whites and whipped cream.

Turn into baked tart shell and chill well before serving.

RUM CHIFFON PIE

1 tablespoon (envelope) gelatin	Pinch salt
4 tablespoons dry white wine	½ cup heavy cream, whipped
1½ cups top milk	3 tablespoons Jamaica rum
¾ cup brown sugar	Baked 9-inch TART SHELL
3 eggs, separated	Grated sweet chocolate

Soak gelatin in the wine for 5 minutes.

Combine milk, sugar, egg yolks, and salt in top of a double boiler and cook over boiling water, stirring, until mixture coats the spoon.

Add softened gelatin and stir until thoroughly dissolved, then stir over cracked ice until custard is thick and cool.

Fold in stiffly beaten egg whites and whipped cream alternately with the rum.

Fill baked tart shell and grate a little sweet chocolate over top.

Chill thoroughly before serving.

STRAWBERRY CHIFFON PIE

1 tablespoon (envelope) gelatin	Pinch salt
¼ cup cold water	1 cup strawberry pulp and juice
4 eggs, separated	Baked 9-inch TART SHELL
1 tablespoon lemon juice	Whipped cream
¾ cup sugar	Whole strawberries

Soften gelatin in cold water.

In top of double boiler combine slightly beaten egg yolks, lemon juice, ½ cup of the sugar, and salt.

Cook over boiling water, stirring, until mixture coats the spoon.

Stir in softened gelatin and the strawberry pulp and juice and cool.

Beat egg whites until stiff.

Gradually beat in remaining sugar and continue beating until meringue is stiff and glossy.

Fold into the cooled strawberry custard and turn into baked tart shell.

Chill.

Before serving, spread the surface with a layer of whipped cream and decorate lavishly with whole hulled berries.

INDIVIDUAL PIES, TARTS, AND TURNOVERS

Small pies, tarts, and turnovers are individual desserts just large enough to serve one person.

Small Closed Pies: Pastry for a two-crust pie will make four 3¾-inch two-crust individual pies. Mix and handle the pastry according to directions for two-crust pies. Line tart shells, individual pie pans, or muffin cups with the pastry, flute the edges, and add any fruit filling desired just as you would for a two-crust pie. Cover with the top crust and bake at given temperature, reducing the baking time by about 10 minutes.

Open Small Pies or Tarts: Pastry for a two-crust pie will make eight 3-inch tarts. FLAKY PASTRY is especially nice for these little pastries, and variety pastries such as CREAM CHEESE are often suitable. Roll out the chilled dough to about ⅛ inch in thickness and cut it into twelve circles about 5 inches in diameter. Line plain or fluted tart shells, being careful not to stretch the dough. Trim the edge to about ½ inch beyond the edge of each pan. Moisten the rims of each pan with a little cold water, fold the overlapping edge back, and flute with the fingers or press with a fork. Use any of the fillings given for one-crust pies, such as CUSTARD, PUMPKIN, or LEMON CAKE, and bake at given temperature, reducing baking time by about 15 minutes.

To Bake Tart Shells: Line tart pans in the regular way. With a fork, prick small holes generously over the sides and bottom of each tart to prevent puffing and bake at 425° F. for 10 to 12 minutes, or until lightly browned. Attractive tart shells may be made by fitting the rounds of dough over the backs of muffin tins, pricking the dough thoroughly, and making six pleats at regular intervals around the shell.

Fresh Fruit or Berry Fillings: Pile fresh sliced fruit or berries into baked tart shells. Soften a little jelly over hot water, adding about 1 tablespoon of hot water to every 4 tablespoons of jelly used. Currant jelly is good for dark fruits such as blueberry or strawberry; a light-colored jelly should be used for peaches or apricots. Pour a little melted jelly over the fruit and place the tarts in the refrigerator. As the jelly sets again, it will give a shiny glaze to the fruit. Decorate with whipped cream before serving. Or fill the baked shells with sweetened and flavored whipped cream, place sliced fruit or berries on top, and glaze with jelly. Another day, spread 1 tablespoon whipped cream cheese in each shell and top with sugared fruit or berries.

Fruit and Cream Fillings: Baked tart shells may also be partially filled with PASTRY CREAM. The fruit is placed on top and glazed with melted jelly. A little whipped cream piped around the edge of each tart before serving adds an attractive touch.

Cream Fillings: The various creams, custards, meringue, and chiffon fillings used for large baked pastry shells are all suitable for tarts. Make the fillings according to the recipes in the chapter. The filling for a 9-inch baked pastry shell will fill eight 3-inch baked tart shells.

Turnovers: Roll out pastry ⅛ inch thick and cut into 4-inch rounds or squares. This is an excellent way to use leftover trimmings of pastry. Place marmalade, jam, chutney, or fruit fillings on half of each pastry, fold it over to form half a circle or a triangle, moisten the edges with a little water, and seal the edges by pressing them together with the tines of a fork. Prick small steam vents and bake at 425° F. for 15 minutes.

TARTES AUTRICHIENNES

8 large tart apples	½ teaspoon cinnamon
½ cup water	¼ pound butter
1¼ cups sugar	½ cup shredded blanched
½ cup seedless raisins	almonds
Juice of 1 lemon	Pastry for two-crust pie
Grated rind of 1 lemon	Heavy cream

Peel, quarter, and core apples and place them in a saucepan with water and sugar.

Bring to a boil and cook until apples are tender.

Put apples and juice through a fine sieve and add to the resulting purée the raisins, lemon juice, rind, cinnamon, and butter.

Return mixture to the heat and simmer for 15 minutes, or until thick, stirring occasionally.

Roll out pastry and line small tart pans.

Fill the lined pans with the apple mixture and bake at 425° F.

for 10 minutes. Sprinkle with almonds and bake for 10 minutes longer.

Serve hot with heavy cream.

BLACK CHERRY TARTS

3 tablespoons cornstarch	1 teaspoon vanilla
1¼ cups sugar	½ cup water
Pinch salt	2 cups black pitted cherries
½ cup cold milk	½ cup heavy cream, whipped
1½ cups hot milk	8 baked flaky pastry TART
3 egg yolks, beaten	SHELLS

In the top of a double boiler mix together the cornstarch, ¼ cup of the sugar, and salt.

Stir in cold milk to make a smooth mixture and then gradually add the hot milk, stirring constantly.

Stir mixture over low heat until thickened and smooth, place over boiling water, and cook for 10 minutes.

Stir a little of this hot thick mixture into the egg yolks and then gradually stir them into the rest of the thickened mixture. Continue to cook over boiling water for 2 minutes, stirring constantly.

Remove from heat, stir in vanilla, and cool.

In a saucepan combine remaining sugar and the ½ cup water. Bring to a boil and cook for 5 minutes.

Add cherries, cover, and simmer gently for 15 minutes.

Remove cherries from syrup with a slotted spoon and spread on a platter to cool.

Continue to cook syrup gently until very thick.

When custard is cool, fold into it the whipped cream and spread a layer of custard in each tart shell.

Cover custard with cherries and pour a teaspoon of the thickened syrup over the top of each.

FRESH PEACH TARTS

Fill baked TART SHELLS level with whipped cream sweetened and flavored to taste. Place over the cream slices of fresh peaches and brush the surface of the sliced peaches with a little apricot or peach jam, which has been heated with an equal amount of water. Sprinkle over all some blanched almonds, shredded and baked in the oven to a golden brown.

APRICOT RUM TARTS

⅓ cup brown sugar	2 tablespoons Jamaica rum
2 tablespoons cornstarch	12 baked TART SHELLS
1¼ cups apricot juice	12 apricot halves, fresh,
2 tablespoons butter	cooked, or canned
6 ounces cream cheese	1 cup heavy cream, whipped

Combine sugar and cornstarch.

Gradually stir in apricot juice and add butter.

Bring to a boil and cook for 15 minutes, stirring constantly, until smooth and thickened.

Beat cream cheese with the rum until smooth and whipped and place about 2 tablespoons in each tart shell.

Place a half apricot, rounded side up, on top of the cream cheese and pour over a good tablespoon of the thickened apricot juice.

Make a fluted edge of whipped cream around the edge of each tart.

STRAWBERRY TARTS

3 tablespoons all-purpose flour	½ cup heavy cream, whipped
3 tablespoons sugar	2 tablespoons Jamaica rum
1 egg	6 baked flaky pastry TART SHELLS
1 egg yolk	Strawberries, whole or halved
2 teaspoons gelatin	2 tablespoons currant jelly
¾ cup hot milk	¼ cup heavy cream
2 egg whites, stiffly beaten	

In a saucepan combine flour, sugar, egg, and egg yolk and beat until smooth.

Stir in gelatin and gradually add the hot milk.

Stir over low heat until almost boiling.

Place saucepan over a bed of cracked ice and stir until cool and beginning to set.

Stir in egg whites, ½ cup whipped cream, and rum.

Fill tart shells with this rum pastry cream.

Cover top with strawberries and glaze strawberries by brushing with currant jelly melted over a little warm water until thin enough to spread.

Whip the ¼ cup cream and use to pipe a line around edge of each tart.

RAISIN TARTLETS

FLAKY PASTRY *for two-crust*   1 *dozen walnut halves*
  pie   3 *tablespoons lemon juice*
1 *pound raisins*   ¼ *cup brown sugar*

Line twenty small tartlet pans with flaky pastry.

Put raisins and nuts through a food chopper, using a medium blade, and moisten with lemon juice.

Stir in 2 tablespoons of the brown sugar and place 1 tablespoon of the mixture in each prepared tartlet pan.

Sprinkle surface of each tart with a little of the remaining brown sugar and bake at 400° F. for 15 to 20 minutes.

TRANSPARENT TARTS

Pastry for two-crust pie   5 *eggs*
½ *cup butter*   3 *tablespoons lemon juice*
2 *cups sugar*

Line twelve tart pans with pastry.

Cream butter until soft, add sugar gradually, and cream together until light and fluffy.

Beat in eggs one at a time.

Stir in lemon juice and turn into prepared pans.

Bake at 400° F. for 5 minutes.

Reduce temperature to 350° F. and bake for about 10 minutes longer, or until firm.

FRUIT TURNOVERS

⅔ *cup cooked prunes*   ¼ *teaspoon salt*
⅓ *cup cooked apricots*   1 *tablespoon lemon juice*
¼ *cup sugar*   *Pastry for two-crust pie*
1 *tablespoon cornstarch*

Combine all filling ingredients and stir over a low flame for 5 minutes.

Roll out pastry ⅛ inch thick and cut into 4-inch squares.

Place a spoonful of filling on half of each square, moisten the edges, and fold the pastry over to form triangles.

Seal the edges by pressing them together with the tines of a fork, prick the surface to allow for the escape of steam, place on baking sheet, and bake at 425° F. for 15 minutes.

JAM-FILLED TURNOVERS

Roll pastry ⅛ inch thick and cut it into 4-inch circles. Place a tablespoon marmalade, jam, chutney, or fruit preserve on half of each round. Fold pastry over to form half a circle and seal by pressing together with tines of a fork. Prick small steam vents, place on a baking sheet, and bake at 425° F. for 10 to 12 minutes.

MARMALADE JALOUSIE

Roll one-half pastry for a two-crust pie ⅛ inch thick into a rectangle about 4½×15 inches. Transfer to a baking sheet and spoon a wide band of marmalade down the center. Roll other half of pastry to same dimensions, fold in half lengthwise, and cut slashes 1½ inches deep across the fold. Unfold, place over filling, and crimp edges. Bake at 400° F. for 12 to 15 minutes, or until browned.

CHERRY TURNOVERS

¼ cup sugar	1 cup red sour cherries,
1 teaspoon cornstarch	drained
⅛ teaspoon cinnamon	LEMON SAUCE
Pastry for a two-crust pie	

Combine sugar, cornstarch, and cinnamon.

Roll pastry ⅛ inch thick and cut into 4-inch squares.

Place a tablespoon of cherries on each square and sprinkle with 1 teaspoon sugar mixture.

Fold pastry over into triangles and seal.

Prick or slash top, place on baking sheet, and bake at 425° F. for 10 to 12 minutes.

Serve with lemon sauce.

APRICOT TURNOVERS

FLAKY PASTRY   Brown sugar
Apricot halves   Butter

Roll pastry ⅛ inch thick and cut it into 4-inch squares.

Place an apricot half on half of each pastry square and fill each hollow with 1 teaspoon brown sugar and ½ teaspoon butter.

Fold pastry over to make a triangle and seal.

Prick surface of each turnover and bake at 400° F. for 12 to 15 minutes.

PEACH TURNOVERS

To make peach turnovers cut pastry into 6-inch squares. Bake according to instructions for APRICOT TURNOVERS.

LEMON CURD TARTLETS

Grated rind from 1 lemon   Dash salt
Lemon juice from 1 lemon   ¼ cup butter
3 eggs, lightly beaten   8 baked 3-inch TART SHELLS
⅔ cup sugar   Whipped cream, optional

In top of a double boiler combine lemon rind, lemon juice, eggs, sugar, salt, and butter.

Cook over hot water, stirring frequently, until thickened. Cool. Spoon into tart shells.

Top with a large rosette of whipped cream, if desired. *Serves 8.*

CHOCOLATE PRALINE TARTLETS

½ cup semi-sweet chocolate   3 tablespoons cream
   pieces   ¼ cup (½ stick) soft butter
2 tablespoons boiling water   ¾ cup PRALINE POWDER
1 tablespoon dark rum   12 baked 2-inch TART SHELLS
2 egg yolks   Whipped cream

Into container of an electric blender put chocolate pieces and boiling water.

Cover and blend on high speed for 10 seconds, or until chocolate sauce is smooth.

Add rum, egg yolks, cream, butter, and praline powder.

Cover and blend on high speed for 10 seconds longer, stopping to stir down if necessary.

Fill tart shells with the chocolate cream and decorate each tartlet with a rosette of whipped cream. Chill until serving time. *Makes 12.*

CHAPTER 16

Fruit Desserts,
Hot and Cold

No man-made dessert in the world can surpass the beauty and flavor of a basket or bowl of fresh fruit to pass at table after a substantial main meal. It is simplicity itself, but is only a treat if the fruit are at their peak of perfection. You may feel it is something extra special to serve fresh persimmons or pomegranates, and so it is, but only if these imported specialties are perfectly matured and ready to eat. A basket of fresh Concord grapes in mid-September are equally as good as a slice of chilled honeydew melon in January, or a wedge of red, ripe watermelon in May.

Fruit or berries stewed with a small amount of water and sugar to taste are equally good to serve as a simple dessert, but the compote is only as good as the fruit you start with. Again, fruits for stewing should be fully ripe and full of juice and flavor.

The following chart is a guide to when fruits are in season to serve out of hand, stewed, baked, cooked in pies, made into puddings, or for use in various other kinds of desserts.

SEASONAL CHART FOR FRESH FRUIT

FRUIT	SEASON	USES
Apples		
Yellow Transparent	July–Aug.	Cooking
Gravenstein	July–Sept.	Eating, cooking
Wealthy	Aug.–Dec.	Eating, cooking
King David	Oct.–Nov.	Eating, cooking
Winter Banana	Oct.–Dec.	Eating, cooking
McIntosh, Grimes Golden	Oct.–Jan.	Eating, cooking
Spitzenberg, Jonathan, York Imperial	Oct.–Feb.	Eating, cooking
Rhode Island Greening, Northern Spy	Oct.–Mar.	Eating, cooking
Delicious, red and yellow	Oct.–Apr.	Eating
Stayman, Baldwin	Nov.–Apr.	Eating, cooking
Rome Beauty	Nov.–May	Cooking (especially good for baking)
Winesap, Yellow Newton	Jan.–May	Eating, cooking
Apricots	June–Aug.	Eaten out of hand, stewed, or fresh in fruit cups, puréed in creams, baked in pies and puddings, used to top ice cream.
Bananas	All year	Eaten out of hand, sliced fresh in fruit cups, on ice creams, and custards, baked with rum.
Berries		
Blackberries	June–Aug.	Fresh with sugar and cream, stewed, baked in pies and puddings, puréed for sauces and ices.
Blueberries and Huckleberries	May–Aug.	Fresh with sugar and cream, stewed, baked in pies and puddings.
Boysenberries	May–July	Fresh with sugar and cream, stewed, baked in pies and puddings, cooked and puréed for sauces.

FRUIT	SEASON	USES
Cranberries	Sept.–Feb.	Baked in cakes and pies, fresh puréed for whips and ices.
Dewberries	May–July	Fresh with sugar and cream, in fruit cups, or with custards and creams.
Elderberries	July–Aug.	Baked in pies and puddings.
Currants, red, white, and black	June–Aug.	Fresh, dipped in sugar, stewed, and baked in pies and puddings.
Gooseberries	June–Sept.	Baked in pies or puddings, stewed.
Loganberries	July–Aug.	Stewed or baked in pies and puddings.
Mulberries	July–Aug.	Stewed or baked in pies and puddings.
Raspberries	May–Aug.	Fresh with cream and sugar, in fruit cups, sherbets, and ice creams, baked in pies and puddings.
Strawberries	Dec.–Sept. Peak: June –July	Fresh with cream and sugar, in fruit cups, tart shells, puréed in sherbets, ice creams, molded desserts, and custards, as garnish for many desserts.
Youngberries	July–Aug.	Fresh with cream and sugar, in fruit cups, or baked in pies and puddings.
Cherries	May–Sept. Peak: June	Sweet, eaten from hand, pitted in fruit cups, stewed as topping for puddings and ice creams. Sour, baked in pies and puddings.
Dates		
Fresh	Sept.–Dec.	Eaten out of hand or halved, pitted, and served with cream.
Dried	All year	Baked in cakes, puddings, muffins, puréed as filling for cakes and cookies.
Figs		
Fresh	June–Aug.	Eaten out of hand, sliced and served with cream or marinated in wine.
Dried	All year	Baked in cakes, puddings, muffins.
Grapefruit	All year Peak: Nov. –Feb.	Fresh in fruit cups, broiled, or baked.

Grapes

Catawba	Aug.–Sept.	Eaten out of hand, juiced for jams and preserves.
Concord	Sept.–Nov.	Eaten out of hand, juiced for jams and preserves.
Emperor	Nov.–Dec.	Eaten out of hand, sliced in fruit cups.
Flame Tokay	Sept.–Nov.	Eaten out of hand, sliced in fruit cups.
Niagara	Sept.–Nov.	Eaten out of hand, juiced for jams and preserves.
Red Malaga	Aug.–Sept.	Eaten out of hand, sliced in fruit cups.
Ribier (imported most of the year)	Aug.–Oct.	Eaten out of hand, sliced in fruit cups.
Thompson Seedless	July–Oct.	Eaten out of hand, halved or whole in fruit cups.
White Malaga	Aug–Sept.	Eaten out of hand, halved in fruit cups.
Kumquats	Dec.–Jan.	Eaten out of hand, in fruit cups, cooked in puddings, puréed for sauces, and stewed.
Lemons	All year	Juiced for flavoring pies, puddings, creams, and sauces.
Limes	All year Peak: Sept.	Juiced for flavoring pies, puddings, creams, and sauces.
Mangoes	May–Aug.	Eaten out of hand or sliced in fruit cups, marinated in wine, or stewed, chilled, halved, and eaten like a melon.

Melons

Cantaloupe	April–Oct.	Halved or sliced, in fruit cups.
Casaba	July–Dec.	Halved or sliced, in fruit cups.
Honeydew	Feb.–Nov.	Halved or sliced, in fruit cups.
Persian	June–Oct.	Halved or sliced, in fruit cups.
Santa Claus	Nov.–Dec.	Halved or sliced, in fruit cups.
Watermelon	May–Aug.	Halved or sliced, in fruit cups, candied rind.
Nectarines	July–Aug.	Eaten out of hand, sliced with cream and sugar, stewed, baked in pies and puddings, puréed for ice cream and creams.

Oranges

Navel	Dec.–May	Eaten out of hand, sections in fruit cups, juices as flavoring for puddings, creams, ice creams, stewed for preserves and marmalades.

Temple	Dec.–Jan.	Eaten out of hand, sections in fruit cups, juices as flavoring for puddings, creams, ice creams, stewed for preserves and marmalades.
Valencia	May–Nov. (Calif.) Mar.–June (Fla.)	Eaten out of hand, sections in fruit cups, juices as flavoring for puddings, creams, ice creams, stewed for preserves and marmalades.
Other Varieties	Locally, year-round	Eaten out of hand, sections in fruit cups, juices as flavoring for puddings, creams, ice creams, stewed for preserves and marmalades.
Peaches	June–Sept.	Eaten out of hand, sliced with cream and sugar, stewed, baked in pies and puddings, puréed for ice cream and creams.

Pears

Bartlett	July–Oct.	Eating, cooking
Flemish Beauty	Sept.–Nov.	Cooking
Howell	Sept.–Nov.	Eating, cooking
Seckel, Bosc	Sept.–Dec.	Eating, cooking
Comice	Oct.–Feb.	Eating
Anjou	Oct.–April	Eating
Keiffer	Oct.–Dec.	Cooking
Winter Nelis	Jan.–June	Eating, cooking
Persimmons	Oct.–Feb.	Whole or halved on dessert plate, served with knife and spoon. Puréed in mousses and gelatin desserts, baked in pies and puddings.
Pineapple	All year	Fresh in fruit cups, marinated in wine, baked in puddings and cakes.
Plums	June–Oct.	Eaten out of hand, stewed, baked in pies, cakes, and puddings.
Pomegranates	Oct.–Dec.	Whole on dessert plate, served with knife and spoon. Juiced for flavoring sauces, puddings, and creams.
Quince	Sept.–Nov.	Stewed in compotes, or baked in pies and puddings.
Rhubarb	April–July	Stewed in compotes, or baked in pies and puddings.
Tangerines	Nov.–Mar.	Eaten out of hand, in fruit cups, sections good for garnish.

MARINATED FRUIT

Fresh fruit or berries or a mixture of fruit and berries, lightly sugared and allowed to soak for an hour or longer in a favorite liqueur, liquor, or wine make excellent desserts after a rich meal.

Following are suggested wines and liquors which may be used to marinate fruit, or you may use a combination of a liquor and a wine.

Sweet liqueurs should be used cautiously, or the flavor will be overpowering. When sliced fruit or berries are sugared they usually draw enough juice upon standing to blend with and dilute the liqueur, otherwise the liqueur should be mixed with a little fruit juice or white wine. Favorite liqueurs to serve with fruit are: apricot liqueur, anisette, Benedictine, Chartreuse, cherry liqueur, Cointreau, crème de cassis, crème de menthe, curaçao, Drambuie, Grand Marnier, kümmel, strega, maraschino, triple sec, Van der Hum,. or Vieille Cure.

Brandies and other spirituous liquors are not sweet like the above liqueurs. Their sugar content is less than 2½ per cent. Again, these liquors should be used lightly, and slightly more sugar can be used than with the liqueurs. Excellent brandies and liquors for marinating fruit, alone or in combination with fruit juice or white wine are: cognac, armagnac, fine champagne, kirsch (cherry brandy), slivovitz and mirabelle (prune brandies), eau-de-vie de framboise (raspberry brandy), aquavit, and rum.

Fortified wines may be used more generously to marinate fruit than liqueurs or brandies. Marsala, Madeira, port, sherry, or Dubonnet are all excellent and should be used with very little sugar. The red wines are apt to discolor such fruit as melons or peaches and are best used for the dark fruit and berries—strawberries, raspberries, cherries, prunes, or plums. Again they may be combined with a white wine or champagne.

Wines. Usually only the white wines or a vin rosé are used to marinate fruit and may be used generously and combined with fruit or berries and sugar to taste. Sweet wines such as a Sauternes are excellent, so, too is champagne, which should not be too dry. White wine or champagne with a dash of brandy or liqueur as marinating liquid for fruits and berries is delicious.

Spices. A whisper of a spice may be added to marinating fruit, but the choice should be carefully considered. Cinnamon is good with white wine; a pinch of nutmeg may be used with cognac; ginger is a delightful addition to many combinations of wine and liquors, and candied ginger minced and mixed into the fruit is excellent—try it with white wine and rum. Fresh, chopped mint leaves are also delicious with white wine or liquor.

STRAWBERRIES AND PINEAPPLE WITH KIRSCH

1½ cups strawberries, rinsed and hulled	½ cup sugar
	½ cup water
1½ cups fresh diced pineapple	2 tablespoons kirsch

Mix fruit, put into serving bowl, and chill.

Combine sugar and water, bring to a boil, and simmer for 5 minutes.

Chill.

About 1 hour before serving, add kirsch to the syrup, pour it over the fruit, and garnish with fresh mint leaves. *Serves 4.*

BERRIES CHANTILLY

1 quart strawberries or raspberries	1 cup heavy cream
	3 tablespoons kirsch
½ cup confectioners' sugar	

Prepare the fruit. Leave raspberries whole, but cut strawberries in half.

Sprinkle with sugar and chill for 30 minutes.

Whip cream until stiff and fold in the kirsch.

Fold berries into the cream and keep cold until ready to serve.

This dessert looks attractive served in sherbet glasses and garnished with a few whole berries. *Serves 6.*

PINEAPPLE WITH RUM AND WHITE WINE

1 large fresh pineapple	¼ cup light rum
1 cup sugar	1 cup white wine

Cut top from the pineapple and remove pulp, leaving a shell.
Dice pulp and return it to the shell in layers alternately with the sugar.

Pour over fruit the rum and white wine.

Chill for 2 hours before serving. *Serves 4 to 6.*

MIXED FRUIT IN BRANDY · *Mélange des Trois Fruits*

1 cup fresh raspberries	½ cup brandy
1 cup fresh strawberries	1½ cups sugar
1 cup fresh Bing cherries, halved and pitted	

Combine all ingredients in a stone crock or large glass jar.

Stir thoroughly and cover tightly.

Let stand in a cool place or refrigerate for several days to let the flavors blend, stirring at least once each day. It will keep for 3 to 4 weeks.

Serve over ice cream. *Makes 1½ pints.*

STRAWBERRIES ROMANOFF

1 pint strawberries, fresh or partially defrosted frozen	¼ cup curaçao or Grand Marnier
1 cup orange juice	1 pint vanilla ice cream

Pour orange juice over berries and let steep at least 30 minutes in refrigerator.

Stir in liqueur.

Serve ice cream on chilled plates; top with flavored berries.

Serves 6.

FIGS IN CURACAO

12 fresh figs, peeled and quartered	1 cup sour or sweet cream
1 tablespoon cognac	⅓ cup curaçao

Marinate figs in the cognac 30 minutes or longer.

Mix cream and curaçao.

Fold in figs and any cognac which they have not absorbed.

Serves 6.

ORANGE COMPOTE

6 *oranges*	1 *cup crushed pineapple*
1 *cup orange marmalade*	¼ *cup rum*

Peel oranges so that no white remains.

Cut into segments, discarding seeds.

Simmer marmalade and pineapple 5 minutes, add rum, pour over oranges.

Chill. *Serves 6.*

PEACHES MELBA • *Pêches Melba*

1 *package frozen raspberries*	1 *tablespoon cold water*
½ *cup currant jelly*	6 *canned peach halves*
1½ *teaspoons cornstarch*	*Vanilla ice cream*

Place raspberries in a saucepan and allow to thaw.

Mash berries with a spoon, add jelly, and bring to a boil over low heat.

Add cornstarch mixed with water and cook, stirring, until clear.

Strain, if desired, and cool.

Place a canned peach half, cut side up, in each of 6 individual dessert dishes.

Top each with a scoop of ice cream and pour the cooled sauce over the top. *Serve 6.*

PEACHES IN COINTREAU

2 *pounds fresh peaches*	¼ *cup lemon juice*
1 *cup sugar*	½ *cup slivered blanched*
½ *cup (1 stick) butter*	*almonds*
½ *cup Cointreau*	

Peel, halve, and stone peaches.

Arrange cut side up, one layer deep in a shallow baking pan.

Cream together sugar and butter, spread mixture over peaches.

Pour over the Cointreau and lemon juice.

Sprinkle with almonds.

Bake in 375° F. oven for 25 minutes. *Serves 6.*

FRUIT BAKED IN WINE

4 apples or pears
⅔ cup red wine
½ cup sugar
1 small stick cinnamon

4 whole cloves
Pinch salt
½ lemon, thinly sliced

Place fruit in a buttered baking dish.

Combine and heat the wine and sugar with the cinnamon, cloves, salt, and lemon slices.

Pour hot wine over fruit, cover, and bake in a preheated 350° F. oven for about 40 minutes, or until fruit is tender. *Serves 4.*

FIGS ROYALE

8 large fresh figs
1½ cups water
½ cup chopped walnuts

3 tablespoons honey
½ cup port wine
½ cup heavy cream, whipped

In a saucepan combine figs and water. Bring to a boil, cover, and simmer for 30 minutes, or until figs are very plump.

Remove figs from heat, drain, and cool.

In a small bowl combine nuts and honey.

Make a slit in each fig and stuff with some of the nut mixture.

Arrange figs in buttered baking pan and pour port wine over them.

Bake in a preheated 325° F. oven for 15 minutes, or until hot.

Serve hot with whipped cream. *Serves 4.*

PRUNES IN PORT WITH CREAM

1 pound dried prunes
2 cups port wine
1 cup sugar

1 teaspoon vanilla
1 cup cream, whipped
6 macaroons, crushed

Soak prunes overnight in half the port wine.

Next day add sugar, remaining wine, vanilla.

Bring to a boil, simmer 30 minutes.

Cool and chill.

To serve, cover with whipped cream, sprinkle with macaroon crumbs. *Serves 6.*

BANANAS FLAMBE · *Bananes Flambées*

4 medium bananas	¼ teaspoon cinnamon
¼ cup brown sugar, packed	½ cup sherry
½ cup fresh orange juice	1 tablespoon butter
¼ teaspoon nutmeg	2 tablespoons light rum

Peel bananas and split in half lengthwise.
Place in a buttered 10×6×2-inch baking dish.
Combine brown sugar with orange juice, spices, and sherry.
Heat and pour over bananas.
Dot with butter and bake in a preheated 450° F. oven for 15 minutes. Remove from oven, pour over rum, and flambé.

Serves 8.

CHERRIES JUBILEE

1 can pitted black cherries	1 quart vanilla ice cream,
1 tablespoon sugar	optional
1 tablespoon cornstarch	
¼ cup warmed kirsch or cognac	

Drain cherries, reserving juice.
Mix sugar with cornstarch and add one cup of reserved juice, a little at a time.
Cook three minutes, stirring constantly.
Add cherries and pour kirsch over the top.
Ignite kirsch and ladle the sauce over the cherries.
Serve over vanilla ice cream if desired. *Serves 6.*

PEARS BORDELAISE · *Poires à la Bordelaise*

6 fresh pears	1 3-inch piece stick cinnamon
Lemon juice	1 small piece lemon peel
½ cup red Bordeaux wine	2 tablespoons warm rum or
1 cup sugar	cognac, optional

Peel and core pears, cutting each into lengthwise halves. To prevent pears from darkening, brush with lemon juice or drop into water containing a little lemon juice.
In a saucepan combine wine, sugar, cinnamon, and lemon peel.

Bring to a boil, stirring.

Add 2 or 3 pear halves at a time and cook gently until tender. Repeat the process until all pears have been cooked.

Cook syrup until reduced to about one-half the original quantity. Pour over pears and chill.

If desired, add rum before serving. Pour over the pears and ignite at the table. *Serves 6.*

PEARS MARY GARDEN • *Poires Mary Garden*

4 table pears	1 teaspoon cornstarch
1 cup sugar	1 tablespoon kirsch
Water	¼ cup candied cherries
½ cup raspberry jam	1 cup whipped cream

Peel pears, cut in half, and remove cores.

Boil sugar and one cup water together three minutes, stirring until sugar has dissolved.

Add pears, lower heat, and simmer until pears are tender.

Cool pears in syrup, then drain.

Heat jam, stirring, until softened. Strain.

Mix cornstarch with one tablespoon cold water and add to the strained jam. Bring to a boil and cook, stirring, for a few minutes.

Cook and add kirsch.

Pour warm water over candied cherries and let stand until soft. Drain and dry. Add to jam mixture.

To serve, turn raspberry-cherry sauce into a serving dish, arrange the cooled pears over the sauce and garnish with the whipped cream, using a pastry tube if desired. *Serves 4.*

PEARS MELBA WITH KIRSCH • *Poires Melba au Kirsch*

Water	1 teaspoon cornstarch
Sugar	Kirsch, optional
½ teaspoon vanilla extract	Slivered blanched almonds
3 peeled ripe pears, halved	
1 package frozen raspberries, defrosted	

Combine 1½ cups each water and sugar and boil 5 minutes. Add vanilla and pears and simmer until fruit is tender. Drain and chill.

Combine raspberries with 1 tablespoon sugar.

Mix cornstarch with 2 tablespoons cold water and combine with raspberries. Simmer 3 minutes and mash through a sieve. Chill and add kirsch to taste.

Spoon over the pears and sprinkle with almonds. *Serves 6.*

PEARS HELENE · *Poires Hélène*

3 *ripe pears*	6 *rounds of spongecake,*
2 *cups water*	*optional*
⅔ *cup sugar*	*Crystallized violets*
1 *teaspoon vanilla extract*	*Hot fudge sauce*
1 *quart vanilla ice cream*	

Peel, halve, and core the pears.

Combine water and sugar and bring to a boil.

Add pears and reduce heat.

Simmer, covered, for about 5 minutes, or until pears can be pierced easily with a fork.

Add vanilla and let pears cool in the syrup.

At serving time, divide ice cream on six dessert plates.

If desired, set the ice cream on rounds of spongecake.

Drain the syrup from the pears.

Place a half pear, rounded side up, on each portion of ice cream and garnish with violets.

Serve the hot fudge sauce separately. *Serves 6.*

NOTE: Canned pear halves may be substituted. Omit the cooking and flavor the syrup from the can to taste with vanilla. Let the pears stand in the syrup three hours before serving.

PEARS WITH GINGER

6 *firm cooking pears*	⅛ *teaspoon powdered ginger*
Water	1 *slice lemon*
¾ *cup sugar*	

Peel pears, cut in half, and remove cores.

Drop pears into 2 cups boiling water, cover, and simmer 10 minutes.

Add sugar, ginger, and lemon, cover and cook until tender, or 10 to 15 minutes.

Cool. *Serves 6.*

PRUNE WHIP WITH PORT

½ pound dried prunes	*1 cup heavy cream*
Water	*3 tablespoons confectioners'*
⅔ cup granulated sugar	*sugar*
Lemon rind	*Slivered blanched almonds*
1 cup port wine	

Soak prunes overnight in water to cover. Drain.

Add sugar, lemon rind, and fresh water to cover. Bring to a boil and cook until prunes are tender.

Drain, add port, and cook 10 minutes longer.

Remove stones and put prunes through a sieve, or purée in an electric blender. Add a little more port if necessary to make the prunes moist; add sugar, if needed, to taste.

Whip cream and mix half of it with prunes. Sweeten remaining cream with confectioners' sugar and use as a garnish.

Top with almonds. *Serves 4.*

STRAWBERRIES CARDINAL • *Fraises Cardinal*

1 quart fresh strawberries	*1 tablespoon kirsch*
¼ cup raspberry jam	*¼ cup slivered blanched*
2 tablespoons sugar	*almonds*
¼ cup water	

Wash and hull strawberries.

Combine jam, sugar, and water in a saucepan and simmer about 2 minutes.

Add kirsch and chill.

Arrange strawberries in 4 individual serving dishes.

Pour chilled raspberry sauce over the fruit and sprinkle with the slivered almonds. *Serves 4.*

STRAWBERRIES JUBILEE · *Fraises Jubilé*

½ cup water
⅓ cup sugar
2 teaspoons arrowroot or
  cornstarch

1 pint strawberries, washed
  and hulled
2 ounces kirsch
1 quart vanilla ice cream

Mix water, sugar, and arrowroot.
Bring to a boil, stirring, and add strawberries.
Return to a boil, stirring only enough to blend.
Add kirsch and ignite.
Serve the flaming sauce and strawberries over ice cream. *Serves 6.*

AMBROSIA

2 large oranges, peeled and
  sectioned
3 bananas, thinly sliced

¼ cup confectioners' sugar
  or to taste
1½ cups shredded coconut

Arrange alternate layers of oranges and bananas in serving bowl, sprinkling each layer with sugar and coconut.
Top with coconut and chill thoroughly before serving. *Serves 4.*

STEWED APPLES · *Pommes Etuvée*

2 pounds (about 6 medium)
  tart cooking apples
¾ cup water
1 tablespoon grated lemon
  rind

½–¾ cup sugar, depending
  on tartness of apples

Peel, core, and thinly slice apples.
Combine in saucepan with water, lemon rind, and sugar.
Bring to a boil, stirring until sugar dissolves; reduce heat, cover tightly, and simmer for 20 minutes, or until tender.
Serve warm or cold, plain or with cream or whipped cream.
Serves 6.

APPLESAUCE

4 pounds tart cooking apples,
  peeled, cored, and quartered
1½ cups water

½–1 cup sugar
½ teaspoon cinnamon or
  nutmeg if desired

In saucepan combine apples and water.

Bring to a boil, cover tightly, and simmer for 20 minutes, or until apples are tender, stirring occasionally.

Press apples through food mill or blend apples and liquid in an electric blender.

Sprinkle sugar to taste over hot applesauce and stir until dissolved.

Stir in cinnamon or nutmeg if desired.

Serve warm or cold, plain or with cream, or spoon over hot gingerbread. *Serves 8.*

GLAZED BAKED APPLES

6 large tart baking apples
¾ cup seedless raisins
¼ cup brown sugar
1 teaspoon cinnamon

1 tablespoon grated lemon
  rind
1 cup granulated sugar
½ cup hot water
2 tablespoons butter

Wash, core, and peel apples halfway down from stem.

Place in shallow buttered baking dish.

Combine raisins, brown sugar, cinnamon, and lemon rind, and fill centers of apples with the mixture.

Combine granulated sugar and water. Bring to a boil, remove from heat, and stir in butter. Pour hot syrup over apples.

Bake in a preheated 350° F. oven for 45 to 60 minutes, or until apples are tender, basting frequently with the syrup in pan.

Serve hot with cream or cool, basting frequently with syrup in pan as apples cool to make a thick glaze. *Serves 6.*

SAUTEED APPLES • *Pommes Sautées*

3 large tart cooking apples
½ cup brown sugar
1 teaspoon cinnamon

⅛ teaspoon salt
6 tablespoons butter or
  margarine

Wash and core apples and cut into ½-inch-thick slices.

In small bowl combine brown sugar with cinnamon and salt.

In large frying pan melt butter or margarine and in it arrange a few apple slices. Sprinkle each slice with a little sugar-cinnamon mixture and sauté over low heat for about 5 minutes; turn; sprinkle with more sugar and cinnamon and continue to cook until apple slices are tender.

Keep warm until all apples are fried, and serve with sour cream. *Serves 4.*

APRICOTS MELBA • *Abricots Melba*

1 cup sugar	1 teaspoon vanilla
½ cup water	1 quart vanilla ice cream
Pinch salt	RASPBERRY SAUCE
8 whole fresh apricots, peeled,* halved, and pitted	

In saucepan combine sugar, water, and salt. Bring to a boil, stirring, and cook until sugar is dissolved.

Add apricots and simmer for 3 to 5 minutes, or until barely tender. Cool, add vanilla, then chill in the syrup.

Spoon ice cream into individual serving dishes or glasses.

Arrange 4 drained apricot halves over each serving and top with raspberry sauce. *Serves 4.*

GLAZED PEACHES

4 large peaches, peeled, halved, and stoned	2 tablespoons light corn syrup
½ cup water	1 tablespoon lemon juice
½ cup sugar	Pinch salt
	1 tablespoon butter

Slice peaches into a 1-quart buttered baking dish.

In small saucepan combine remaining ingredients. Bring to a boil, stirring until sugar is dissolved.

Pour hot syrup over peaches and dot with butter.

Cover tightly and bake in a preheated 325° F. oven for 30 minutes.

Serve warm with plain or whipped cream. *Serves 4.*

* To peel apricots, drop into simmering water for 1 to 2 minutes, then remove peel.

GINGERED PEARS

1½ cups sugar
1 cup water
Grated rind of 1 lemon
3 tablespoons lemon juice

2 slices candied ginger,
  chopped
1½ pounds cooking pears,
  pared, quartered, and cored

In saucepan combine sugar, water, lemon rind and juice, and ginger.

Bring to a boil, stirring until sugar is dissolved.

Add pears, reduce heat, and simmer for 30 minutes, or until pears are tender.

Serve warm or cold, plain or with cream. *Serves 6.*

After a rich or heavy meal, one of the most satisfying desserts is a bowl or basket of fresh fruit served with cheese.

FRUIT AND CHEESE

While any cheese which you prefer is a suitable cheese to serve for dessert, the ones that complement fruit best are any of the blue-veined cheeses such as Danish blue, Roquefort, Gorgonzola, or Stilton; the soft-ripening cheeses such as Brie, Camembert, or Liederkranz; the semi-soft such as Bel Paese, Pontina, Muenster, Oka, Pont-l'Evêque, Port du Salut, or Reblochon, or any one of the firm cheeses such as a really fine, aged Cheddar, Edam, Gouda, Gruyère, Provolone, or Swiss.

The most suitable cheeses to serve with berries are the cream varieties such as American cottage or cream cheese, crema Danica, crème Chantilly, petit Suisse, ricotta, or triple crème.

With the cheese or with the cheese and fruit, always serve a loaf of crusty French or Italian bread—never crackers.

Here are a few cheese and fruit desserts which you may wish to try:

HOMEMADE PETIT SUISSE

2 packages (3 ounces each)
    cream cheese
2 teaspoons confectioners'
    sugar
2 tablespoons cream

Beat cheese until soft.
Beat in the sugar and cream.
Pack into a small round-bottomed dish and chill.
When ready to serve, unmold and serve with fresh berries. *Serves 4.*

HEART OF CREAM · *Coeur à la Crème*

1 pound cottage cheese
1 pound cream cheese
Pinch salt

2 cups heavy cream
Bar-le-Duc, wild strawberry
    jam, or strawberries

Thoroughly combine cottage cheese, cream cheese, and salt.
Gradually add the heavy cream, beating constantly, until mixture is smooth.
Turn cheese into a heart-shaped basket lined with moist cheesecloth and place basket on a deep plate in the refrigerator to drain overnight.
When ready to serve, unmold the heart onto a chilled serving platter and serve with jam or surround with fresh strawberries. *Serves 6.*

CHEESE AND FRUIT PARFAIT

1 cup cream-style cottage
    cheese
1 cup heavy cream, whipped
1 egg white

Pinch salt
Stewed fruit or sweetened
    fresh fruit or berries

Press cottage cheese through a fine sieve and beat until smooth.
Fold in whipped cream.
Beat egg white with salt until stiff and fold in.
Alternate spoonfuls of the cheese mixture and the fruit in a glass serving bowl or in parfait glasses.
Chill thoroughly before serving. *Serves 8.*

BERRIES IN CHEESE SAUCE

1 *quart strawberries or raspberries*	4 *tablespoons heavy cream*
2 *packages (3 ounces each) cream cheese*	⅓ *cup confectioners' sugar*

Wash berries; hull strawberries, or pick over raspberries, and chill.

Beat cream cheese until soft and smooth. Beat in cream and sugar and chill.

About 1 hour before serving, set aside a few of the best berries for garnish. Fold remaining berries into the cream-cheese sauce and keep cold until ready to serve.

Garnish with the reserved berries.

Serve with crusty French bread. *Serves 4.*

CHAPTER 17

Ice Creams, Ices,
and
Frozen Desserts

In 1786, a Mr. Hall of Chatham Street, New York City, advertised ICE CREAM FOR SALE. Americans were quick to approve the frozen cream, and today we are the largest ice-cream-eating nation in the world. Ice cream is as American as Pike's Peak, and yet honor for its invention goes, once again, to a Frenchman, chef to the Duc de Chartres, who, one hot day in 1774, set before the duke a dish of cool, smooth cream.

A fancy ice was served to Louis XIV as early as 1660 by a Florentine, Procope, but this was probably a variation of one of the highly esteemed Italian ices, whose secrets followed Catherine de'Medici to France, and was not ice cream as we know it today.

Concluding a meal with a cold dessert was not a new idea even in the seventeenth century. Poet Chaucer gathered freshly fallen snow, sweetened it with honey, and flavored it with rosemary to refresh his palate and aid digestion. Chaucer's "Dishe of Snowe" was no novelty. The extravagant Romans had discovered—as they discovered many another sensuous delight—that a dish of ice, served between the highly seasoned courses of their banquets, brought grateful coolness to mouths burned with an overabundance of pepper and spice, and revived the appetite. Under Nero, "ice houses" were constructed for the more opulent epicures, and ice was transported from the Alps for the fashionable tables of the Imperial City.

Millions of gallons of ice cream are frozen commercially each year in America, but none can compare in smoothness of texture and richness of flavor with that made at home either in an old-fashioned crank freezer or in the tray of the refrigerator. Homemade ice cream means real cream sweetened and flavored to taste, or it may mean thick heavy cream yellow with egg yolks, filled with fruits or nuts, spiked with chocolate or spices or liqueurs. It means honest goodness combined to cool, velvety perfection.

HOMEMADE ICE CREAM IN A HAND FREEZER

Prepare an ice-cream mixture and chill in the refrigerator for at least an hour before freezing. Scald the freezer container, rinse in ice water, and fill two thirds full of the cream. Fit the dasher into place, adjust the top, and put the container into a large, deep tub. Fill the tub to slightly above the cream in the container with from 3 to 5 parts ice to one part rock salt. The more salt used the faster the cream will freeze, but the coarser will be the texture of the cream.

Turn the crank slowly and steadily at first, adding more ice and salt to the tub as the ice melts. After about 15 minutes the cream will be frozen to a mush and the crank may be turned more quickly without injuring the fine texture of the cream. When the crank turns with difficulty, the cream is frozen.

Remove the freezer from the tub and wipe the top. Take off the lid and remove the dasher. Pack the ice cream down solidly into the container and cover it with a solid cover, or with the freezer lid with a cork in the crank opening. Repack the freezer with a mixture of 4 parts ice to 1 part rock salt, cover with a heavy cloth, and let stand for 1 to 2 hours before serving.

HOMEMADE ICE CREAM IN A REFRIGERATOR

Set the temperature of the refrigerator to VERY COLD. Prepare an ice-cream mixture, turn it into a deep refrigerator tray, and freeze until the cream is mushy. Spoon the cream into a chilled bowl and beat with a rotary or electric beater until smooth. Return to the tray, beat it again just before it solidifies, and finally freeze for about 3 hours, or until firm. Cover the cream with waxed paper to prevent the formation of ice crystals on top.

FROZEN CREAM · *Glace au Vanille*

1 two-inch piece of vanilla bean	1 quart heavy cream
	¾ cup sugar

Slit the piece of vanilla bean in half and scrape pulp into the cream.

Scald cream, stirring to distribute the particles of vanilla, stir in sugar, and cool.

Chill and freeze.

FROZEN FRUIT CREAM · *Glace aux Fruits*

¾ cup sugar
1 quart heavy cream
1 tablespoon lemon juice or
vanilla
1 cup crushed fruit or berries

Combine sugar and cream and stir until sugar is dissolved.

Stir in flavoring and the crushed fruit and freeze.

The best fruits to use are raspberries, strawberries, peaches, apricots, or pineapple, but almost any fruit, even unusual ones such as papaya or cherimoya, will make interesting and delicious ice creams.

FRENCH VANILLA ICE CREAM · *Glace à la Crème au Vanille*

½ cup sugar	1 one-inch piece of vanilla
¼ cup water	bean
¼ teaspoon cream of tartar	3½ cups heavy cream
4 egg yolks	

In a saucepan combine sugar, water, and cream of tartar, bring to a boil, and cook until syrup spins a light thread.

Beat egg yolks until fluffy and gradually pour syrup into them, beating constantly until mixture is thick and pale in color.

Scrape pulp from vanilla bean and add to eggs with the cream.

Stir until mixture is thoroughly blended, chill, and freeze in a hand churn or in a quart-size refrigerator tray.

FRENCH CHOCOLATE ICE CREAM · *Glace à la Crème au Chocolat*

Substitute 6 ounces semi-sweet chocolate melted until smooth with 4 tablespoons strong black coffee for the vanilla in FRENCH VANILLA ICE CREAM.

FRENCH COFFEE ICE CREAM · *Glace à la Crème au Café*

Substitute strong coffee for the water in recipe for FRENCH VANILLA ICE CREAM. Omit the vanilla and add a few drops of coffee essence.

PRALINE ICE CREAM · *Glace à la Crème au Praline*

Omit vanilla in recipe for FRENCH VANILLA ICE CREAM, and stir in ¾ cup PRALINE POWDER before freezing.

CHESTNUT ICE CREAM

Stir 1 cup chilled CHESTNUT PURÉE into FRENCH VANILLA ICE CREAM before freezing.

STRAWBERRY ICE CREAM · *Glace à la Crème aux Fraises*

Stir 1 cup cold strawberry purée into FRENCH VANILLA ICE CREAM before freezing. Lemon may be used instead of vanilla.

WALNUT ICE CREAM

Stir 1 cup ground walnuts into FRENCH VANILLA ICE CREAM before freezing.

PISTACHIO ICE CREAM · *Glace à la Crème aux Pistaches*

Stir 1 cup brown pistachios and a few drops of green food coloring into FRENCH VANILLA ICE CREAM before freezing.

MADELEINE ICE CREAM · *Glace Madeleine*

Omit vanilla in recipe for FRENCH VANILLA ICE CREAM. Stir in ¾ cup mixed candied fruits, finely diced and steeped in 2 tablespoons kirsch for 30 minutes before freezing.

EGGNOG ICE CREAM

4 egg yolks	1 cup hot milk
Dash salt	2 tablespoons bourbon
Dash nutmeg	2 cups heavy cream, whipped
⅓ cup sugar	

Mix together in a saucepan the egg yolks, salt, nutmeg, and sugar.

Gradually stir in hot milk. Cook over very low heat, stirring constantly, until slightly thickened, making certain that the custard does not boil.

Strain.

Stir in bourbon and chill.

Fold into the whipped cream.

Turn into refrigerator trays.

Freeze.

Beat until smooth and return to trays to freeze. *Makes just over 1 quart.*

COFFEE ICE CREAM · *Café Liégeois*

¾ cup boiling water	⅔ cup sugar
½ cup ground coffee	1 cup heavy cream
4 egg yolks	Whipped cream

Pour water over the coffee and chill for 1 hour.

Strain coffee through cheesecloth, pressing well to remove all moisture.

Turn into a small saucepan.

Combine egg yolks, sugar, and cream and stir into the coffee in saucepan.

Cook over low heat, stirring constantly, until custard coats the spoon.

Strain into refrigerator tray.

Freeze until ice crystals have formed.

Remove from tray and beat until smooth.
Return to tray and freeze 2 to 3 hours.
Serve in parfait glasses topped with whipped cream. *Makes 1 pint.*

CARAMEL ICE CREAM · *Glace à la Crème au Caramel*

1 cup sugar	Dash salt
3 tablespoons water	2 egg yolks, beaten
1 cup milk	2 cups heavy cream, whipped

In a small saucepan combine sugar and water.
Stir until sugar is dissolved.
Cook until caramel color.
Gradually add milk and continue cooking, over low heat, until caramel is dissolved.
Remove from heat and beat in salt and egg yolks.
Strain and chill.
Fold in whipped cream.
Turn into refrigerator trays.
Freeze.
Remove from trays and beat until smooth.
Return to trays and freeze. *Makes 1½ quarts.*

BUTTER PECAN ICE CREAM

1 cup brown sugar	Dash salt
½ cup water	3 tablespoons butter
1 one-inch stick vanilla bean, split	1 tablespoon brandy
	1 cup heavy cream, whipped
3 egg yolks	½ cup coarsely chopped pecans
1 cup light cream	

In a saucepan combine sugar, water, and vanilla bean.
Bring to a boil and boil hard for 2 minutes.
Remove from heat. Discard vanilla bean.
Combine egg yolks, cream, and salt, and gradually stir into the syrup in the saucepan.
Return to low heat and cook, stirring constantly, until slightly thickened, do not let boil.
Remove from heat and add butter, stirring until the butter is dissolved.

Strain.
Add brandy and chill.
Fold in whipped cream and pecans.
Turn into refrigerator tray and freeze.
Beat ice cream until smooth and return to tray.
Freeze. *Makes 1 quart.*

ELECTRIC BLENDER FRENCH VANILLA ICE CREAM

⅓ cup sugar   *1½ teaspoons vanilla*
3 tablespoons water   *1½ cups heavy cream,*
4 egg yolks   *whipped*
Dash salt

Combine sugar and water into small saucepan.
Bring to a boil and boil for 3 minutes.
Into blender container put the eggs, salt, and vanilla.
Cover container and turn motor on high. Remove cover and, with motor on, gradually pour in the hot syrup in a steady stream.
Turn off blender motor.
Fold yolk mixture into whipped cream.
Spoon into a refrigerator tray.
Cover with waxed paper.
Freeze 2 to 3 hours, or until firm. *Makes about 1 quart.*

ELECTRIC BLENDER FRENCH CHOCOLATE ICE CREAM

¼ cup sugar   *3 egg yolks*
½ cup water   *1½ cups heavy cream,*
1 6-ounce package semi-sweet   *whipped*
* chocolate pieces*

In a small saucepan mix sugar and water.
Bring to a boil and boil rapidly for 3 minutes.
Into blender container put chocolate pieces and hot syrup.
Cover and blend on high speed for 6 seconds, or until chocolate mixture is smooth.
Turn off motor, remove cover, and add egg yolks.
Cover and blend on high speed for 5 seconds, or until well blended.
Fold chocolate mixture into cream.

Turn into refrigerator tray.

Cover with waxed paper.

Freeze 2 to 3 hours, or until firm. *Makes about 1 quart.*

ELECTRIC BLENDER WALNUT ICE CREAM

1 *cup walnut halves*	1 *teaspoon vanilla*
1 *cup heavy cream, whipped*	3 *egg yolks*
¼ *cup sugar*	½ *teaspoon ginger*
2 *tablespoons water*	*Dash salt*

Into blender container put walnut halves.

Cover and blend on high speed for 15 seconds, or until nuts are ground.

Turn into a large bowl with whipped cream.

In a small saucepan combine sugar and water.

Bring to a boil and boil rapidly for 3 minutes.

Into blender container put vanilla, egg yolks, ginger, and salt.

Cover container and turn motor on high.

Remove cover and, with motor on, gradually pour in the hot syrup in a steady stream.

Turn off motor.

Fold egg yolk mixture into cream and walnuts.

Spoon into a refrigerator tray.

Cover with waxed paper.

Freeze 2 to 3 hours, or until firm. *Makes about 1 quart.*

ELECTRIC BLENDER FRESH STRAWBERRY ICE CREAM

2 *tablespoons water*
1 *pint fresh strawberries*
⅔ *cup sweetened condensed
    milk*
1 *cup heavy cream, whipped*

Into blender container put water and strawberries.

Cover and blend on high speed for 10 seconds, or until smooth.

Remove cover and, with motor on, pour in condensed milk.

Turn off motor and fold strawberry purée into whipped cream.

Turn into refrigerator tray.

Cover with waxed paper.
Freeze 2 to 3 hours, or until firm. *Makes 1 quart.*

Fruit juices or FRUIT PURÉES, sweetened with syrup and frozen to a mush in a hand freezer or in a refrigerator tray, are usually served in chilled sherbet glasses, a perfect background for a topping of berries, sliced fruit, or a spoonful of rum, kirsch, Cointreau, curaçao, or crème de menthe, according to the flavor of the ice.

LEMON ICE · *Glace au Citron*

Make a syrup by combining 2 cups sugar and 4 cups water, bring to a boil, and boil for 5 minutes. Cool. Stir into the cooled syrup ¾ cup lemon juice and 1 tablespoon grated lemon rind and freeze according to directions at the beginning of the Chapter.

ORANGE ICE

Make the same syrup as for Lemon Ice. Stir in 2 cups orange juice, ¼ cup lemon juice, and the grated rind of 2 oranges, and freeze.

CITRUS ICE

Make the same syrup as for Lemon Ice. Stir in 1 cup grapefruit juice, 1 cup orange juice and ¼ cup lemon juice and freeze.

APRICOT ICE · *Glace à l'Abricot*

Combine 1 cup sugar and 2 cups water, bring to a boil, and cook for 5 minutes. Cool, stir in 2 cups apricot nectar and ¼ cup lemon juice, and freeze.

Peach, pineapple, blackberry, blueberry, or grape juice may be used instead of the apricot juice.

STRAWBERRY ICE · *Glace aux Fraises*

Make syrup as for APRICOT ICE. Cool. Stir in 2 cups strawberry purée, sieved, the juice of ½ lemon, and a few drops of red food coloring. Freeze acording to directions at the beginning of the Chapter.

RASPBERRY ICE · *Glace à la Framboise*

Substitute raspberry purée for the strawberry purée in STRAWBERRY ICE and omit the red coloring.

TANGERINE ICE · *Glace à la Mandarine*

Infuse the peel of 4 tangerines in 3 cups boiling syrup (1½ cups sugar and 3 cups water boiled for 5 minutes). Add juice of 6 tangerines, 2 oranges, and 1 lemon. Strain and freeze.

Ices can be made from the fresh purée of plums, peaches, apricots, or pineapple in the same way.

Granités are similar to ices and served in sherbet glasses. They are not stirred during freezing and have a somewhat granular or *granite* texture. They are quickly made with fresh fruit, sugar, and water in an electric blender.

PEACH GRANITE · *Granité aux Pêches*

1 cup water	Lemon juice
¾ cup sugar	White corn syrup
4 cups ripe peach slices	

Bring water and sugar to a boil.

Cook rapidly 5 minutes; cool.

Pour syrup into container of an electric blender; add peach slices. Cover and blend on high speed 5 seconds or until puréed.

Taste the purée and add lemon juice and/or white corn syrup to taste.

Pour mixture into a refrigerator tray and freeze thirty minutes to 1 hour, until firm but not frozen solid.

If the dessert becomes too frozen, spoon it into the blender container and blend at high speed until softened to a sherbet consistency. *Serves 4 to 6.*

WATERMELON GRANITE • *Granité au Melon*

4 cups watermelon meat, without seeds	2 tablespoons lemon juice
	½ cup sugar

Place watermelon in container of an electric blender and blend five seconds or until puréed.

Add lemon juice and sugar and continue blending until sugar is dissolved.

Pour mixture into a refrigerator tray and freeze 30 minutes to 1 hour, until firm but not frozen solid.

If the dessert becomes too frozen, spoon it into the blender container and blend on high speed until softened to a sherbet consistency. *Serves 4 to 6.*

NOTE: Cantaloupe or honeydew may be substituted for the watermelon.

RASPBERRY GRANITE • *Granité à la Framboise*

¾ cup sugar	Lemon juice
1 cup water	White corn syrup
3 cups red, ripe raspberries, free from blemishes (about 2 pints)	

Bring sugar and water to a boil.

Cook rapidly 5 minutes; cool.

Pour berries into container of an electric blender and add sugar syrup.

Cover and blend 20 seconds or until puréed.

Strain.

Taste the purée and add lemon juice and/or white corn syrup to taste.

Pour the purée into a refrigerator tray and freeze 30 minutes to 1 hour, until firm but not frozen solid.

If the dessert becomes too frozen, spoon it into the blender container and blend on high speed until softened to a sherbet consistency. *Serves 4 to 6.*

RASPBERRY MILK GRANITE

> 1 cup milk
> 1 can (6 ounces) frozen
>   raspberry lemon punch
>   concentrate
> 1½ cups crushed ice

Put all ingredients into blender container.
Cover and blend on high speed for 15 seconds, or until smooth.
Turn into refrigerator tray and freeze. *Makes 1 pint.*

To serve granités in semi-frozen form, cut the frozen granités into cubes. Put about 1 cup frozen cubes into container of the electric blender. Add about 1 tablespoon boiling water and blend on high speed until the granité is the consistency of fine snow. Pile into sherbet glasses and spoon over the top a little favorite liqueur, rum, cognac, or sweet wine.

MARQUISE

Blend a fruit granité in the electric blender until the consistency of fine snow. Fold in an equal quantity of whipped cream and pile into sherbet glasses. Spoon a little kirsch over top.

CHAMPAGNE MARQUISE • *Marquise au Champagne*

> 1½ cups water
> ¾ cup sugar
> Grated rind of ½ orange
> Juice of 2 lemons
>
> Juice of 2 oranges
> 1 pint chilled champagne
> 2 cups heavy cream
> Cognac

Combine water and sugar.
Bring to a boil and boil for 5 minutes.
Add grated orange rind and fruit juices and cool.
Add champagne and strain into refrigerator tray.
Freeze for 1 hour, or until set around sides but still mushy.
Turn into a chilled bowl and beat with rotary beater until frothy.

Return to refrigerator tray and freeze for 3 to 4 hours, or until frozen.

Whip cream until stiff and stir into the *marquise* along with 1½ tablespoons cognac.

Pile into sherbet or champagne glasses and pour over each 1 teaspoon cognac. *Serves 6.*

Sherbets are a form of ice made of fruit juice or fruit purée and syrup and frozen. About an hour before the sherbet is to be served, stiffly beaten egg whites or ITALIAN MERINGUE is folded into the frozen mixture.

RASPBERRY SHERBET

2 boxes (10 ounces each)
   frozen raspberries
Water
1 cup sugar
1½ cups water
Juice of 1 lemon

1 cup dry white wine
2 tablespoons eau de vie de
   framboise
1 egg white ITALIAN
   MERINGUE

Crush raspberries and add enough water to make 2 cups thin purée. Or blend to a purée in an electric blender and add water to make 2 cups thin purée.

Combine sugar and the 1½ cups water, bring to a boil, and boil rapidly for 5 minutes. Cool syrup.

Combine syrup and raspberry liquid.

Add lemon juice, white wine, and framboise, and mix thoroughly.

Pour into refrigerator tray and freeze for about 1 hour, or until frozen around the sides but still mushy in the middle.

Turn into a chilled bowl and beat with a rotary beater until frothy.

Return to refrigerator tray and freeze for 2 hours, stirring every half hour until it sets in small crystals.

About 1 hour before serving, stir in the Italian meringue.

Serve in chilled sherbet glasses. *Serves 6.*

ORANGE SHERBET · *Sorbet à l'Orange*

2 cups water
1 cup sugar
Grated rind of 1 orange
1 cup orange juice

2 tablespoons lemon juice
1 egg white ITALIAN
   MERINGUE
Cointreau

Combine water and sugar, bring to a boil, and boil rapidly for 5 minutes.

Add grated orange rind, orange and lemon juice.

Cool syrup and strain into refrigerator tray.

Freeze for 1 hour, turn into a chilled bowl, and beat with a rotary beater until frothy.

Return to freezer tray and continue to freeze for 2 hours, stirring every half hour until it begins to set in small crystals.

About 1 hour before serving, stir in the Italian meringue and continue to freeze.

Just before serving, stir in the ½ cup chilled Cointreau.

Spoon into chilled sherbet glasses and pour 1 tablespoon Cointreau over each serving. *Serves 6.*

ELECTRIC BLENDER PINEAPPLE SHERBET

1 egg white
2 tablespoons orange juice
Rind of ½ orange

1 can (13½ ounces) frozen pineapple chunks, cut into 4

Put into blender container the egg white, orange juice, and rind.

Cover and blend on high speed for 10 seconds.

Turn off motor and add pineapple.

Cover and blend on high speed for 20 seconds, or until smooth.

Spoon into refrigerator tray and freeze until just set. *Makes about 1 pint.*

LEMON SHERBET • *Sorbet au Citron*

2 cups water
1¼ cups sugar
Dash salt
½ cup lemon juice
2 teaspoons grated lemon rind

Few drops yellow food coloring
3 egg whites, stiffly beaten

Combine water with sugar in a saucepan.

Bring to a boil and boil rapidly for 5 minutes.

Stir in salt, lemon juice, rind, and food coloring, and chill.

Fold into beaten egg whites.

Turn into refrigerator trays and freeze. *Makes 1½ quarts.*

GINGER RUM SHERBET

1 cup sugar
1½ cups water
Juice of 1 orange
Juice of 1 lemon
¼ cup dark rum

2 tablespoons finely chopped
  preserved ginger
1 egg white ITALIAN
  MERINGUE

In a saucepan combine sugar and water.
Bring to a boil and boil rapidly for 5 minutes.
Strain juices.
Combine syrup, fruit juices, rum, and ginger.
Turn into refrigerator tray.
Freeze until consistency of fine snow, stirring occasionally.
Make Italian meringue and stir in the rum mixture.
Spoon into parfait glasses and freeze until serving time. *Makes 2 quarts.*

Punch glaces are similar to sherbets, but are generously laced with wine or rum.

ICED ROMAN PUNCH • *Punch Glace à la Romaine*

¾ cup sugar
Juice of 2 lemons
Juice of 1 orange
1 strip each of lemon and
  orange peel
2 cups champagne or dry

  white wine
½ cup strong tea
1 egg white ITALIAN
  MERINGUE
1 cup rum

In saucepan combine sugar, fruit juices, and fruit peel. Bring to a boil and boil rapidly for 5 minutes. Cool and strain.
Add champagne or dry white wine and tea.
Pour mixture into refrigerator tray and freeze for 1 hour, or until set around sides but still mushy in middle.
Turn into a chilled bowl and beat with a rotary beater until frothy.
Return to refrigerator tray and freeze for 2 hours, stirring every 30 minutes until it begins to set in tiny, smooth crystals.
About 1 hour before serving, stir in the Italian meringue and continue to freeze.
Just before serving beat in the rum.
Spoon into chilled sherbet or punch glasses. *Serves 6.*

Spooms are a kind of sherbet made with sherry, port, madeira, champagne, or a combination of any dry white wine and sweet fortified wine. They contain a much larger proportion of Italian meringue than a sherbet.

PORT WINE SPOOM • *Spoom au Porto*

2 cups water	¼ cup strained lemon juice
1 cup sugar	4 egg white ITALIAN
Pinch salt	MERINGUE
2 cups port	

In saucepan combine water, sugar, and salt. Bring to a boil and boil rapidly for 5 minutes.

Add port and lemon juice to the hot syrup and cool.

Pour into refrigerator tray and freeze for 1 hour, or until it is set on sides but is still mushy in the center.

Turn into chilled bowl and beat with a rotary beater until frothy.

Continue to freeze for 2 hours, stirring every 30 minutes until it begins to set in tiny, smooth crystals.

About 1 hour before serving, stir in the meringue. Serve in chilled sherbet glasses. *Serves 12.*

Mousses, the richest of all frozen creams, are simple to freeze, for they need no beating or stirring. They may be frozen in the refrigerator tray, in fluted paper cups set into the tray, or in large or individual molds. Fill molds with the mixture, cover with waxed paper, then with the mold cover. In order to keep the salt water out of the cream, spread the seam with butter or wrap the mold tightly in aluminum foil. Pack the mold or molds in 2 parts crushed ice to 1 part rock salt and freeze for 2½ to 3 hours, depending on the size of the mold. To serve, unpack the mold and wipe it with a cloth wrung out of hot water. Remove the cover and invert the mousse on a serving dish.

VANILLA MOUSSE

¾ cup sugar	1 one-inch stick of vanilla
½ cup water	bean
4 egg yolks	2 cups heavy cream

Combine sugar and water, bring to a boil, and cook for 5 minutes. Cool.

Beat egg yolks in top of a double boiler.

Stir in syrup gradually, add pulp from vanilla bean, and cook over hot, but not boiling, water, stirring constantly until mixture is thick and creamy.

Rub cream through a fine sieve and cool.

Whip cream until it is stiff and fold it into the other mixture.

Freeze in a refrigerator tray or in a mold buried in equal parts of rock salt and ice. *Serves 6.*

VANILLA CUSTARD MOUSSE

1 *cup milk*	4 *egg yolks*
1 *cup light cream*	½ *cup sugar*
1 *one-inch stick of vanilla* *bean*	2 *cups heavy cream, whipped*

In top of a double boiler scald milk, cream, and pulp from piece of vanilla bean.

Beat egg yolks and sugar until light and pale in color and stir into the hot liquid.

Cook over hot, but not boiling, water, stirring constantly, until custard is thick, strain through a fine sieve, and cool.

Fold in whipped cream and freeze in a refrigerator tray or in a mold buried in 2 parts crushed ice to 1 part rock salt. *Serves 8.*

CHOCOLATE MOUSSE

Omit vanilla from VANILLA MOUSSE and stir in ½ cup melted semi-sweet chocolate.

COFFEE MOUSSE

Omit vanilla from VANILLA MOUSSE and flavor mixture to taste with coffee essence.

FRUIT MOUSSE

Omit vanilla from VANILLA MOUSSE and fold in 2 cups sweetened fruit purée and juice of ½ lemon.

BANANA-RUM MOUSSE

Omit vanilla from VANILLA MOUSSE and fold in 2 cups sweetened banana purée and 2 tablespoons dark rum.

COEUR GLACE

Turn a mousse mixture into individual heart-shaped molds or a large heart-shaped mold, cover, and seal with butter to prevent salt water from entering. Freeze for 2½ to 3 hours, depending on size, in a home freezer or in a tub filled with 2 parts crushed ice to 1 part rock salt. Unmold, pour a fruit sauce around it, and decorate with chocolate leaves, sliced fruit or berries, or blanched grilled almonds.

SOUFFLE GLACE

Turn a mousse mixture into a soufflé dish with a 2-inch band of paper tied around the top so that when mousse is frozen the paper can be removed and frozen cream will extend above dish to give the illusion of a hot soufflé. *Soufflés glacés* cannot be submerged in ice and salt but can be frozen only in a home freezer or refrigerator compartment. Freeze for 2 to 3 hours, remove paper rim, and serve in the soufflé dish.

SOUFFLE GLACE AUX FRAISES

Tie a rim of paper around top of a soufflé dish and place a tall tin in the center. Pour VANILLA CUSTARD MOUSSE between can and dish, and freeze for 2 hours. When ready to serve, remove both paper rim and tin can. If can is difficult to remove, fill it with warm water and it will slip out easily. Fill cavity with strawberries sweetened to taste and flavored with kirsch. Other fruits or berries may be substituted for the strawberries.

BISCUIT TORTONI

¾ cup sugar
¼ cup water
5 egg yolks
¼ cup sherry

2 cups heavy cream, whipped
½ cup ground toasted almonds

Combine sugar and water, bring to a boil, and cook for 5 minutes.

Add hot syrup gradually to egg yolks, beating constantly, and stir over hot, but not boiling, water until thick.

Stir in sherry, strain through a fine sieve, and cool.

Fold whipped cream into egg mixture and turn into paper cases.

Sprinkle the top of each little cup with ground almonds, put the cases in a refrigerator tray, and freeze for 3 hours. *Serves 6 to 8.*

ELECTRIC BLENDER BISCUIT TORTONI

⅓ cup toasted almonds	2 tablespoons water
2 tablespoons sherry	⅓ cup sugar
3 egg yolks	1 cup heavy cream, whipped

Put toasted almonds into blender container.

Cover and blend on high speed for 5 seconds, or until nuts are ground.

Turn out onto waxed paper.

Into blender container put sherry and egg yolks.

Into a small saucepan put water and sugar. Bring to a boil and boil rapidly for 3 minutes.

With cover off blender container turn on motor to low speed and gradually pour in the syrup.

Turn off motor as soon as all syrup has been added.

Fold into heavy cream, whipped.

Arrange 8 individual paper cases in a refrigerator tray.

Pour cream mixture into paper cases.

Sprinkle tops of each with ground nuts.

Freeze 2 to 3 hours. *Serves 8.*

BISCUIT MONT BLANC

Make BISCUIT TORTONI, substituting ¼ cup rum for the sherry, and sprinkling with ½ cup chopped chestnuts.

BISCUIT MARQUISE

Make BISCUIT TORTONI, omitting sherry. Divide mixture in half. To one half stir in 2 teaspoons vanilla. To other half fold in 1 cup strawberry purée. Alternate strawberry layer with vanilla layer. Sprinkle with ½ cup crushed vanilla wafers.

BISCUIT EXCELSIOR

Make BISCUIT TORTONI, omitting sherry. Divide mixture in half. Into one half stir 2 tablespoons sherry. Into other half stir 1 cup raspberry purée. Alternate raspberry layer with vanilla layer. Sprinkle with ½ cup ground pistachios.

The parfait, like the mousse, needs no churning. The mixture is turned directly into an especially designed parfait mold and is frozen in a deep freeze or in 2 parts crushed ice and 1 part rock salt. Parfaits may have vanilla, chocolate, fruit, nut, liqueur, praline, or other flavors, and may be served garnished with fruits or nuts. A final touch is a topping of whipped cream prettily forced through a pastry bag fitted with a small fluted tube.

PARFAIT AU CAFE

1 cup sugar	8 egg yolks, beaten
½ cup strong black coffee	3 cups heavy cream, whipped

Combine sugar and coffee, bring to a boil, and cook until syrup spins a thin thread.

Pour hot syrup gradually into egg yolks, beating constantly until mixture is thick.

Continue to beat until cold.

Stir in whipped cream and turn into a parfait mold.

Freeze in a home freezer or in 2 parts crushed ice and 1 part rock salt for 2½ to 3 hours.

If frozen in ice and salt, the cover of the mold must be sealed hermetically by covering the seam with butter to prevent the salt water from seeping into the cream. *Serves 8.*

Bombes are the very last word in frozen desserts. The sophisticated, seductive combination of a smooth mousse interior wrapped in a coat of fruit ice or ice cream is the perfect frigid climax to a flawless repast at any time of the year. Special *bombe* molds are needed, and they may be round, square, or timbale-shaped. Imagination is the only limitation to the variety of *bombes* that can be made. Any combination of mousse and ice may be used, harmonizing flavors the sole prerequisite.

HOW TO LINE, FILL, AND FREEZE A BOMBE

Chill the mold thoroughly. Spread the interior with a layer of firmly frozen water ice or ice cream about 1 inch thick, spreading it as evenly as possible with the back of a spoon. Fill the center with a chilled mousse mixture and cover the mousse with a layer of buttered paper. Adjust the mold cover and spread a little butter around the seam to hermetically seal it, and freeze in a home freezer or in a mixture of 2 parts crushed ice to 1 part rock salt for 2½ to 3 hours. When ready to serve, wipe the mold with a cloth wrung out of hot water, unseal, and invert the *bombe* on a chilled serving plate. Garnish with whipped cream, or serve plain with a dessert or fruit sauce on the side.

BOMBE MALTAISE

Line a mold with ORANGE ICE and fill interior with a mousse mixture flavored with either vanilla or curaçao. Freeze, unmold, and garnish with orange sections cooked in syrup until glazed.

BOMBE JAVANAISE

Line a mold with COFFEE ICE CREAM and fill interior with a BANANA-RUM MOUSSE flavored with coffee liqueur.

BOMBE FALSTAFF

Line a mold with PRALINE ICE CREAM and fill interior with STRAW-BERRY MOUSSE. Freeze, unmold, and sprinkle with PRALINE POWDER.

BOMBE A LA COMTESSE-MARIE

Line a square *bombe* mold with VANILLA ICE CREAM and fill interior with STRAWBERRY MOUSSE, or line with STRAWBERRY ICE and fill with VANILLA MOUSSE.

BOMBE A LA MARIE-THERESE

Line a square mold with CHOCOLATE ICE CREAM and fill interior with whipped cream mixed with ladyfingers soaked in kirsch. Freeze, unmold, and garnish with strips of pineapple.

BOMBE CARDINAL

Line a mold with RASPBERRY ICE and fill interior with a mousse mixture flavored with kirsch.

BOMBE MAROCAISE

Line a mold with CHOCOLATE ICE CREAM and fill interior with a mousse mixture flavored with rum and mixed with chopped dates.

BOMBE SINGAPOUR

Line a mold with STRAWBERRY ICE and fill the interior with PINE-APPLE MOUSSE. Freeze, unmold, and garnish with strips of pineapple.

BOMBE ESPERANZE

Line a mold with PISTACHIO ICE CREAM and fill with ORANGE ICE mixed with chopped preserved fruits.

BOMBE SORCIERE

Bake a GENOISE in a *flan* ring and cut it into small triangles. Line a half-spherical *bombe* mold with the *génoise* triangles and fill the interior with CHOCOLATE MOUSSE. Freeze, unmold, and quickly mask it with warm CHOCOLATE FONDANT. Insert slivers of grilled almonds in the fondant.

BOMBE BOULE DE NEIGE

Marinate ¾ cup mixed candied fruits, diced, and ¼ cup sultana raisins in ¼ cup kirsch for 1 hour, stirring often. Stir fruit and kirsch mixture into a cold VANILLA MOUSSE mixture and turn into a spherical *bombe* mold. Freeze and unmold onto a chilled serving platter. Cover the *bombe* closely with tiny rosettes of whipped cream, sweetened and flavored with kirsch, pressed through a pastry bag fitted with a small fluted tube. Decorate with crystallized violets and serve with chilled SABAYON GLACE AU KIRSCH sauce.

NEAPOLITAN BOMBE

1 pint chocolate ice cream
1 pint vanilla ice cream
1 pint strawberry ice cream
½ cup sugar
2 tablespoons water
2 egg whites
½ cup heavy cream, whipped

¾ cup chopped mixed
  candied fruits
¼ cup chopped almonds
¼ cup rum
Whipped cream
Glacé cherry halves

Line a 2-quart mold with an even layer of chocolate ice cream. Freeze until firm.

Repeat, lining mold with a layer of the vanilla ice cream and then the strawberry ice cream.

In a small saucepan bring sugar and water to a boil and boil hard for 2 minutes.

Beat egg whites until stiff and gradually beat in the hot syrup. Fold in whipped cream, mixed fruits, almonds, and rum.

Turn this into center of ice-cream-lined mold.

Cover with buttered paper and seal.

Freeze until firm, 3 to 4 hours.

Unmold onto chilled plate and decorate with whipped cream and cherries. *Serves 12.*

SPUMONI

¾ cup sugar
5 egg yolks
2 cups milk
1 one-inch stick of vanilla
  bean
⅓ cup chopped glacé cherries

¼ cup chopped candied
  orange peel
¼ cup sugar
¼ cup chopped walnuts
2 tablespoons sweet sherry
1 cup heavy cream, whipped

In the top of a double saucepan combine ¾ cup sugar, egg yolks, milk, and vanilla.

Cook over hot water until thickened, stirring occasionally.

Remove vanilla bean and freeze for 1 hour.

Line a 1-quart mold with custard.

Freeze until ready to fill.

Fold cherries, orange peel, ¼ cup sugar, walnuts, and sherry into whipped cream.

Spoon into center of mold.

Cover with buttered paper.

Freeze until firm, 3 to 4 hours.

Unmold on chilled serving plate. *Serves 8.*

CHAPTER 18

Cake Fillings, Frostings, and Dessert Sauces

A FILLING or frosting can be that special touch that changes a plain cake into a party spectacular, just as a dessert sauce can add the finishing touch, that missing flavor or texture, to another type of dessert.

What, for instance, would a savarin or baba be without its bath of warm fruit or rum-flavored syrup? What would plum pudding be without hard sauce?

Some sauces are traditional to serve with certain desserts, others can be used to give variety or to make a dish still sweeter, still richer. Only a few of the best are included here. You undoubtedly have many more family favorites to add to the endless number of sweet garnishes that make a dessert your specialty.

All frostings are sufficient to frost top and sides of an 8- or 9-inch layer cake. Fillings make a generous spread between two layers.

VANILLA PASTRY CREAM · *Crème Pâtissière*

4 cups milk	1 teaspoon cornstarch
1 one-inch stick vanilla bean	1 cup sugar
¾ cup flour	8 egg yolks

Heat milk with vanilla bean to boiling.

In a saucepan combine flour, cornstarch, sugar, and egg yolks, and beat thoroughly. Gradually stir in hot milk and cook over low heat, stirring rapidly, until thickened. The cream should be the consistency of thick mayonnaise.

CHOCOLATE PASTRY CREAM • *Crème Pâtissière au Chocolat*

Mix 1 cup VANILLA PASTRY CREAM with 2 ounces (squares) melted sweet chocolate.

CUSTARD FILLING

½ cup sugar	2 cups hot milk or cream
⅓ cup flour	4 egg yolks lightly beaten
Pinch salt	2 teaspoons vanilla

In top of double saucepan combine sugar, flour, and salt.

Gradually stir in hot milk or cream and cook, stirring, until sauce is smooth and thickened.

Pour a little of the hot sauce into egg yolks, then stir egg yolks into sauce.

Cook over steaming, not boiling, water for about 5 minutes, stirring frequently, until eggs are cooked. Remove from heat, cool, and stir in vanilla.

BANANA CUSTARD FILLING

Prepare CUSTARD FILLING. Just before spreading between cake layers, fold in 2 bananas, thinly sliced.

CUSTARD CREAM FILLING

1 tablespoon gelatin	2 cups milk
4 tablespoons cold water	2 teaspoons vanilla extract
4 egg yolks	2 cups heavy cream, whipped
6 tablespoons sugar	¼ cup Cointreau, optional
2 tablespoons cornstarch	

Soften the gelatin in water.

Combine egg yolks, sugar, cornstarch, and milk in top of a double saucepan.

Stir and cook over simmering water until smooth and thickened.
Remove from heat and add gelatin and vanilla.
Stir until gelatin is dissolved.
Stir until cool.
Fold in whipped cream and Cointreau.
Pour the mixture into two 9-inch cake pans and chill until firm.
Makes two 9-inch custard layers.

LIME CUSTARD FILLING

4 egg yolks	Pinch salt
¼ cup lime juice	2 cups cream, whipped

In top of double saucepan combine egg yolks, lime juice, and salt.
Cook over simmering water, stirring constantly, until custard is thick.
Cool and fold in whipped cream.

ORANGE CUSTARD FILLING

⅓ cup sugar	1 cup milk
5 tablespoons flour	½ cup orange juice
Pinch salt	1 egg, lightly beaten

In top of double saucepan combine sugar, flour, and salt.
Stir in milk and orange juice.
Cook over simmering water for about 10 minutes, stirring frequently.
Beat about ⅓ of sauce into egg. Stir egg mixture into cream in pan and continue to cook, stirring, for 2 minutes longer. Cool.

BUTTERSCOTCH FILLING

¾ cup brown sugar	½ cup milk
¼ cup butter	Pinch salt
1½ cups milk	2 eggs, beaten
5 tablespoons flour	1 teaspoon vanilla

In saucepan combine sugar and butter.
Cook over low heat until butter is melted and syrup is clear.
Stir in the 1½ cups milk and heat to boiling.

Combine flour, the ½ cup milk, and salt. Stir into brown sugar mixture and cook for 15 minutes, stirring frequently.

Mix eggs with a little of the hot sauce and stir into remaining sauce. Continue to cook over low heat for about 3 minutes, stirring constantly, or until eggs are cooked. Do not let mixture boil.

Cool and stir in vanilla.

CHOCOLATE FILLING

4 egg yolks	1 ounce unsweetened choco-
½ cup sugar	late, grated
1 cup milk	Pinch salt
1 tablespoon butter	1 teaspoon vanilla

Beat egg yolks until light, and gradually beat in sugar.
Slowly stir in milk.
Add butter, chocolate, and salt.
Cook over simmering water, stirring frequently, until filling is thick.
Cool and stir in vanilla.

MOCHA FILLING

2 ounces unsweetened choco-	¼ teaspoon salt
late, chopped	1½ cups sugar
⅔ cup cream	2 teaspoons cornstarch
1⅓ cups strong coffee	2 tablespoons water
4 egg yolks	1 teaspoon vanilla or 1 table-
1 egg	spoon rum

In saucepan combine chocolate, cream, and coffee.
Cook over low heat, stirring occasionally, until mixture is smooth.
Combine egg yolks, egg, and salt.
Gradually beat in sugar.
Combine cornstarch and water and stir into sugar mixture.
Add all these ingredients to the chocolate milk and cook, stirring constantly, until filling is thick. Do not let mixture boil.
Cool and stir in vanilla or rum.

ALMOND ORANGE FILLING

½ cup sugar
1 tablespoon grated orange
  rind
½ cup orange juice
3 tablespoons flour

¾ cup water
2 cups chopped seedless raisins
Pinch salt
1 cup slivered blanched
  almonds, toasted

Combine sugar, orange rind and juice, flour, water, raisins, and salt.

Bring to a boil and simmer for 5 minutes, stirring constantly.

Remove from heat and stir in almonds.

FIG FILLING

½ pound figs, chopped
⅓ cup sugar
⅓ cup water

1 tablespoon lemon juice
1 teaspoon grated lemon rind
1 tablespoon cornstarch

Combine all ingredients, bring to a boil, and simmer until thick, stirring constantly.

WALNUT FILLING

½ cup sugar
3 egg yolks
3 tablespoons strong black
  coffee

½ cup chopped walnuts
1 tablespoon sugar

Combine sugar, egg yolks, and coffee and stir briskly over a low flame until mixture is thick and creamy. Do not let it boil.

Cool.

Mix walnuts with sugar and stir over the fire until browned.

Fold walnuts into the coffee cream.

SOUR ORANGE FILLING

2 tablespoons lemon juice
6 tablespoons orange juice
⅓ cup water
½ cup sugar

2 tablespoons flour
Pinch salt
1 teaspoon grated lemon rind
3 egg yolks, beaten

Combine all ingredients in top of double saucepan. Cook over simmering water until thick, stirring frequently.

APRICOT FILLING

Make ORANGE FILLING and when thick stir in ½ cup stewed apricot purée. Add sugar, if desired, to taste.

DECORATOR'S BUTTER CREAM

1 cup light colored butter or margarine	1 pound confectioners' sugar (sift if lumpy)
1 cup white shortening	Almond or vanilla extract

Both butter and shortening should be at room temperature.

Put butter and shortening into bowl and beat until smooth and fluffy.

Gradually beat in sugar and flavoring.

Use an electric beater for this if possible.

NOTE: This BUTTER CREAM can be made with all butter or margarine, but not unless you are very expert in cake decorating. The shortening gives it a stability which makes it much easier to work with than if made with all butter or margarine. The shortening also results in a whiter butter cream, so that when you tint it with food colors, the colors are more true than if the butter cream has a yellow cast. In such cases all your blues will be slightly greenish and your pinks will lean toward the salmon shade.

BUTTER CREAM FILLING AND FROSTING

¾ cup sugar	5 egg yolks, beaten
¼ cup water	1 cup unsalted butter
⅛ teaspoon cream of tartar	Flavoring

In saucepan combine sugar, water, and cream of tartar.

Bring to a boil and boil rapidly until syrup spins a light thread (238° F.).

Beat syrup gradually into egg yolks and continue to beat until cream is thick and cool.

Beat in butter, bit by bit.

Flavor with vanilla, almond, rum, brandy, kirsch, or any desired liqueur.

CHOCOLATE BUTTER CREAM

Melt 3 ounces semi-sweet chocolate with 1 tablespoon water and stir into BUTTER CREAM FILLING AND FROSTING.

WALNUT BUTTER CREAM

1¼ cups finely ground walnuts	1 egg white
	4 tablespoons sugar
2 tablespoons rum	¾ cup soft butter

Moisten walnuts with rum.

Beat egg white and sugar over boiling water until the consistency of heavy cream.

Stir in walnuts and gradually beat in softened butter.

CHESTNUT BUTTER CREAM

4 cups glacéed chestnuts, finely chopped	½ cup water
	¼ teaspoon cream of tartar
¾ cup butter	2 teaspoons vanilla
1⅛ cups sugar	

Thoroughly mix chestnuts and butter.

In saucepan combine sugar, water, and cream of tartar.

Bring to a boil and boil rapidly until syrup spins a long thread (238° F.).

Gradually beat syrup into nut-butter mixture and continue to beat until thick and cool.

Stir in vanilla.

ELECTRIC BLENDER CHOCOLATE BUTTER CREAM

1 package (6 ounces) chocolate pieces	4 egg yolks
	½ cup (1 stick) soft butter
⅓ cup boiling water	1 tablespoon dark rum

Into container of electric blender put chocolate pieces and boiling water.

Cover and blend on high speed for about 10 seconds, or until mixture is smooth.

Add egg yolks, butter, and rum.

Cover and turn motor on high.

If vortex ceases, remove cover and, with a rubber spatula or bottle scraper, break surface of mixture, folding cream from sides of container to center. Be careful not to dip too deeply into the blades.

Blend until smooth.

CREAMY FROSTING

6 tablespoons butter
5 tablespoons cream or evaporated milk

1 box confectioners' sugar
1½ teaspoons vanilla extract

Cream butter until fluffy.

Beat in sugar alternately with cream and vanilla. If an electric beater is used it is not necessary to sift the sugar. If hand beaten, a smoother frosting will result if the sugar is sifted.

CREAMY DECORATOR'S FROSTING

To use CREAMY FROSTING for decorating cakes with pastry tubes, beat in from ½ to 1 cup additional sugar.

To Color Creamy Frosting: Beat in a few drops of food coloring. For true pinks and blues, use half white vegetable shortening and half butter in the above recipe and beat until shortening is very fluffy and white.

CREAMY CHOCOLATE FROSTING

1 package (6 ounces) semi-sweet chocolate pieces
¼ cup water or cold coffee
2 egg yolks

½ cup (1 stick) butter
2 cups sifted confectioners' sugar

Put chocolate pieces and water or coffee into a small saucepan and stir over simmering water until chocolate is melted and mixture is smooth.

Remove from heat and beat in egg yolks.
Beat in butter, bit by bit.
Stir in sugar.

ELECTRIC BLENDER PRALINE CREAM

2 eggs
1 cup milk
1 cup heavy cream
3 tablespoons cornstarch

1 tablespoon instant coffee
    powder
1 cup PRALINE POWDER

Into container of an electric blender put eggs, milk, cream, cornstarch, and coffee powder.
Cover and blend on high speed for 5 seconds.
Pour into small saucepan and cook over low heat until thickened, stirring constantly.
Cool, stirring occasionally.
Stir in praline powder.

MOCHA CREAM FROSTING

1 cup sugar
⅓ cup water
¼ teaspoon cream of tartar
3 egg yolks
½ cup butter or shortening
4 ounces semi-sweet choco-
    late pieces, melted

1 teaspoon instant coffee
    powder
1 tablespoon hot water
1 teaspoon vanilla

In a saucepan combine sugar, ⅓ cup of water, and cream of tartar.
Bring slowly to a boil and boil rapidly to 236° F., or until syrup spins a light thread.
Beat egg yolks until creamy, and very gradually beat in the hot syrup.
Beat in shortening and chocolate.
Dissolve instant coffee in 1 tablespoon of hot water and add with vanilla.

CHOCOLATE CREAM FROSTING

1 cup sugar	½ cup butter or shortening
⅓ cup water	4 ounces semi-sweet choco-
¼ teaspoon cream of tartar	late pieces, melted
3 egg yolks	1 teaspoon vanilla

In a saucepan combine sugar, water, and cream of tartar.

Bring slowly to a boil and boil rapidly to 236° F., or until syrup spins a light thread.

Beat egg yolks until creamy and very gradually beat in the hot syrup.

Beat in shortening, chocolate, and vanilla.

LEMON FROSTING

3½ cups sifted confectioners' sugar	¼ cup lemon juice
	1 tablespoon cream
¼ cup butter or shortening	

Blend 2 cups sugar into shortening alternately with lemon juice and cream.

Beat until smooth.

Add 1½ cups sugar and beat until smooth and creamy.

COCOA FROSTING

½ cup butter or shortening	4 cups sifted confectioners'
½ cup cocoa	sugar
¼ teaspoon salt	4–6 tablespoons hot milk
1 teaspoon vanilla	

Blend shortening, cocoa, salt, and vanilla.

Stir in sugar alternately with milk and beat until frosting is smooth and creamy.

ORANGE FROSTING

⅓ cup butter or shortening
3½ cups sifted confectioners'
  sugar
1 tablespoon grated orange
  rind

1 egg
¼ cup orange juice

Blend shortening, 1½ cups sugar, orange rind, and egg until mixture is fluffy.

Gradually stir in 2 more cups sugar alternately with orange juice and beat until smooth and creamy.

VANILLA FROSTING

⅓ cup butter or shortening
3½ cups sifted confectioners'
  sugar

1 teaspoon vanilla
6–11 tablespoons cream or
  milk

Blend shortening with 1½ cups sugar and vanilla.

Add 3 tablespoons cream or milk and mix until smooth.

Stir in 2 more cups sugar alternately with 3 to 5 tablespoons cream or milk and beat until smooth and creamy.

FUDGE FROSTING

3 cups sugar
1 cup water
2 tablespoons corn syrup
2 tablespoons butter or
  shortening

4 squares (ounces) unsweetened chocolate
1½ teaspoons vanilla

In a saucepan combine sugar, water, corn syrup, shortening, and chocolate.

Stir until ingredients are mixed, cover, and bring to a boil.

Uncover and cook without stirring to the soft-ball stage (234° F.).

Remove from heat and let stand until cool.

Add vanilla and beat until frosting is thick enough to hold its shape.

If frosting becomes too thick to spread, stir in a little cream; if too thin to spread, stir in about ½ cup sifted confectioners' sugar.

FONDANT

> 3 cups sugar
> 1 cup hot water
> ⅛ teaspoon cream of tartar

In a heavy 2-quart saucepan combine sugar, water, and cream of tartar.

Stir over a low flame until sugar is dissolved.

Increase heat and cook rapidly, without stirring. As the syrup boils, wash down the crystals that form on the sides of the saucepan with a fork wrapped in a damp cloth or with a wet brush.

When a few drops of the syrup form a soft ball in cold water (238° F. on a candy thermometer), pour the syrup onto a marble slab, an enamel-top table, or a large, flat, smooth platter to cool.

When the center of the batch feels just warm to the hand (110° F.), work the mixture vigorously with a spatula until it becomes white and solid. Let it rest for a few minutes, then knead until it is creamy.

Store the fondant in a tightly covered jar at room temperature for two days before using it.

CHOCOLATE FONDANT • *Fondant au Chocolat*

Melt 2 squares chocolate and let it cool. Add it to 1 cup FONDANT and stir the mixture over a low flame until it is warm to the touch. Add ½ teaspoon vanilla and thin the chocolate fondant to the right consistency with a little warm water.

COFFEE FONDANT • *Fondant au Café*

Flavor warm FONDANT with coffee extract and stir in a drop or two of brown food coloring.

CARAMEL GLAZE

Combine and mix thoroughly ¼ cup dark corn syrup, 1 tablespoon melted butter, 1 teaspoon lemon juice, and the grated rind of 1 lemon, if desired.

PECAN TOPPING

Combine 4 tablespoons melted butter, ½ cup light brown sugar, 1 cup chopped pecans, and 2 tablespoons milk. Spread on top of baked cake as soon as cake is taken from oven and place under broiler heat for 4 minutes, or until topping is bubbly.

MERINGUE FROSTING

2 cups sugar	4 egg whites
⅔ cup water	1 teaspoon vanilla
½ teaspoon cream of tartar	

In a saucepan combine sugar, water, and cream of tartar. Bring slowly to a boil, then boil rapidly to 236° F., the soft-ball stage.
Beat egg whites until stiff.
Pour syrup very slowly over egg whites, beating constantly.
Add vanilla and continue beating until frosting holds its shape.

STRAWBERRY MERINGUE FROSTING

When frosting is finished fold in ¾ cup strawberry preserves.

FOR A 2-EGG WHITE FROSTING

Make half the recipe above.

SEVEN-MINUTE ICING

2 egg whites	5 tablespoons cold water
1½ cups sugar	⅛ teaspoon salt
¼ teaspoon cream of tartar	1 teaspoon vanilla extract

Combine all ingredients except vanilla in top of double boiler.
Cook over rapidly boiling water, beating constantly with a rotary beater until mixture holds a stiff peak—about 7 minutes with hand beater, 3 minutes with an electric beater.
Remove from heat and beat in vanilla, and a few drops of food coloring if desired. Continue to beat for 30 seconds, or until icing is the right consistency to spread.

QUICK MERINGUE ICING

⅓ cup water	¼ teaspoon salt
¼ teaspoon lemon juice	1 egg white
¾ cup sugar	1 teaspoon vanilla extract
¼ teaspoon cream of tartar	

Combine water, lemon juice, sugar, cream of tartar, and salt in a saucepan.

Stir over heat until sugar is dissolved and syrup is hot.

Beat egg white until almost stiff.

Gradually pour hot syrup into egg white, beating constantly. Use an electric rotary beater if possible.

Add vanilla and continue to beat until frosting holds a peak.

Tint with food coloring if desired.

BUTTERSCOTCH MERINGUE FROSTING

1¼ cups brown sugar	3 egg whites
¾ cup white sugar	1 teaspoon vanilla
⅔ cup water	

In a saucepan, combine brown sugar, white sugar, and water.

Bring to a boil and boil rapidly to firm-ball stage (244° F.).

Beat egg whites until stiff.

Pour syrup very slowly over egg whites, beating constantly.

Add vanilla and continue beating until frosting holds its shape.

COFFEE MERINGUE FROSTING

2 egg whites	5 tablespoons water
1½ cups sugar	1 tablespoon instant coffee
½ teaspoon salt	powder
¼ teaspoon cream of tartar	

Combine all ingredients in top of double boiler.

Beat over boiling water until frosting holds a soft peak.

Remove from heat and beat 1 to 2 minutes longer.

ITALIAN MERINGUE

1 cup sugar	1/4 teaspoon cream of tartar
1/3 cup water	4 egg whites, stiffly beaten

Dissolve sugar in water.

Add cream of tartar, cover, and bring to a boil.

Uncover and boil rapidly until syrup spins a long thread (240° F.).

Pour gradually into egg whites, beating constantly, until meringue is cool and thick.

Flavor with vanilla, kirsch, rum, or any liqueur.

ONE EGG WHITE ITALIAN MERINGUE

1/2 cup sugar	Pinch cream of tartar
1/4 cup water	1 egg white, stiffly beaten

In saucepan combine sugar, water, and cream of tartar.

Bring to a boil and boil rapidly until syrup spins a light thread (240° F.)

Beat hot syrup gradually into beaten egg white and continue to beat until meringue is stiff, glossy, and cool.

Stir in desired flavoring.

APRICOT GLAZE

1/4 pound dried apricots
1 cup water
1/3 cup sugar

Soak apricots in water for 2 hours or overnight.

Cook them with sugar until soft and strain through a fine sieve.

Pour the glaze, while hot, into a small sterilized jar and seal.

When ready to use, dilute the glaze with a little hot water to the proper spreading consistency.

ROYAL ICING · Glace Royale

1½ cups sifted confectioners' sugar	1 egg white
	1 teaspoon flavoring

Work sugar gradually into egg white until icing is stiff enough to hold its shape when forced through a pastry tube.

Stir in almond or vanilla flavoring.

This icing, often used for a decorating icing, will not remain soft and creamy like DECORATOR'S BUTTER CREAM. It will harden on standing and icing will chip when cut.

CONFECTIONERS' SUGAR ICING

Combine 1 cup sifted confectioners' sugar and 2 tablespoons warm milk or cream. Beat until smooth and flavor with vanilla, almond, or rum.

HARD SAUCE

2 tablespoons soft butter
1 cup confectioners' sugar
   (sift if lumpy)
Pinch salt

1 teaspoon vanilla, rum, bourbon, brandy, anisette, or other flavoring

Beat butter until fluffy.
Gradually beat in sugar and salt.
Beat in flavoring and chill.

FLUFFY HARD SAUCE

2 tablespoons butter
1 cup confectioners' sugar
   (sift if lumpy)

3 tablespoons cream
2 egg whites, stiffly beaten
1 teaspoon flavoring

Beat butter until fluffy.
Gradually beat in sugar alternately with about 1 tablespoon of the cream.
Fold in egg whites.
Add remaining cream and flavoring and beat well.
Pile into serving dish and chill.

FOAMY SAUCE

½ cup butter
1 cup confectioners' sugar
   (sift if lumpy)
1 egg yolk

1 tablespoon sherry
1 egg white, stiffly beaten
Pinch salt

Beat butter until soft and fluffy and gradually beat in sugar.

Beat in egg yolk and sherry and beat over simmering water until egg has thickened slightly.

Fold in lightly the egg white with the salt.

Serve hot or cold.

LEMON SAUCE

1 tablespoon cornstarch	2 tablespoons butter
½ cup sugar	2 tablespoons lemon juice
½ cup water	

Combine cornstarch, sugar, water, and butter in a saucepan.

Bring to a boil, stirring constantly.

Remove from heat and stir in the lemon juice.

HOT CARAMEL SAUCE

1¼ cups sugar	1 teaspoon vanilla
⅓ cup hot cream	Chopped nut meats, optional

In a heavy saucepan or skillet heat sugar over very low flame until it turns light gold in color.

Stir in cream very slowly and cook, stirring, until sauce is smooth.

Remove from heat and stir in vanilla.

If desired, add chopped nut meats.

BUTTERSCOTCH SAUCE

⅓ cup white corn syrup	2 tablespoons butter
½ cup plus 2 tablespoons light brown sugar	Pinch salt
	⅓ cup cream

In saucepan combine corn syrup, sugar, butter, and salt.

Bring to a boil and boil to a heavy syrup.

Cool and stir in cream.

CRIMSON SAUCE

½ cup currant jelly
2 tablespoons hot water
2 teaspoons lemon juice
⅛ teaspoon salt
2 tablespoons chopped raisins

4 maraschino cherries,
chopped
1 teaspoon maraschino cherry
juice

Combine all ingredients and serve hot or cold.

SABAYON SAUCE · *Sabayon Glacé au Kirsch*

6 egg yolks
¾ cup sugar
¾ cup Marsala

2 tablespoons kirsch
1 cup heavy cream, whipped

Beat egg yolks and sugar until light and pale in color.
Stir in Marsala and cook over hot, but not boiling, water, whipping constantly, until cream is thickened.
Remove from heat and stir in kirsch.
Continue to whip until cool.
Chill and, just before serving, fold in whipped cream.

APRICOT RUM SYRUP OR SAUCE

1½ cups sugar
3 cups apricot juice

3 teaspoons lemon juice
¾ cup rum

Combine sugar and apricot juice.
Bring to a boil and boil rapidly for 10 minutes.
Remove syrup from fire and stir in lemon juice and rum.

PLAIN RUM OR KIRSCH SYRUP

1 cup sugar
1½ cups water
½ cup rum or kirsch

Combine the sugar and water.
Bring to a boil and boil rapidly for 5 minutes, or until a candy thermometer registers 218° F.
Remove the syrup from the stove and stir in the rum or kirsch.

SPICED RUM OR KIRSCH SYRUP

2 cups sugar
2 cups water
1 teaspoon anise
1 two-inch stick cinnamon

Pinch of coriander
Pinch of mace
1 cup rum or kirsch

Combine the sugar and water and bring to a boil.

Add the anise, cinnamon, coriander, and mace.

Boil for 5 minutes, remove from the heat, and stir in the rum or kirsch.

Index